How to Find Your
Soulmate
Without Losing Your Soul

---

21 *Secrets for Women*

How to Find Your
Soulmate
Without Losing Your Soul

21 Secrets for Women

By Jason and Crystalina Evert

Totus Tuus
P R E S S

San Diego

Published by Totus Tuus Press
P.O. Box 1702
Spring Valley, CA 91979

Cover design by Devin Schadt
Typesetting by Loyola Book Composition
Printed in the United States of America
ISBN 978-0983092-30-8
Library of Congress Control Number: 2010917344

Dedication

FOR MARY

CONTENTS

INTRODUCTION

Jason

While driving to the beach with my roommate several years ago, I spotted a neon banner hanging from the roof of a shopping mall: "Grand Opening! Haircuts: $2.99." Any woman would run from such an invitation, but I couldn't resist. A few days later I found myself sitting in the stylist's chair, smug about the fact that I was getting such a deal. As you may have predicted, she mauled my hair.

So what did I do? Thirty days later, I pulled up to the store thinking, "This time it will be different. I'll get another person to cut it. For three bucks, it's worth a shot. Besides, it'll grow out." Again, a budding stylist practically scalped me. You can imagine what I did after this horrendous experience. That's right: I drove to the store a month later, knowing that it was nearly impossible that a third hairstylist could do as much damage as the first two. You would have thought that I'd feel suspicious about the fact that the sale was still on after three months. Nope.

You can guess what happened. But you'll be proud to learn that I didn't go back a fourth time. Although most women would rather cut their own hair with a pair of sharp rocks than let someone groom it for three dollars, the bargain was irresistible to a single guy just out of college.

In one way or another, we all do this. Because of an enticing offer, we return to what is least likely to satisfy us. In terms of our relationships, how often have we sought love where we know it won't be found?

Everyone longs for love, and nearly every girl grows up imagining the ideal mate—a true gentleman who stands out among today's modern men like a knight among boys. When he doesn't show up, her dream begins to fade. Although the thirst for authentic love is ingrained in her heart, she may begin to settle for less, imposing her hopes on guys who fall far short of them. One woman remarked:

> If I really stop to think about it, I'm getting hung up on men I never wanted in the first place. And all the women I know feel the same way. We've collectively lowered our standards without even realizing it.[1]

The reason I have spent several years writing this book is because I want you to know that you don't need to settle in your current relationships, and you certainly don't need to settle in your future marriage. I have written each word to you as I would to a sister and a friend. Since we males aren't exceptional communicators, I'm hoping to offer to you a glimpse into our intentions, our fears, and our desires when it comes to relationships.

Since I'm not a woman, I can only imagine how challenging it is to grow up in a culture that perpetually undermines your womanhood and your desire to be loved. From a guy's perspective, it seems that the average teen girl magazine has an occasional article bashing anorexic models, followed by a hundred pages of advertisements that glorify them. They'll warn against the dangers of eating disorders, then remind girls that they should start working toward the perfect bikini body because summer is on its way. The headlines read, "10 Ways to Make Him Want You!" "How to Get Perfect Abs in 20 Minutes!" and "How to Look Perfect for Your Prom!" Whether you realize it or not, each headline is appealing to the deepest desire of a woman—to be lovable.

Even when a girl graduates from teen magazines, the literature for women isn't much better. Take, for example, books targeting singles. In one book on relationships, under the heading, "Raise Your Standards and Reach for Love," relationship expert Ian Kerner, PhD, recommends, "Use the booty: Guys are using you, so use back. Look at casual sex as a way to work on identifying your sexual wants and needs."[2] Dr. Ian doesn't fully explain how such advice raises a woman's standards and helps her reach for love.

His notion of love is a far cry from what stirs within the soul of a woman. I know this because on her powdery blue stationery with clouds and a rainbow, an eighty-two-year-old woman wrote to me about her love story. In the 1940's she was a "lively nursing student" in San Diego. She recalled her college life:

> All of us were constantly and happily "dating" young navy and marine men. In those days, chastity was a given. Most of us received many more than one or two marriage proposals. Going back to when I first started dating in 1940, by 1945 my own count was a ten. All during 1946, the days past graduation were followed by marriages for almost all of us in our fifteen-person class. These were marriages that lasted through our lifetimes.

Not long after her fiftieth wedding anniversary, her husband became ill. After years of caring for him with the tenderness of a bride, she said he "passed peacefully away in my arms."

Ten wedding proposals, a fifty-five-year marriage, and holding her lover as he passed into eternal life. Not bad.

It's hard to believe that less than a century ago, men considered chastity to be "a given" and leapt at the chance to offer women their hand in marriage. Nowadays some guys are frustrated if a woman expects so much as a text message after a hookup. Is it possible to restore reverence for women and to rekindle a sense of wonder and anticipation in the realm of human sexuality? If it weren't, we wouldn't have bothered to write this book.

My wife's contribution to the creation of this book cannot be measured. For the past decade, she has accompanied me across the globe, courageously opening her heart and sharing her testimony with countless singles. As you will read, she understands what weighs upon your heart—both the fears about the future and the anxieties about the past. She knows how difficult it can be to look for love in a world that seems to offer you only the opposite.

In the pages to come, our goal is to offer you the vision of godly love, the hope that it exists, the confidence that you deserve it, and the means by which you can find it. As you will soon discover, we are not afraid to challenge you. Think: How many great achievements have you accomplished with little effort? Then why put less effort into the one thing you want most, which is love?

If you decide to follow the principles of this book, I can't promise that you'll meet your soulmate next month. I can't guarantee you'll receive ten marriage proposals, let alone one. But I can guarantee that if you never give these twenty-one secrets a try, you'll always wonder what might have happened if you did.

Crystalina

After breaking off the worst relationship a woman can imagine, I sat alone in my room feeling as if I had already lived through two divorces—at the age of eighteen. Broken, used, and confused, I knew that there had to be another way to live. I had invested so much of my identity into my ex-boyfriends and was now faced with a choice: Do I go back to the familiar routines of my old life, or do I set out to find the love that I feared only existed in my imagination?

Standing at a crossroad, my mind was filled with self-doubt: Why do I deserve love, after all I've done? There aren't any good men left, and even if there were, why would they want me? Can I really change? If I do change, will it last? Is love even worth the risk?

I had grown so accustomed to the security of a relationship that singleness seemed like a sentence. But then again, it couldn't be much worse than all the abuse, infidelity, and drama that had stained my last two relationships.

Now that I was on the outside looking in, I began to remember who I was before I began dating. So much had changed, yet the process of lowering my standards had been so gradual and subtle that I hardly noticed. I entered high school innocent and naïve, but graduated jaded, angry, and bitter toward men. One friend summed up my frustration with guys by calling them "chocolate covered pigs." I suppose you could say I had a few issues to sort through.

During her single years of life, a woman can either find herself or lose herself. Because I didn't find myself before finding a man, I established my identity in them. Over time, I forgot who I was because I was always trying to find new ways to keep the guys interested. I had always thought of myself as a strong and independent woman, but I had become weak and utterly dependent upon their approval for my sense of worth.

The time had come for things to change. If I wanted to find love, I would need to make a sobering assessment of all the ways I had settled for less. Without doing this, I would have been doomed to repeat the same mistakes. In time, I was able to learn that as long as I could respect and love myself, I wouldn't settle for less from others.

I knew the love I wanted to find but I had no idea where to look. I dreamed about it and longed for it but had no living examples of it in my life. As a teen, I read a quote that said, "It is not moments of unleashed passion that prove our love, but the countless hours of commitment spent between." Upon reading such things, my heart would rise up, as if it were being called toward the only type of love that would satisfy its deepest longing.

Although I had seen much darkness, I knew that in order for things to improve I needed to give myself permission to hope. So on a lonely summer night soon after my eighteenth birthday, I sat in my room and wrote my first love letter to a man I had never met:

> This is the first of many letters I will write to you. As you can see, I am not sure who to address this to or what to call you. So I will take this step-by-step. I know somewhere in this huge world you are out there. As hard as that may seem at times to believe, I know it's true. . . .

With these words, I began writing letters to my future husband. I didn't know if I would ever meet him, or if he even existed. But after all I had been through, I could only hope in love. Every time I was tempted to return to my former life, I would read these letters and add to them.

On the first night of my honeymoon, I presented them all to Jason. The scribbled stack of love notes from my late teens and early twenties were my way of showing him that even though I hadn't lived the perfect past, I did start thinking of him. Throughout this book, I want to share with you not only the trials I faced before my lifestyle change and the challenges that followed, but also the rewards of choosing to hope when you have every reason not to.

Jason brings a unique male perspective to this work because he has spoken to more than a million singles across the globe. Following his presentations, women often line up for hours on end to share their stories with him. On more occasions than I can count, I've watched him stand for hours in the hallways of high schools, universities, and churches listening to them pouring their hearts out to him. They trust him as a friend, and have given him a rare glimpse into the daily struggles we all face. Much of this book is the fruit of those thousands of conversations.

We wanted to create a manual that could be used throughout a woman's single years: from the turbulent teens, through college, and well into her years as a single professional—or a professional single. Therefore, some portions of this book target issues for teens, while other sections deal with challenges faced by older women. Every woman's situation is unique, yet so many of us stumble over the same things regardless of our age. Let's be honest: Countless teens struggle with adult problems, and just as many adults wrestle with daily drama that should have ended with high school. In our quest for love, we sometimes grow weary and need reassurance. Sometimes we just need someone to tell us, "You—and your standards—are not the problem!"

As you read the following pages, be assured of our prayers that you will not only find, but also give, the love you have been created for.

No Missionary Dating

Walking between classes one day, my friend Paul blurted out to me, "Jason, did you hear what Jerrod got his girlfriend to do with him?" I knew the girl he was talking about because she sat next to me in an afternoon class. She and I would often joke around during class, and she seemed like she'd be a fun girl to date, had she not been attached at the hip to Jerrod for as long as I could remember.

As we walked across campus, my jaw dropped in disbelief as Paul filled me in on the sordid details. From that day on, I wondered, "What does she see in that guy?" Unfortunately, until she wanted something better for herself, no one could give it to her. No doubt she cared about him. The problem was that she didn't care enough about herself.

Every woman knows when something's not right in a relationship; there's a lack of peace. But she has only two options: Fix it or get out. Many women think, "After investing so much in the relationship, the last thing I want to do is throw it all away." In order to avoid the heartache, they remain emotionally married and forever postpone the divorce. Instead of leaving the relationship in search of a healthy one or enjoying a time of independence, they stay put and try to rehabilitate it. In other words, they begin "missionary dating."

In order to avoid the pitfalls of missionary dating, a woman would do well to avoid committing to such guys in the first place. After all, it's hard to find a soulmate when you're clogging up your dating life trying to convert a frog into a prince. Therefore, before we offer twenty chapters of dating advice, we thought it would be helpful to begin by pointing out which guys you should avoid like the plague.

Do you know when to pass on a potential boyfriend? Here's our top ten list:

The Top Ten Guys to Avoid

1. The Flip-Flopper
2. The Problem Child (aka: The Fixer-Upper)
3. The Walking Hormone
4. The Smooth Criminal
5. The Control Freak
6. The Older Guy
7. The Potty Mouth
8. The Tearful Cheater
9. The Spiritual Midget
10. Mr. I-Don't-Have-Enough-Social-Skills-to-Meet-Girls-without-the-Internet

1. The Flip-Flopper

A flip-flopper might waver between being an ex-boyfriend or a current boyfriend, but at least one thing is for sure: He's always a future ex-boyfriend. He can't live without you, but he's got a girlfriend. It's the saga of a guy who can't make up his mind, and a girlfriend who sits and waits for him like a puppy on the back porch waiting for her master. When he opens the door, she wags her tail and gleefully runs into the house. But it's only a matter of time before he rolls up the newspaper and sends her back outside.

Often he will have difficulty making up his mind because he likes more than one woman at a time. He'll be desperate for one girl as soon as he's not busy with another. In an effort to win his love, the woman who dates a flip-flopper may hook up with him after they've already broken up, hoping it will ignite a spark and remind him of what he's missing. Her efforts will always backfire because what she's really reminding him of is why he won't commit to her in the first place: She doesn't respect herself.

When a woman dates a flip-flopper, she is like someone trapped in a revolving door: Now she's in. Now she's out. The drama of the relationship is enough to make all her friends dizzy. While they're trying to keep track of her ever-changing relationship status, she's trying her best to ignore the pattern of instability.

Thankfully, flip-floppers are easy to detect. They will drag on a physical relationship without bothering to make a clear commitment. When anyone asks the woman if the two of them are dating, she can only reply, "Kind of." Because he's immature and she's infatuated and desperate, the guy is unable to maintain a lasting interest in her. Instead of committing to her, which is a true mark of love, he leaves her hanging. Any woman who commits (or tries to commit) to such a guy is not ready for a relationship herself, regardless of how much she may want one.

Women who fall for flip-floppers are often masters of denial. One girl pondered to me (Jason) in an e-mail about her dilemma: "We are soulmates and will be bound together for the rest of our lives. Why is he afraid to accept our status right now and keep squeezing in as many random hookups as possible?"

He's not afraid of their status. He knows their status and he enjoys it. She's the one who is afraid to accept her status with him. He refuses to commit to her. That's the status, and it hurts to admit it. She may wonder, "Why does he need these other girls? Am I not enough for him? Is there something wrong with me that he would rather be with them?" She wants to believe him when he says they're "meant to be," but if their destiny is inevitable, why is he hooking up with other girls in the meantime? He's basically saying, "Wait for me while I use other women. When I'm done with them, I'll fall hopelessly in love with you forever." Sure.

Guys are simple creatures. If we want to be with a woman, we'll be with her. End of story. If we need to storm a castle and kill the dragon to win her heart, we'll do it. Women often create excuses for why the guy won't commit to them. For example, "He's just really busy." "He's not ready for the label of a relationship." "He's afraid of commitment." "He's under a lot of stress," and so on. These are all coping mechanisms for the girl to avoid accepting the fact that he's not interested in her. Such excuses are simply distractions. When a guy really loves a woman, she doesn't have to plead with him to commit. He'd commit to her if she lived on the moon.

Remember when you were in eighth grade and you tried to turn down boys without hurting their feelings? "Sorry, I can't go out. I'm washing my hair tonight, or . . . um . . . rearranging my sock drawer." It's pretty much the same thing. If you have to convince yourself that he cares for you, then he does not. If he's not asking you out, don't try to make up reasons for his decision. (Note that I am not calling it indecision.)

To ask a woman out means that a man would rather risk rejection than not have had the opportunity to be with her. If a guy never asks you out, he obviously doesn't feel this way. Sure, there may be women we find attractive who we never ask out. But if a friendship develops and the opportunity for a relationship arises, a guy who wants to be with a girl will not miss the chance to make the relationship official.

The fear of commitment is something all guys are notorious for feeling. But our love for freedom is not as strong as our desire for love itself. There comes a point in a man's life when he finds a woman he loves more than his own personal freedom. And he surrenders it because freedom exists to be given away for the sake of love.

You don't need to beg for anyone's attention. Make him work to win your heart instead of simply handing it to him. If you like a guy, stay friends with him and it will become obvious to him if you're interested. If a guy likes a woman, he'll easily pick up on her subtle clues. If the feelings aren't mutual, you could put a billboard in front of his face and he'd probably miss it.

Chasing after a flip-flopper takes its toll on a woman's heart. One girl described her experience to me:

> One day he's hanging out with me and all nice and so fun to be with and the next I just want to yell at him and just sit in front of him and bawl my eyes out. I know I have so much going for me but he's just

meant so much to me for so long that it's so hard. I'm just so sick of his games that he plays with me and I can't take much more of it. It's like he's saying, "No, Emily,* you can't go and be with other guys. I only want you to want me even though I don't want you anymore."

Love thrives in the presence of commitment. So don't waste years of your life dragging on a relationship that exists only in your imagination. Such advice might be hard to hear but it will be more painful to ignore. Besides, do you really want to spend your life with a man who is too passive and afraid to ask you out?

Because a flip-flopper is immature and indecisive, he'll offer you nothing but emotional instability. Such a guy does not deserve a girlfriend, let alone several. If you try to break things off and he gets emotional and sappy, don't take the bait and hope he really means it this time. Stay away and don't give him the pleasure of dumping you again. You're better than that.

I will predict, though, that the more you pull away, the more he'll want you back. But the more you cling to him, the more he'll lose interest. You can't win. Realize from this pattern that you're not the problem. He is. You may be tempted to wait patiently for him, hoping he'll come around. Don't do this. He does not know how to love you. It is not that you are unlovable, but that he has no idea what love is.

Reflecting upon her habit of dating such men, one woman remarked:

> When we are with the wrong man and he is clearly lacking the qualities we want in a partner, we gladly supply them for him. We fill in the blanks instead of realizing he's wrong to begin with. . . . And it dawned on me . . . the whole time I worried about why he didn't like me, I forgot to ask myself whether or not I liked him.[1]

Instead of waiting on an indecisive guy, realize that you're better off with someone who can't wait to commit to you. Don't wait around for a flip-flopper, hoping he'll want you. Walk away and let him wish he deserved you! Be brave. Love awaits you.

---

* Throughout the book, names and minor details have been changed in order to preserve the anonymity of individuals.

2. *The Problem Child (aka: The Fixer-Upper)*

The problem child is a guy who typically comes from a troubled family and has either had trouble with the law, difficulties at school or work, addictions to drugs and alcohol, a history of violence, or all of the above. Countless girls fall in love with such "bad boys." But once a woman forms an attachment to him, she begins to feel sorry for him and to "see in him what nobody else does." She dreams about his potential while downplaying the fact that he refuses to grow up and improve his life. As a result, she may drag out the relationship for years, ignoring her intuition to leave.

Have you ever seen one of those TV shows in which a team of decorators takes a run-down house and transforms it overnight? Many women are hoping for the same kind of miracle makeover in their boyfriends. However, relationships are not the place to fix a guy. When women ignore this reality, they often spend ungodly amounts of time trying to rescue their man from himself. They wish that they could admire him, but they don't. They long for the day that they can look at him and see everything they hope he can be.

When a woman falls in love with a problem child, she'll ignore his present problems and spend her time thinking about how great he'll be in the future—when he becomes completely different. It's like moving into a dilapidated home because you plan to remodel it as soon as you win the lottery.

After years of trying to make these relationships work, some girls open their eyes. One such woman e-mailed me to say, "I didn't want to be used as an object to cure his depression, problems, or physical 'needs.' I felt like I was being used like a medication." I remember meeting another young woman who was dating an older guy—who just happened to be in prison. When I asked the reason for his incarceration, she said, "I asked him why he was in jail and he said, 'They caught me on surveillance cameras, but all I was doing was standing there.'" I pointed out to her that most people don't get arrested for "standing there." But she was convinced of his innocence.

A fifteen-year-old girl wrote to me:

My boyfriend used to smoke pot and do meth a lot, but he's really gotten better. He still does it once in a while when he gets stressed, and you're probably thinking I'm crazy for not dumping him. But his dad and step-mom are really mean to him, and I'm afraid what he'll do to himself if I leave. He said he can't live without me. I'm not sure what to do.

If a guy ever tells you that he can't live without you, trust me: He doesn't need a girlfriend. He needs a therapist. Until both people are whole, they cannot create a healthy relationship. In this guy's case, he wants his girlfriend to feel responsible for him so that she'll stay. He wants her to think that if she leaves, he'll have no choice but to build a methamphetamine lab in his closet!

Don't believe it. It's just one way that immature guys manipulate insecure girls. It is not the woman's job to save her man. Only he can change himself, and the longer a girl tries to mother him the more drawn out the process becomes.

The age at which a man begins using drugs or alcohol to deal with life's problems is the emotional age at which he remains. If a guy uses drugs, violence, or alcohol as a way to cope with stress, then he'll use the stress as an excuse to misbehave. Such emotional immaturity can be devastating to a future marriage, because marriage and adulthood involve plenty of stress.

Any woman who is trying to mother a guy should also consider the long-term impact this will have on her romantic relationship. A man does not want to marry his mother. He wants to marry his soulmate. When a guy begins to see his girlfriend as his mom, you can kiss his romantic feelings toward her goodbye.

Worse, when a woman insists on playing the role of messiah, she often ends up being pulled into her boyfriend's problems instead of pulling him out of them. She's so concerned about him that she forgets to take care of herself. He may temporarily improve, but the change is rarely permanent. Deep down she knows that she's not going to change him. He is changing her, though, into someone she never wanted to become.

If a girl really wants to help a problem child boyfriend, the most effective way to do this may be to do what she fears most: Let go of him. This teaches him the priceless lesson that his poor behavior has negative consequences. By breaking up, she is doing what is best for him. She is loving him by leaving him.

Even if he comes back saying that he's a changed man, she must stand her ground and not go back. He needs time to get on his feet, and she needs to find out why she liked him in the first place. Perhaps it was the fact that he liked her. Maybe she fell for him before she realized how troubled he was. Or maybe she wanted the challenge and adventure of saving a bad boy. Perhaps it was something deeper. Maybe she was trying to win the affection of a man who resembles her troubled father. If she was unable to win her dad's love and rescue him from his problems, perhaps she can save someone like him. Whatever the cause of her fascination with a troubled guy, she would do well to step back and open her life to the possibilities of a more peaceful relationship.

3. The Walking Hormone

During the teenage years, males can have twenty times more testosterone in their bodies than females have.[2] For this reason, most girls probably think that "teenage boy" and "walking hormone" are synonymous. Unfortunately, many women will testify that some adult men still haven't outgrown this phase.

But a distinction is needed here: Although men have ample amounts of testosterone, some control the hormones while others are controlled *by* them. We'll be looking at the latter of the two.

The walking hormone has one thing in mind: self-gratification at the expense of women. To reach his goal, he'll often manipulate women with pressure or guilt. He may be congratulated in the locker room as a player, but he's nothing more than a slave to his weakness.

Usually, such guys are easy to recognize because of the lines they use. For example:

- "You're such a tease."
- "If you loved me, you'd show me."
- "What's the problem? We've done it before."

- "Don't you like me?"
- "I feel like you're not attracted to me if you don't do this stuff with me."

Some walking hormones can be pretty creative in their tactics. For example, a newspaper article in California reported that a twenty-eight-year-old soccer coach manipulated several of his female players into sleeping with him. He showed them a red amulet filled with fluid and said that it was his "life essence." It would dwindle if he did not have sex, and once it disappeared he would die. Several of the young women believed him and slept with him. Thankfully, he was arrested, and now both he and his life essence are in prison.[3]

While most guys won't try to convince a girl that abstinence is lethal to them, the walking hormone won't hesitate to make her feel like she's a cruel, heartless, and stingy prude for denying him his "needs." If she's already done certain sexual things with him, he'll remind her as an attempt to convince her that it's not a big deal. In other words, her body isn't a big deal. And neither is her soul.

If she respects herself, she has no choice but to dump him. In fact, the only way he'll stop using her is if she stops letting him. However, this is easier said than done. Consider the struggles of these two young women:

> He would come over, and though I'd try to talk or to watch a movie all he ever wanted to do was physical activity. I was somewhat uncomfortable with this, but rather than lose a friend, shut my mouth. I knew I was being used, but I kept making excuses so that I wouldn't feel as horrible as I did. However, feeling so bad was inevitable.

> I always kept telling myself, "No, he really cares about you. . . . He's going through a very tough time right now and he's just confused. . . . No, he's not really using you," and just like that I lied to myself for months on end.

You'll notice that the common thread between these women is the use of excuses that only prolong their problems. Buried under these rationalizations is a God-given intuition that serves as a compass to find authentic love. When women begin to doubt or ignore the voice of their conscience, they become their own worst enemies. They then wonder why love seems so elusive.

Walking hormones have certain preferences when it comes to women. For example, easy prey is someone with lower-than-average self-esteem. Because of her fear of rejection, she's less likely to say no to his desires. She may even initiate the affection in hopes that he'll like her more. However, while such a girl would be fun for him to date, he'll never take her home to mom, much less marry her. He'll just fool around with such women until he grows up. Then he'll start looking for a nice, pure one. Needless to say, you want to avoid these guys and their double standards.

If you won't avoid them for the sake of yourself, at least stay away for the sake of your future children. Such men make deadbeat dads, and your kids deserve a better father. That's why I would go so far as to say that sleeping with a player is asking for child abuse. He might seem charming now, but ask the last twelve girls he's abandoned how charming they think he is after he left them in the morning.

Included in the "walking hormone" category is any guy who looks at porn or asks you to send him a racy photo of yourself. If a guy asks you for a revealing photo, go ahead and send him a picture of your bare hand, waving goodbye to him.

If you're inclined to tolerate this behavior in a man, allow me—as a guy who viewed plenty of porn as a teen—to explain to you what it does to the male mind. Neurologically, porn trains a man's brain to associate sexual joy with trashy forbidden fantasies. No wife can compete with this, because marriage requires respect and reverence, not to mention monogamy. But even if a bride did try to conform to such a warped image of womanhood to win his interests, the victory would be short-lived. Remember, such a man hops from web site to web site. He grows bored of each supermodel within a matter of seconds! He has destroyed his ability to be captivated. Instead of sexually liberating a guy, pornography enslaves him.

Such a man has warped his capacity to love because he has trained himself in selfishness and lust. Instead of making love within marriage, such a man will see his wife as an outlet for what he thinks are his sexual needs. Because he lacks the self-control that makes love possible, he is unable to make a gift of himself to her.

One man admitted, "Long before my first sexual relationship, porn was my sex education."[4] Can you imagine what happens to a guy's outlook on human sexuality when porn producers are his professors? At a Midwest all-girls high school, a religion teacher told me that she invited a panel of college guys to answer chastity-related questions in front of her classroom of teenage girls. Prior to inviting the young men, she had been under the impression that they were practicing their faith in college. When one of them admitted to viewing porn on a regular basis, the teacher inquired, "Don't you think that might cause problems in your future marriage?" The young man looked puzzled, and replied, "Well, isn't that what your wife is for?" Judging by the seething reaction he received from the classroom of young women, he learned that this is actually not what a wife is for.

When a man's expectations of a woman's body and behavior are shaped by the porn industry, it causes immeasurable harm to his future marriage. A frustrated wife wrote to me:

> He had been reassuring me and swearing and promising me that nothing of the sort was going on and I believed him. In hindsight, I think I just wanted to believe. I am so frustrated and sick of it. I am so suspicious of him. I don't trust him at all when it comes to other women. But all I see anywhere we go is his eyes on other girls. It bothers me because I am thinking that he must be thinking perverted sexual thoughts because of the porn. I am so sure he is and it makes me sick.

I met one ex-wife who found a stack of porn magazines under their bed after she and her husband had separated. She knew they had struggled with intimacy and now she knew why: He used her body to make love to the women in his imagination.

When a husband looks at porn, it not only reveals that he sees women as objects, it also reveals that he has a warped notion of fidelity. Another wife wrote to me, saying:

> My husband of a little over one month is in love with pornography. I've tried to speak with him about it before, but I get nervous and

flustered and end up nodding to whatever he says. He does not believe his indulging this desire is cheating or harmful or anything to
be ashamed of. He knows I disagree with him, but I doubt he even
begins to comprehend how devastating and heartbreaking it is for me.

Unless you want your marriage to resemble these, never date a
guy who looks at porn. When it infects a relationship, the woman is
the one who pays the highest price. A psychologist named Douglas
Kenrick performed famous studies on the effects of pornography.[5]
In a pair of experiments, he showed images of *Playboy* models, aver-
agely attractive women, and abstract art to separate groups of male
students. He then asked them to rate the attractiveness of an average
female student. Those who had looked at the porn rated her as less
attractive than the others. But they also rated their actual girlfriends
the lowest in terms of attractiveness and how much they loved them!

Some girls realize that the problem of porn is widespread among
men and have no desire to address it. Instead, they use a man's weakness to get his attention. They descend into the pornographic culture by becoming billboards for porn companies, adorning themselves
with anything from *Playboy* earrings and purses to belly button rings
and bumper stickers. Such women may even agree to a guy's invitation to watch porn with him. He hopes that she'll be aroused by the
images and will want to act it out with him. But she should know
that child molesters routinely use the same tactic with their victims.
Real romantic.

A porn addict may try to blame you for being a prude or claim
that it's natural for guys to have erotic moments with their laptops,
but don't back down on this. It is your future that is at stake. Do not
allow yourself to be enslaved by the fear that a guy will dump you
if you insist that he have faithful eyes and an undivided heart. If he
leaves you in search of a less "demanding" girlfriend, you should do
one thing: Thank God. If he prefers porn to the love of an actual
woman, then let him commit to his imaginary girlfriends.

We should add that porn is not exclusively a male problem. Because of the availability of porn and sensual chats on the Internet,
many women stumble across it and eventually find themselves seeking it out. If it weren't for the Internet, they would never venture

into an adult bookstore to buy a pornographic magazine. Although they often feel ashamed of their habit, they're not sure how to stop. Most of these women are not thirsting for smutty images or seedy conversations. More often than not, they're curious and yearning for intimacy. The illusion of porn, cybersex, or sensual novels traps them, and they are left to wonder why they feel so empty afterward.

One man described the love you seek when he wrote, "The wife must love her husband as if there were no other man in the world, in much the same way as the husband should love her as if no other woman existed."[6] Obviously, if a person fosters an attachment to porn, such love does not exist in his or her heart.

Believe it or not, there are good guys out there. One young man confided in me why he refused to view porn:

> It's like it would cheapen everything that I like in the few pure-hearted girls I know. If I watched porn, I wouldn't be able to honestly say to myself that the reason I am attracted to any woman is the reason that God wants. Or I might not even be able to tell if it really was love.

He rejected porn because he knew that it threatened his ability to love a woman. Don't settle for a guy who is unwilling to do the same for you.

If you want a true man, you need to know what one looks like. For starters, a guy cannot be considered a man unless he treats a woman with dignity. When a boy learns how to forget himself for the good of another, he becomes a man. This transition does not occur at puberty; it comes when he learns the meaning of sacrifice. As you can imagine, walking hormone guys are locked into a mentality of using instead of loving. For this reason, stay far away from them. Instead of wasting your time on guys who see your purity as a problem or a neurotic condition, hold out for a guy who values you for more than your body.

4. The Smooth Criminal

The smooth criminal is similar to the walking hormone but he has enough intelligence to make him especially dangerous. He understands women well enough to know that most of them are not likely to become physical with guys who don't care for them. He knows that while most guys need a reason *not* to have sex, a woman usually needs one.

Such a man will use any number of tactics to convince the woman of his good intentions. For example, after speaking at an all-boys high school, a young man approached me before I left to give the assembly at the nearby all-girls school. He asked me, "Do you ever tell the girls that a guy will say that he's okay not having sex, so that she'll give it to him?"

As if it were needed, scientists have published research papers to prove that college guys admit that they pretend to be more kind, sincere, and trustworthy than they really are, as a ploy to become more sexually desirable to women.[7] Be careful with a guy whose words sound too sweet to be true. All too often, women fall in love with a man's speech and overlook who he actually is. If you think you might already be dating such a guy, take a step back and ask yourself: "Is my boyfriend doing what's best for me, or just doing what feels good for him?"

While the walking hormone will clearly pressure a woman into sexual activity, the smooth criminal will be suave enough to convince her that the choice is entirely up to her. Because she feels that he is being a gentleman by waiting until she's "ready," she becomes more vulnerable. In fact, it won't feel like pressure at all. It will seem like she's freely making the decision herself. Meanwhile, he will take from her everything sexual she is willing to give him. He's not leading her to purity, he's wearing it down. But because women today live in a culture in which so many men are sexually aggressive and irreverent, it seems attractive when a man seems relaxed about the matter. In the case of the smooth criminal, however, his indifference is manipulative.

One young man e-mailed me, sharing how devastated he was when he discovered that the girl he loved had been cheating on him for six months. After this, he changed:

The way I saw it, I gave myself to one of them and she played with me and hurt me. Then I figured that guys go through this all the time and I figured that I would stand up for all of us. I would be the one who did it to girls. It's amazing how easy it is to do that when you have enough confidence. This, of course, led me to parties and drinking, since those and sex, to a young man, always seem to go together. I lost myself in this, and after three years of it, I felt no better. I just wanted to keep doing it in hopes of gaining satisfaction.

Many girls were drawn to his confidence and he knew it. After all, it's normal for a girl to find confidence attractive. It's a quality that every man should possess, as opposed to the extremes of insecurity or cockiness. But like all good things, it can be twisted and used for selfish motives.

Most guys don't have such scheming intentions. Usually when a guy says, "I'm okay not having sex," he'll mean it. If she doesn't want to do anything, he's fine with that. But be careful: In the case of a smooth criminal, although he won't pressure you to do anything, he certainly won't pressure you to remain chaste either. If you're willing to give, he's ready to take. Because he doesn't understand the point of chastity and doesn't care about guarding his own innocence, he certainly won't be concerned about preserving yours. But if you hope to find real love, look for a guy who has morals, not one who simply tolerates them.

One young woman said to me, "I feel like I owe it to him to do some stuff because he's such an understanding person about my decision not to have sex." Don't be impressed by the fact a guy doesn't pressure you. He doesn't get any points for that. It's his duty as a gentleman. Besides, he should be encouraging you to be pure, not waiting for you to give in.

Stay away from such men, because there will be days when you'll feel tempted to toss aside your commitment to be pure. At such moments of temptation, when you feel weak, the character of a man is revealed. If he has a pure heart, he will remind you of your standards when the two of you are about to forget them. However, if he's a smooth criminal, the innocence of the relationship will disappear the moment you consent. Think of him as one of those dogs that have been trained to balance food on its nose. As soon as the trainer gives the dog the signal, it devours the treat. It will work the same way if you date a smooth criminal. As soon as you give him the green light, he'll take everything you'll offer.

If you want lasting love, begin your love story by refusing to date the smooth criminal. Keep your distance from such men, because the closer you get to them, the weaker you become.

5. The Control Freak

When a relationship begins, a girl may feel flattered if the guy is possessive or jealous. She may think to herself, "Wow. It's kind of nice that he cares so much about what I'm doing." But it doesn't take long before she begins to see that his "devotion" is unhealthy. Is this the case with you? Here are more than two dozen warning signs to watch out for:

- He interrogates you: "Did you talk to any other guys while you were out?"
- He behaves badly and then blames it on other people or events.
- He emphasizes or exaggerates how bad his life is (while doing nothing to improve it).
- He hits things to deal with his anger.
- He has a jealousy problem, but says it's because he loves you.
- He insults you, and then tells you he's kidding.
- He makes you feel like you have to apologize for things that are not your fault.
- He makes you feel like he can't live without you.
- He tries to control the amount of time you spend with your friends or family.
- He makes you feel guilty for being with other people.
- He tries to control the way you dress.
- He always needs to know where you're at or what you're doing.
- His mood swings from extremes of sweetness to selfishness.
- He expects you to answer your phone or return his messages immediately.
- He sets one standard for how he expects you to live, but another for himself.
- He makes you feel like it's your job to keep him from getting angry.

- He accuses you of flirting with others or being unfaithful (while he's the one who's probably guilty).
- He pressures you to do sexual things.
- He acts like a victim instead of taking responsibility for his life.
- He makes you feel like you're lucky to have him, instead of making you feel like he's lucky to have you.
- He makes you feel like his problems in life would be solved if you loved him enough.
- You feel like you need to hide the truth about this relationship from those who love you. You fear that otherwise you would not be allowed to see him.
- You don't have peace about the relationship and you often feel sad about it.
- Your self-esteem has suffered because of the relationship.
- You always feel like you're living according to his moods and wishes.

The more items you recognizeded on this list, the faster you should get away from this guy. Any one of these can be damaging to a future marriage. If you noticed several items, don't stick around hoping he'll improve. But watch out! Controlling guys have all kinds of tricks to make you stay. For example:

- He might try to detach you from all your loved ones so that you'll have nobody but him. You'll think you have nowhere to go.
- When you want to leave he may become sweet as a lamb, which is what you've been waiting for. You won't want to leave him while he's being nice. You want to believe that he has changed. But don't be fooled. It will only last until his next mood swing.
- He may be verbally or physically abusive, making you feel unlovable. His goal is to make you feel as if no one else would want you. In reality, I bet nobody else wants him.
- He may use guilt to keep you on a leash, making you feel like he'd die without you. Putting on a pouty party, his tears of unmitigated sorrow may flow as he manipulates your feminine emotions. Don't let empathy get the best of you.
- He may try to rush engagement or give you a "promise ring" without a wedding date. Or he'll commit to marrying you . . . sometime during the next presidency. His talk of "forever" gets you to dream about the future and forget about the present problems.
- When all else fails, he may threaten you or your loved ones and pets, hoping you will stay out of fear.

In all these cases, he is trying to stay in control at your expense.

Where is all this control freak behavior coming from? He is probably insecure. Even if he appears cocky and assertive, he's covering up a lack of confidence. A confident man is not afraid that you'll talk to male and female friends or spend time with your family. He knows that loving relationships never require you to hide the truth from others who love you. A confident man will make you make you feel confident and free, but an insecure guy will try to make you feel insecure so that he can control you.

Although he's insecure, do yourself a favor and don't feel sorry for him. He's not a victim. He chooses how to act. What's sad is that a girl may fall for these tricks and repeatedly go back to an abusive or controlling relationship. She may gravitate toward such strong-willed guys because she lacks a will of her own. If she does not know her identity, she'll find a man to give her one. As one young woman said, "After I got over him, which took a pretty long time, I realized what I was looking so hard for before I met him: myself."

When I (Crystalina) felt trapped in an abusive and controlling relationship, I always felt the need to apologize for things that were not my fault. Can you relate? If so, why are we always apologizing? Why do we take it upon ourselves, as if we always have to make up for what is wrong around us? Offering a superficial "sorry" won't change a thing. Does apologizing for everything make anything better or change your circumstances? No. You and I both know it doesn't, but by announcing to everyone that we're sorry, we take the blame upon ourselves and inflict a false guilt that is not our own. Always taking the burden of blame gives us unspoken permission to think, feel, and be insecure.

If you do this, begin to face the truth in every situation and see things for what they are. In the future, do not allow another to hold you down, or make you feel bad or weak. Refuse and renounce the lie of false blame. Apologize only when you've actually done something wrong, and not because of harbored guilt that is not your own. Your apologies will begin to mean something and will acknowledge that you hurt someone you care about. That is what "sorry" really means, and you need to stop using the term lightly.

If you're finding it hard to get away from the relationship, make yourself a "control freak calendar." Here's how to do it: Get a blank calendar and write down each time he's controlling, possessive, jealous, or abusive. Women often go back to unpromising relationships because they "forget" how bad he is. Having a written record of his behavior will keep this amnesia from occurring. Make sure to keep the relationship pure, because sexual activity will bond you to him, increase your trust of him, make you less critical of him, and impair your memory of bad experiences with him. Take the sexual element out so that you can see more clearly.

Then, after a few weeks, take a good look at the calendar and listen to your gut. I'll bet you've been ignoring it for some time. You may fear abandonment and you may struggle with self-doubt. We're all afraid of being alone, but perhaps the thing you fear the most —not having a boyfriend—may be the thing that will give you the independence you need in order to find real love.

Like him, you are not a victim. You can't change his behavior but you can change yours. If you're dating him, get out. If you're not yet committed to him, don't even think about it.

6. The Older Guy

When it comes to age discrepancies in relationships, the older a couple is, the less an age gap matters. Nobody really cares if a thirty-six-year-old man is dating a thirty-year-old woman. But when a high school junior is chasing after an eighth grade girl, we've got problems. As a rule of thumb, if you're interested in an older guy, ask yourself one thing: "When I'm *his* age, would I consider dating a guy who is *my* age?" If such a thought makes you laugh out loud, you're better off ending this relationship before it starts.

"Something is keeping me with him," Madison explained to us, regarding her inability to end an unhealthy relationship with her older boyfriend. "Maybe it's just the fact that I can say that I am 'with' someone. I'm looking for compassion, love, a confidant, someone to hold me, make me feel safe and take care of me."

You may have noticed that all the things that Madison longed for in a relationship (compassion, love, a confidant, someone to hold her, make her feel safe and taken care of) are things that a father is supposed to give to his daughter. It's no surprise, then, to learn that she was still looking for these things long after her dad had abandoned her as a child. Even if the father is physically present, he may be emotionally distant from his daughter. When a girl does not receive masculine approval within her home, she'll be fascinated by such approval when it finally appears. If she finds a devoted man, she'll be quick to give her heart away.

As one expert put it:

> One primary result of growing fatherlessness is more boys with guns. Another is more girls with babies. . . . A father plays a distinctive role in shaping a daughter's sexual style and her understanding of the male-female bond. A father's love and involvement builds a daughter's confidence in her own femininity and contributes to her sense that she is worth loving. This sense of love-worthiness gives young women a greater sense of autonomy and independence in later relationships with men.[8]

A girl is supposed to be able to admire her dad and compare all other guys to him. This helps to weed out troublesome guys because the daughter will know how she ought to be treated. Beyond his example, his love gives her strength. In broken English, one teenager from Brazil shared with us her thoughts on her dad, saying: "My father is my mirror, it is my base, is everything to me. I love him very much." Similarly, a twenty-four-year-old wrote:

> When a man gives up on me because I won't sleep with him, because he "needs to know if we're compatible," it's easy to doubt myself, and at such times there's really no substitute for a booming male voice at the other end of the line.[9]

When a girl lacks the "booming male voice" of a loving dad and does not feel valued by her father, she will seek male affirmation elsewhere. What's dangerous is that older guys—who typically lack the social skills to date women their own age—know how to make younger girls feel wanted. In a world where every billboard and magazine cover makes a girl feel as if she's not gorgeous enough, it's refreshing to meet a man who finds her desirable. What the girl does not realize is that she's probably not in love with the guy. She's in love with the feeling of being wanted, because she doesn't even want herself sometimes.

One researcher said that girls without dads often ask themselves, "What do I need to do, and who do I need to be, to find a man who won't abandon me, as the men in my life and my mother's life have done?"[10] Her deep fear of abandonment may influence her to settle for terrible relationships either out of fear that nothing better will come along or out of despair that she would not deserve it if it did.

One young woman wrote us about a number of difficulties in her life, including a distant, abusive, and hard-to-please father:

> I realized what the relationship with my dad had set me up for—the desire to please others and count on them to fill me up. I realized that if I didn't make a conscious decision otherwise, I would let boys do the same thing my father did. I knew that unless I did something, I would do anything to please a boy and keep his so-called "love."

While all this offers an insight into why some younger women prefer older men, it doesn't explain why the older guy is bad. Generally speaking, older guys know one very important fact: Younger girls are more likely to consent to sexual advances because they're eager to win a man's approval. A high school female told me (Jason) that she recently heard one of the senior boys at her school say to his friend, "We already got all the seniors and juniors. Let's go de-virginize the freshmen and sophomores!" Granted, most guys are not so heartless. But the ones who are know how to flatter a girl with sweetness and attention. As they earn a woman's trust, they'll simultaneously wear down her innocence.

One male high school senior was interviewed by the *New York Times* on the subject of who hooks up with whom on his campus. He reported that the freshmen and sophomore girls were the main targets. "Some senior girls won't even look at us, but underclassmen, they look at us like we're gods. Which, of course, we are, so it works out well."[11] I can't imagine why the older girls won't look at them.

Our prejudice against dating older guys is not based on theory. Research shows that three out of every four teenage girls who lose their virginity lose it to an older guy.[12] Also, girls who date guys two or more years older are twice as likely to drink and six times as likely to have tried pot.[13]

Certainly not all older guys fit this description. But a further problem with dating an older guy is that it's not realistic. If a high school sophomore girl is dating a senior, hopefully he'll be spending the next two years in college away from her. Since it's unwise for her to pick the same college for the sake of being with him, the two of them will probably spend the next six years apart. This is not the way to build the foundation of a lasting relationship. But because the younger girl is "living in the moment," she won't bother to think about the future. She won't even pause to ask herself, "When he meets all those college women next year, is he still going to keep pursuing a high schooler?"

Not only is it impractical and morally dangerous to date an older guy, it can also become illegal. The laws vary from state to state, but the general rule is that it's against the law to sleep with a girl who is a minor (under sixteen to eighteen years of age). If a man sleeps with her, he may be charged with statutory rape. It may sound strange to call him a rapist when a girl is willing to sleep with him, but there is a reason they call it this. According to one definition:

> Statutory rape laws are based on the concept that a young person may desire sex but may lack the experience possessed by legal adults to make a mature decision as to whether or not to have sexual contact with a particular person. Thus, the law assumes, even if he or she willingly engages in sexual intercourse with a legal adult, his or her sex partner may well have used tactics of manipulation or deceit against which the younger person has not yet developed sufficient discernment or defense.[14]

It's exciting for a young girl when an older guy is interested in her. Because the female brain matures two to three years earlier than its male counterpart, the immaturity of guys her own age may turn her off.[15] It feels exciting to rise above them. But young women must realize that mature guys don't date younger girls. If the guy were so mature, he'd be dating someone his own age.

7. The Potty Mouth

To put it politely, Mr. "Potty Mouth" is a boyfriend who has a real problem with his expressive language skills. It's important to analyze a guy's words because the speech of a man discloses the intentions of his heart. In the case of a guy who has a potty mouth, his nasty habit can manifest itself in a number of ways.

His speech may reveal his wandering eyes and unfaithful heart. For example, a woman e-mailed me to say, "I was walking with my boyfriend and some friends, and he saw another girl and went on and on with his buddies about how 'hot' she was. I felt totally disrespected." If this is how he talks around his girlfriend, one can only imagine what the conversation is like when she's not there!

If her boyfriend were a true gentleman, he would have kept silent and paid closer attention to his girlfriend as the other woman passed by, so that she would be all the more secure in his love. But he's not that mature. He has probably been like this for years and she should have gotten to know him better before she began dating him. That way, she would have known his character (or lack thereof) and could have avoided him. Although he might not physically cheat on her, she can bet what's going on in his mind when he sees other women.

A second type of potty mouth is the man who sounds like he learned his vocabulary from the wall of a guys' bathroom stall. He may joke or talk about sexual things in a casual and perverted manner to his girlfriend in order to see her reaction. If she knows that sex is something that demands great reverence and she knows how a true gentleman should act, she'll be repulsed by his immaturity.

If she doesn't know these things, she may not realize what he's doing. She'll assume he's kidding. But his goal is simple: Fill her mind with sensual thoughts, and perhaps the curiosity of the conversation will lead to action. Things were no different eighteen centuries ago, when an early Christian writer remarked, "Filthy talk makes us feel comfortable with filthy action."[16]

Because a potty mouth values his life, he'll want the conversations to be hidden from the girl's family. These chats may happen in person, over the phone, via texts, or online. But no matter where they take place, they're a huge red flag.

A third type of potty mouth is the guy who is verbally abusive. In such relationships, the verbal attacks usually revolve around three themes: her body, her brains, or her previous sexual behavior. By attacking her intelligence, attractiveness, and lack of innocence, the abuser undermines his victim's self-esteem. This causes her to feel strangely bonded to him, as if no one else would desire her.

One girl said to me, "My boyfriend of two years sometimes calls me fat or stupid, but then he says he's just kidding. What should I do?" He tells her that she's overweight, and then says he's kidding? Wonderful. Tell a woman she's fat and then tell her to forget what you said. To match his wit, perhaps she should run over his foot with her car and tell him that she's kidding as well. Instead of insulting her and saying he's kidding, why can't he compliment her and say he's serious?

The reason a guy tears down the self-esteem of a woman is because his self-image is so low. When a man has a low self-esteem (which may be caused by emotional abuse within his family), he learns to use insults as a form of emotional manipulation. He feels that the only way you would stay with him is if your self-esteem is lower than his. It says nothing about you, your waistline, or your intelligence. It says everything about his own insecurity and interior wounds.

Without realizing it, a woman in such a relationship rewards and validates her abuser's behavior by staying in the relationship. Her presence teaches him that it is acceptable for him to treat women abusively. Meanwhile, she tries to convince herself that they have something worth keeping.

If you have experienced abuse, you owe it to yourself to seek healing. In order to be helped, you need to reach out. If your abusers are within your own family, don't hesitate to talk to someone outside your home who can assist you. As one young woman bravely remarked in an e-mail, "I'm so tired of biting my tongue with everything. I'm done being silent. I'm done faking things. If I don't speak I won't be heard."

The longer a woman stays in an abusive situation the more she begins to think that she deserves it. This is because it is a quality of abusive men to make the women feel as if their abuse is their fault. His insults reinforce the negative image she already has of herself. On the other hand, when a woman has a high self-esteem, she refuses to be a doormat.

How do you build self-esteem? You get it by making smart decisions, surviving painful moments, and coming out a stronger woman. For starters, dump anyone who doesn't treat you with respect and avoid such guys in the future. You'll be surprised how good this feels. Every time you walk away from the counterfeits of love you get one step closer to the real thing. Whatever you do, do not remain in such a relationship or go back to him out of pity, in an effort to save him from his emotional problems. He needs to learn to bless instead of to curse, and the only way he might learn this is if his attitude ends up costing him the friendships and love he desires.

If you are in a verbally abusive relationship, realize that you have chosen to put up with it. It's been said regarding abusive relationships that the first time the abuse happens, you're a victim. The second time it happens, you're a volunteer. Therefore, the question is not: Should you leave him? The answer to that is obvious. The real question is: Why on earth have you stayed with him so long? You need to answer that question for yourself. Take time off to reestablish your boundaries of respect and love. Let go of him and save your love for a guy who will treat you like a queen.

If any man tries to make you feel like you couldn't end up with anyone better than him, realize that you probably couldn't end up with anyone worse. If you want to prove your intelligence to such a guy, just break up with him.

8. The Tearful Cheater

Some people have favorite movie lines. I collect favorite cheater lines. Allow me to share with you some of the most memorable.

When a famous basketball star was caught having an affair, a press conference was scheduled. With his wife at his side, he offered a lengthy apology. Among other things, I remember him saying that she was the wind beneath his wings, the air he breathes, or something else reminiscent of a 1980's slow-dance song. But here's the question: Was his wife the air he breathes while he was in bed with another woman? And would he be saying these flattering things about her on national television if he had never been caught?

Just as a man is seduced through his eyes, women are often seduced through their ears. Some guys can be so smooth with their words that a woman will forget his actions. My favorite example of this was a high school girl who told me that she discovered that her boyfriend cheated on her. She was thinking of letting him back into the relationship because "he said that when he was kissing that other girl, all he could think about was me!"

My question for her was, "Why can't he be thinking about you while being faithful to you?" But I suppose he was telling the truth. Any guy who cheats has to be thinking about the woman he is cheating on. But he's not thinking about being with her. He's thinking about her smacking him if she finds out.

Because of our male pride, we will usually shift the blame when we know we're guilty. For example, when Adam was caught in the Garden of Eden, he not only blamed Eve, he blamed God! In his words, "The woman whom you put here with me—she gave me fruit from the tree, so I ate it."[17]

Therefore, be on the lookout for cheating excuses. There's never an acceptable excuse for cheating, but here are some to watch out for:

"It was an accident."   Exactly how does that happen? Was he skateboarding around a corner and collided with an unsuspecting female jogger? "Whoops! I'm sorry. Did I just cheat with you? I didn't

even see you there! Just wait 'til I tell my girlfriend about this silly mistake." If you hear the "accident" excuse, tell him that because he cheated on accident, you're breaking up with him on purpose.

"She just started kissing me."   When I hear this one I imagine an Amazon woman forcing herself on a helpless and unsuspecting boyfriend. It's tough to believe that he lacks the physical strength to push a girl away from him. As with excuse number one, girls should have enough intuition to see through the lie. Cheating is always mutual and deliberate. After all, women don't typically kiss guys who aren't sending signals.

"I don't know what happened. We started doing stuff and I just couldn't stop."   If it's true that he could not have stopped, what do you think he would have done if you walked in on the two of them? The fact is that he could have stopped whenever he wanted. He just lacked the motivation.

"I was drunk."   The convenient thing about this excuse is that it gives you a reason to dump him whether he's telling the truth *or* lying.

All four of these cheating excuses are almost always followed by, "Baby, you're the only one for me. I've never felt this way about anyone else. Everything with that other girl, I don't even know what I was thinking. It will never happen again." Sometimes, if you listen closely enough, you can even hear a violin playing in the background. If you recognize any of these lines, run.

If he calls back in a week and says he's a changed man, then he'll still be changed in five years. Tell him to come back then. He may have realized what he's losing, but that is very different than him becoming the man you deserve. (By the way, I am serious about taking a five-year break from anyone who cheats on you.) You may think, "Shouldn't I forgive him?" Sure, forgive him. But don't date him.

If someone has cheated on you, don't beat yourself up. When a guy cheats on a girl, she naturally assumes, "I must not be pretty enough.

Otherwise, he wouldn't have done this." But the cause of cheating is not the absence of physical perfection in the girlfriend. It's caused by the presence of infidelity in the heart of the boyfriend. If beauty guaranteed fidelity, why are Hollywood tabloids littered with stories of adultery?

Also included in the cheating category is the type we call the "Flirting Addict." He's the guy who will flirt with you while he's supposedly committed to someone else. Or he'll "commit" to you while leading the rest of the ladies on. If your boyfriend flirts with other girls, he's cheating on you every time he does it. The same goes for you if you flirt with other guys. Faithfulness is not just about your body. If you have committed to a person, then you have committed to them *as* a person. This implies the fidelity of your eyes, your heart, your imagination, your speech, your intentions, and all that makes you up as a person.

Staying away from a flirty charmer isn't always easy. One young woman said in her letter:

> My ex-boyfriend is seeing this other girl, but he called me the other night. It was really cold, and he offered to come over and keep me warm. I told him not to, but I feel torn, because I really want him back. Why do I still feel attracted to him?

Thankfully, this girl turned down his offer to provide his heating services. But it wasn't an easy decision. No matter how much of a cheater or a jerk a guy might be, a girl is always drawn to some extent to the fact that she is desired. There's something flattering in it. But any girl who feels enamored by such attention should remember that he who cheats *with* you will cheat *on* you. Therefore, stay away from any guy who has his eye on you when he's with another girl. His smile may seem cute now, but think about the long term: Who wants to marry a flirty guy?

Wouldn't you prefer that your boyfriend not try to go out of his way to get other girls to notice him? Why does he need their attention anyway? Each time he flirts with someone else it sends the message to you that you are not enough for him. Even if he isn't sleeping with these women, his flirting is still disrespectful to you and it's unacceptable in a loving relationship. He may be sweet and charming to you, but know that unfaithful men tend to be very polite because being a jerk usually doesn't help their chances. It's easy to talk about being boyfriend/girlfriend and to get sentimental over the phone, but the real value of love is proved by being 100 percent faithful.

In the future, remember: If you can't trust the man you are dating, then you're dating the wrong man. When a woman feels a bit hesitant, she's usually on to something. Talk to friends and family to see if it is a reasonable intuition or if it's mistrust that's lingering from a previous experience. Also, don't rush a relationship. Cheating would be almost nonexistent if people took the chance to get to know each other as friends—for a long time—before dating. This way, the unfaithful people would never have the chance to cheat on anyone, because no one would want to date them.

9. *The Spiritual Midget*

Imagine being married someday and walking down the hallway toward your bedroom at about 8:00 at night. You silently peek into your little daughter's room and see your husband kneeling by her bedside as he teaches her how to pray. Leaning your head against the door, you take a deep breath and thank God for both of them.

Or imagine leaving the house on a Sunday morning as you head off to church with your daughter. You sweep her up and look over your shoulder to see your husband in his usual Sunday morning spot: watching TV. At church, you can't help but notice all the other families around you. You say your usual prayers for your husband's conversion, and then return home to find him in the same place.

Both men may be faithful husbands and caring fathers. But if you would prefer the first scenario over the second, then don't date spiritual midgets. The spiritual midget is a guy who may have plenty of other positive qualities but is unable to lead you closer to God. He may even attempt to undermine your faith, asking how you could trust the Bible or believe in God. He may have plenty of questions but he won't spend much time looking for answers.

Faith is hard enough without having to battle your soulmate over it. In the future, know that if a relationship is holding you back spiritually, then that is an unmistakable sign that the relationship is not of God. You may say, "He's not like that. He respects my faith and doesn't try to pull me away from God." But is he capable of leading you closer to Him? For all eternity, that's all that really matters.

10. Mr. I-Don't-Have-Enough-Social-Skills-to-Meet-Girls-without-the-Internet

When the majority of information you know about a guy comes from his Internet profile, it's time to move on. If you think a relationship is becoming serious because you talked online for four hours last night, it's time for you to take up some outdoor hobbies.

Guys who spend vast amounts of time chatting online often do so because they lack the confidence to meet women in public. It also gives them a sense of control because they can present to you whatever image of themselves they desire. (Obviously, these comments also apply to the women who search for guys online.)

Such relationships are usually short-lived and potentially dangerous. Especially in long-distance relationships, the couple often forms a romanticized image of the relationship since they lack the day-to-day interaction that grounds relationships in reality. When a couple begins their relationship online, they have a preconceived notion of the other person's identity. Even after they meet, it's not easy to forget these expectations and to see the real person.

It takes years of seeing each other on a daily basis for two people to truly get to know one another. For example, have you ever noticed how married couples say that they really didn't know the person until years into marriage, while dating couples who are infatuated feel that they know everything about each other? Take your time and you won't be fooled.

In the meantime, if you hope to meet your soulmate, you need to get out of the house. Unless your future spouse is a mailman, he's not likely to come knocking at your door. But be selective in where you meet men. According to a survey of males, their expectations of a relationship differ according to where they meet a woman.[18] If the first meeting takes place at a bar or dance club, men are more likely to expect a short-lived, physically intense fling. In their words, she's less likely to be "marriage material." If they meet online, men rightfully complain of misrepresentation and deception. As a result, in a survey of single men, not one reported a long-term relationship as the result of an Internet contact.[19] However, if the meeting is through a friend, church, or workplace, the potential relationship takes on more potential significance.

With all of this having been said, there are Christian dating web sites that help singles to create healthy relationships and happy marriages. But these services are a far cry from a pair of strangers meeting in a chat room. Nonetheless, there's really no such thing as online dating. You might meet a person online, but any real relationship needs to take place away from the computer, face-to-face.

Who Is Left?

After reading our list of guys to avoid, you may be thinking, "The list makes sense, but there's one minor problem: The only men left are already married or in the seminary . . . or in a nursing home. I would know, because your list just described most of my ex-boyfriends!"

For obvious reasons, many girls feel discouraged by the quality— or lack of it—of modern men. But it is within women's power to remedy the situation. If you study the history of civilizations, you'll notice that women are traditionally the gatekeepers of morality. It has been said that if women do not insist on manners, no one else will. Or, in the words of the nineteenth century philosopher Søren Kierkegaard, "Woman is the conscience of man."[20] Believe it or not, men take your power for granted. One stated:

> The higher the love, the more demands will be made on us to conform
> to that idea. To a great extent the level of any civilization is the level

of its womanhood. When a man loves a woman, he has to become worthy of her. The higher her virtue, the more noble her character, the more devoted she is to truth, justice, and goodness, the more a man has to aspire to be worthy of her. The history of civilization could actually be written in terms of the level of its women.[21]

This does not mean that it is the woman's responsibility to be the chastity cop or that men have a right to pressure a woman until she orders him to stop. There should be mutual respect and accountability. But the fact remains that women possess a unique power to shape cultures. Men look to you to learn how you wish be treated. If a man behaves rudely and women do nothing to reprimand him, he learns that such behavior is acceptable. But when women, as a culture, expect to be treated with dignity, something remarkable happens: Men discover that they'll have to be become gentlemen if they wish to enjoy the company of women.

Our culture did not form its morals (or lack thereof) overnight. Nor will society change in an instant. Men won't passionately respect all women just because you rediscover your dignity. But when a culture of ladies arises, a culture of gentlemen will follow.

Take a look at the list of guys to avoid: Flip-Flopper, Problem Child, Walking Hormone, Smooth Criminal, Control Freak, Older Guy, Potty Mouth, Tearful Cheater, Spiritual Midget, and Mr. Internet. Now imagine a man who has the opposite traits: He would be a faithful, mature, pure, honest, respectful, independent, and sincere spiritual leader. If you consider such a man to be an impossible catch, then you'll never bother to set your standards high enough to attract him. But such men do exist. They come to us and ask, "Where are all the modest girls? If they want to be treated like ladies, how come they don't talk, dress, or dance like ladies?"

Don't ignore your conscience or give up on the deepest desires of your heart. If you're in an unhealthy relationship, get out. Don't squander your life trying to change a guy or hoping he will miraculously improve. You're better than that.

DATE WITH PURPOSE

"Go kiss her!" my friends prodded. "Yeah, all her friends say you should." I (Jason) looked across the schoolyard and saw my sixth grade girlfriend huddling among a band of giggling girlfriends. She was nearly a foot taller than I was, so I wasn't sure how to pull off such a stunt. One of my buddies was less than sensitive about our height discrepancy, and said, "I even went into the P.E. room and flipped a bucket upside-down so you can stand on it to kiss her!" Thankfully, the recess bell rang before any more emotional trauma was caused. She and I dated through the end of the school year and enjoyed a few romantic dates, driven to the mall in my mom's wood-paneled minivan. Eventually, she broke up with me because I forgot that I was dating her. I know, high maintenance.

Such a pointless relationship can be expected from a pair of eleven-year-olds. But nowadays, thirty-year-olds are just as guilty! Never before have there been so many people dating without knowing what they're doing or where they're heading. I remember one young woman saying that she dated a guy because "it was more or less just something new to try." While that's a good reason to taste a new appetizer at a restaurant, it's not an adequate reason to date. She eventually broke up with him because "I basically lost interest." Again, that's a good reason to stop watching a boring commercial on TV, but it's not a reason to end a relationship.

If a woman dates for the sake of experiencing new things and ends a relationship when it gets old, she'll never find love. No matter how perfect a man seems at first, he'll eventually get on your nerves. If you hope to establish lasting love, you must learn to love beyond the feelings.

First Comes Love

Driving back from the beach one day, I turned on the radio and heard the deejay inviting people to call the station and offer him their definition of love. Caller number one talked about "warm fuzzies," and caller number two said something awkward about perspiration and nervousness. Call after call, love was defined by feelings and emotions.

If this is how we understand love, then our relationships are doomed before they even begin. Some may say:

> But isn't there such a thing as love at first sight? Back in high school, my history teacher said that when he first saw his wife across the street, he knew it was love. He walked through the traffic, immediately asked her out to lunch, and proposed to her right there.

Is there such a thing as love at first sight? In order to answer this, one has to define love. Most people think of love as an exhilarating emotion. In that case, lots of people experience "love" at first sight. But if love is a decision to do what is best for the other, then most people don't even think of it when they first meet a person.

Usually, love at first sight occurs when two people are immediately infatuated, and the relationship ends up working out. But the reason it lasts is not because of the mysterious feeling they had when they first laid eyes upon each other. It works out because they choose to love each other through acts of kindness and sacrifice, long after the infatuation fades.

One brain researcher said:

> Many people . . . think the loss of romantic high of early love is a sign that a couple's relationship is going south. In reality, however, the pair may be just moving into an important, longer-term phase of the relationship, driven by additional neurological circuits. Scientists

argue that the "attachment network" is a separate brain system—one that replaces the giddy intensity of romance with a more lasting sense of peace, calm, and connection.[1]

The feelings of "being in love" are exciting, but they should not be confused with love itself. A person can make a promise to love, but no one can make a promise to feel. Emotions come and go. If we equate emotions with love, we'll conclude that when the feelings fade that love has gone away. When this happens, you hear people saying things like, "I love you. I'm just not *in* love with you any more." If this is the case, then that person never loved the other person to begin with. They were in love with their own emotions.

Dating: What's the Point?

When you consider the wrong reasons to date, I (Crystalina) have found that the list is endless. Some girls date to bolster their image or popularity. Others seek commitment because they fear loneliness. Meanwhile, some feel an overwhelming pressure to date or hope to find the intimacy they think everyone else is receiving. But some women don't even know why they're dating. They'll jump into a relationship not so much because they have a good reason to, but because they see no reason not to: "He's cute and he asked me. So why not?"

Although there are a million wrong reasons to date, there's only one right reason: to find a spouse. Such a narrow purpose may seem rigid or old-fashioned, and perhaps it is. But if thousands of cultures throughout history have linked courtship to marriage, their collective wisdom might be worth considering.

It may be old-fashioned to date for the sake of finding a spouse, but a surprising number of people have found it to be a fresh alternative to the stale and mindless dating circus. Those who have spent years dating for superficial reasons often complain about how much of their lives were spent going nowhere. After all, if you're not dating with your eyes on forever, you're just dating to break up. In other words, it's divorce practice.

What is a girl to do? When it comes to dating, the woman is often told of all the things that she shouldn't be doing. Although the guidance is often needed, it still leaves her wondering what she is supposed to do. She feels left alone to find answers to her deep questions about love and intimacy. As a result, she may jump into bad situations because her emotions and attractions are strong while her direction is weak.

Imagine how many painful relationships began because neither person considered the following simple fact: Just because you like a guy, this is not a sign from heaven that you're supposed to date him. Throughout your life, you'll meet countless men with great charm and personality . . . who would be disastrous to date or marry. When girls don't understand this, they blindly follow their emotions into some nightmarish relationships.

How do you know when to say yes to a guy? Here are some principles of courting that have worked for centuries.

1. Begin with a foundation of friendship.   The taller a building is, the greater the foundation must be. Beneath the world's tallest building, the Burj Khalifa, are more than 100,000 tons of concrete and steel. Similarly, the foundation of a relationship determines its stability. If you want to build a lasting love, begin with a long friendship.

When I met Jason, we fell in love the day we met. But because we hoped it would last, we didn't rush forward. Instead, we took the time to build the foundation of a pure and simple friendship. Although I did say that we "fell in love," the virtue of love is not something that just happens to couples. It is a life-long task. Hollywood tells you that love happens in an instant, but Hollywood marriages usually last just about as long. True love takes time. One must have patience, because love itself is patient.

In his book *Boy Meets Girl*, Joshua Harris writes:

> Patience is important not only in waiting for the right time to *start* a relationship, but also in allowing it to unfold at a *healthy pace*. Impatience rushes everything. It urges us to skip the time and attention a healthy friendship requires and to jump straight into emotional and physical intimacy.[2]

How many relationships can you count in which the guy turned out to be entirely different than the girl imagined? Had she taken her time to get to know him better as a friend, she could have avoided such a surprise.

Don't feel stifled by the idea of taking your time to build the foundation of a relationship. The season of pure friendship with a guy should be uncomplicated, free of drama, and enjoyable. If it's not, don't expect anything different by dating him—or marrying him.

2. Only commit to a guy if you can see yourself marrying him. Once you've built the foundation of a lasting friendship, you should be able to determine if the guy is marriage material. If he's not, then don't commit. How do you know what qualities to look for? Here are ten essential questions to ask yourself before dating:

- Can I trust him with all my heart?
- Does he value my goals and dreams in life?
- Does he treat all women with respect, not just the ones he aims to impress?
- Has he recently broken up with another girl? If so, take it extra slow and make sure he's had time on his own for a while.
- What do his ex-girlfriends think of him? Take a serious look at why his last relationship ended.
- Does he care about my happiness, or is he self-absorbed?
- Does he make me a better person, or am I spending my time trying to fix him?
- Would he be a great dad?
- After spending time with him, do I feel cherished instead of used and afraid?
- When it comes to getting to heaven, is he a helpmate or a hindrance?

3. Only commit to a guy if marriage is within reach. There is no point of dating if marriage is a decade away. Therefore, dating in high school is pointless. Beyond the challenges of purity, consider the issue of practicality. If the purpose of dating is to find a spouse, what are the odds of you starting a relationship now that lasts through college and leads to marriage? If you're in high school, realize that long-term, long-distance relationships rarely last, but such friendships often do. Therefore, enjoy time socializing with members of the opposite sex without giving in to the cultural pressure to date prematurely. If you just arrived at college, take your time before jumping into commitment.

4. Be clear about your commitment.   Don't "kinda" date anyone. If the guy isn't enough of a gentleman to communicate his commitment to you clearly, then he doesn't deserve to be with you. When girls let guys "kinda" commit to them, the guy won't respect the girl because she is too timid. You may wonder, "What am I supposed to do? Give him an ultimatum and demand that he make me his girlfriend?" No. Just keep your distance until he makes up his mind. If he doesn't, then don't settle for the kind of quasi-relationship that often leads to being friends with benefits.

5. Involve your family.   You may notice in your own relationships that the more mature and healthy they are, the more you involve your family in them. But to the extent that they are immature and impure, you tend to isolate yourself. Our family members should be our allies when it comes to finding love. If you feel as if they're your rivals, do what you can to heal your family before you begin one of your own.

6. Seek the will of God.   If you want a relationship to have purpose and meaning, it cannot be isolated from your ultimate purpose and meaning in life. God Himself said that it is not good for you to be alone. But that desire for union must first be filled by Him. Before you can truly love a mate, God wants you to be secure and content in His love alone. Only then will you be able to allow Him to love others through you.

Otherwise, a relationship can take the place of God. Instead of being a reflection of God's love, it becomes a replacement for Him. After all, no man's affections can replace the security of knowing the love of God. If your relationship with God is secondary to your relationship with a man, the human relationship can grow into an idol. It will reign over your heart and dictate your level of happiness. Not only is this unfair to the man, it will ultimately end in disappointment. For things to run more smoothly, put God first and let Him worry about the rest.

Love Your Spouse before You Meet Him

"I, Crystalina, take you, Jason, to be my husband. I promise to be true to you in good times and in bad, in sickness and in health. I will love you and honor you all the days of my life."

Just as I spoke these words on the day of our wedding, every bride will do the same for her groom. You may notice in these promises that the couple vow to love one another all the days of their lives. But if you intend to honor your future husband all the days of your life, why not include the days spent prior to meeting him? Have you ever thought about loving your spouse before you meet him?

Because you're not married yet, you're not bound by these promises. You're not being unfaithful to a future spouse by dating others before him. The idea of loving a future spouse might seem illogical to some people because not every woman who wants to get married is going to get married. Therefore, you can't technically love and honor a man who does not exist. Still, you can practice for the love you hope to find. If you hope to marry, then begin thinking about the heart of your future spouse. Consider how the life you lead before meeting him will bring him either joy or sorrow.

Although we are focusing on finding your soulmate, it's not enough to think only of the love you hope to find. A woman must also focus on the kind of love she ought to give. A teenager wrote to us and said that in order to keep her hopes alive and her standards high, she began writing love letters to her future husband, as I had done for Jason before meeting him. The teen wrote:

> Writing things down and imagining someone loving me enough to reach the point of reading them really makes high school a much smaller deal, and also makes me really want to make my future as successful as possible, not only for myself but for him, too.

If you wish to get married, one of the best ways to prepare for marital love is to practice purity of heart, mind, and body. Granted, when most people hear the word "purity" they think of prudishness. It isn't seen as a virtue, but as a neurotic and unhealthy view of sexuality. For example, if we told you that a guy was "pure," you might smile to yourself, and think, "Oh, that's cute. I guess he just can't find a date." But a man's purity has nothing to do with how many women he's dated. When a man is pure, it means that he's free from the selfish attitude of using women and is therefore capable of authentic love. Now we imagine he sounds more appealing to you.

If a woman truly longs for love, she might need to change the way she views chastity. She may need to let go of her old-fashioned idea of purity as something restrictive and boring and open her eyes to the fact that it makes us free to love.

Perhaps the first thing to know about purity is that it is not something that accrues over time, according to how long you've been abstinent. Nor is it the same thing as virginity, because there are plenty of non-virgins who have become pure, and just as many virgins who are anything but innocent. Regardless of your past, you can be pure. But it is something you must choose.

The Point of Purity

A few months before our wedding, I (Jason) received a phone call from England asking if we would be willing to be part of a BBC documentary on chastity. Apparently news had traveled to Europe that there was an American couple who wasn't living or sleeping together prior to marriage. It sounded like a fun opportunity, so we figured, "Why not?" The producer and her camera crew flew out to California and followed us on a date in the Gaslamp Quarter of downtown San Diego. They hung out with a few of my groomsmen and me as we surfed, and accompanied Crystalina as she tried on her wedding dress for the first time. The host of the show asked us all kinds of awkward questions as to why we weren't sleeping together and did her best to comprehend such a strange concept.

A few months after Crystalina and I returned from our honeymoon, we received a package from England containing the footage that was aired for all of the United Kingdom to see. Excitedly, she and I turned on the TV and hopped on the couch together to see how our story would be told. The show was called *Anna in Wonderland,* and featured our interviewer, Anna, who traveled the world experiencing different, bizarre cultures. As the closing credits rolled, a preview of the next episode was advertised: "Join us next week, when Anna visits a colony of vampires!" After a little research—albeit somewhat late on my part—I discovered that Anna had also done shows on female professional wrestlers, psychics, prostitutes, and people who believe they have animals living inside of them . . . and now, my wife and me.

Apparently, the idea that a young couple would wait until they are married to consummate their love is so bizarre that we're on par with a colony of vampires.

If you decide to live a pure life, don't expect the world to understand your decision. Here's why: The sexual revolution of the twentieth century was spawned out of a desire to rebel against an unhealthy, prudish, Victorian notion of human sexuality. As a result, those who buy into the idea of promiscuity as an expression of their freedom naturally associate the idea of chastity with the uptight mentality that was crushed underfoot by the sexual revolution of Margaret Sanger, Alfred Kinsey, and Hugh Hefner. With no desire to turn back the clock and regress toward a rigid and frigid ethos of sexuality, many people have yet to understand that purity renounces prudery.

Chastity is not about repressing one's desires or refusing to acknowledge the goodness and beauty of human sexuality. Instead of giving into the shamelessness of *Playboy* or the shamefulness of the prudes, it rejects and rises above both unbalanced attitudes of intimacy. Chastity does not blush at the sight of a female ankle, nor fail to blush when too much is shown. It frames human sexuality within the context of human love—which is something that both the puritans and the playboys forgot to do.

Although these distinctions are helpful to learn, the most compelling argument for the virtue of chastity is the couples who practice it. Unfortunately, modern women rarely see chaste relationships. They do exist. For example, in their book *A Case for Chastity*, Heather Gallagher recounts a memorable evening from college:

> The night after my college roommate lost her virginity the girls came rushing into our room to celebrate. Beth and her boyfriend had been dating for years; therefore, most agreed, "It's about time!" After Beth described some details, everyone in the room started sharing their first times. Two had lost their virginity with long-term boyfriends, another in the back seat of a car with a guy she never wanted to see again, and then it was my turn. Though I wasn't part of the "club," I shared my most romantic experience.
>
> Ryan and I had been friends for months, talking on the phone for several hours every night. We shared so much with each other and connected on many levels. We were also very attracted to each other. One summer night, he showed up at my house. It was late, so we escaped to a nearby park and walked through the woods together. He was so sweet in the way that he treated me—with total respect. We didn't even kiss that night, but we held hands for the first time . . . and experienced the beauty of being close to someone you care for deeply. The room was silent when I finished describing all the fun and romantic aspects of the night. One friend looked at me and asked, "Heather, why is your story so much better than ours?"[1]

Heather knew from experience that chastity does not merely prevent problems such as unwed pregnancy and STDs. Its deepest allure is not what it prevents, but the blessings it brings.

Ten Benefits of a Chaste Life

1. Chastity weeds out users. "Restricting sex to one married spouse," one man complained, "is like buying a cable package that provides just one channel."[2] Odds are, you've come across men like this. What's so depressing about their mentality is that they enter into relationships for the same reason they subscribe to a cable provider: to be entertained.

One of the beauties of chastity is that you won't have to deal with such men for long. You know—the ones who argue that your morals are spoiling the relationship? In the future, if any man insinuates that your desire for purity is driving a wedge between the two of you, then promptly inform him that this is the very purpose of your morality. Chastity unites lovers and divides those who lust. It's an armor that helps you to defend love from selfishness and aggressiveness. It's a fire that purifies a relationship, burning away all that is false.

Purity invites a man to be one. Many guys will balk at the invitation, but that's their choice. You owe it to yourself at least to extend the challenge. If a woman doesn't rely on purity to sift out unworthy suitors, how is she to know if a man truly loves her? Is she to trust in his flattering words or thoughtful gifts? A more reliable measure of his integrity is his capacity to sacrifice.

One young woman e-mailed us, humored by a teenage boy's attempt to seduce her. In his less-than-romantic invitation, he texted her, "If you do it with me, I'll probably ask you out sooner." If a woman doesn't know how to turn down such offers, consider what happens. One girl lost her virginity to a high school classmate because she hoped he would ask her to the prom. She explained:

> I go over to his house and he basically ignored me except for the hour before I have to leave. And he decided he wanted me to do more stuff with him and then have sex. And I just couldn't say no. Because that's the kind of person I am. I didn't really enjoy it and we stopped talking maybe a week after that, probably sooner. So I didn't even get my date to prom from it. I dunno. I don't really talk to my friends about this because they're all like, "You finally lost it?!?! That's great!" And it's not. My first time doesn't even mean anything to me. It wasn't fun. And I know I didn't want it.

Consider how different her story would have been if she practiced purity. She still might not have had a date for the prom, but she wouldn't have ended up with the heartbreak either. Sometimes a woman learns from such tragic relationships. Other times it takes decades to admit the damage that has been caused. Another woman shared with us that she married a man after becoming pregnant by him. She told us:

> I came to find out when I was nine months pregnant that my husband was a porn addict and generally very immature. But hello? I was stuck now. We have been married now for sixteen years, and my husband still is a porn addict. He has always been emotionally distant, I believe due to his porn addiction, and his "false intimacy" throughout the years with other women. I have cried myself to sleep many nights because of the pain and loneliness of my life choice. He has been laid off from every job he's ever had, in eighteen years. Why did I not notice this in the first few years of our courtship? Because we were too busy having sex, instead of getting to know each other better. I have never ever been really certain if my husband has ever really loved me enough to forego other women, or just loved me period. To this day, I suppose I will never know if he loves me at all, or was ready for marriage.

2. *Chastity brings clarity.* When a woman decides to save sexual intimacy for marriage, she doesn't have to wonder about her standards. In the words of a chaste university student, "I will never have to agonize over how long to wait before having sex with my boyfriend."[3] Such moral clarity frees a couple to focus on more important matters —like discerning marriage while falling in love for the right reasons. When couples become sexually intimate prior to marriage, it's easy to waste months or years before coming to the conclusion that the relationship isn't going anywhere.

Contrary to what many assume, chastity doesn't require the woman to be heartless, untouchable, or cold. Quite the opposite is true. Wendy Shalit, who authored a brilliant defense of purity in her book *A Return to Modesty*, stated:

> First, by not having sex before marriage, you are insisting on your right to take these things seriously, when many around you do not seem to. By reserving a part of you for someone else, you are insisting on your right to keep something sacred; you are welcoming the prospect of someone else making an enduring private claim to you, and you to

him. But more significantly, not having sex before marriage is a way of insisting that the most interesting part of your life will take place *after* marriage, and if it's more interesting, maybe then it will last.[4]

Some people might object, "How do you know if you want to marry a person if you don't sleep with him or her?" But how do you know you should marry him once you've slept together? If anything, you are less objective, because sex isn't supposed to be a pass-or-fail test for potential spouses. Sex doesn't help you to get to know a guy. It clouds your judgment, and often causes unmarried couples to think they have more in common than they really do. If they do marry, their lack of compatibility often comes to the surface later.

Imagine a woman who married a man who felt more lust for her than love. Over time, the sexual values will play a lesser role. Once the fog of lust begins to burn away, a clearer vision of the partner begins to emerge. One of the blessings of purity is that it brings such faults to the surface sooner rather than later.

It's reasonable to want to know a person well before you marry him or her, yet some forms of knowledge need to wait. When intercourse is mentioned in the Bible, the Hebrew word *yada'* is often used, which means to "know" a person. For example, "Adam knew Eve his wife, and she conceived."[5] It's an idiom for the way a wife and husband reveal themselves to one another within marriage.

People who want to know everything about a partner before marriage—including the intimacy of sex—are actually saying that they have little faith in the relationship. Imagine a lover saying to his fiancée, "You know, we really get along, but I need to see how you are in bed before I'll commit to spending my life with you." What does that say? If he marries her and she fails to thrill him sexually, will he love her less? If so, then one can be sure that he never loved her to begin with.

You can never completely know a person before marriage, because it takes a lifetime to fully know a person. Besides, if having intercourse allowed you to know a person completely, then how many women do you want your husband to have known completely? How many men in your life do you want to know completely? We're willing to bet that most women would rather know one.

3. Chastity elevates your attractions.   Chastity will not only shape a man's estimation of you, it will also cause you to look at him differently. One female journalist from London swore off sex for a year in order to take a retreat from the empty relationships and casual hookups that, in her words, "came to define my 20s." She said:

> I soon noticed that I was being drawn to a different type of man. Because sex was out of the question, I wanted someone I could talk to. Instead of flirtatiousness, I looked for unglamorous traits like loyalty and kindness. . . . Back then, I'd have been looking for an instant, lightning bolt connection, rather than the kind that might take a little longer to manifest itself—the kind that might prove more enduring in the long run.[6]

The "lightning bolt" connection she described may be exciting at first. But if such chemistry is expected to sustain a couple, their relationship will collapse under the weight of its own superficiality.

4. Chastity liberates a woman from drama.   Apart from being freed from the obvious risks of disease and pregnancy, chastity affords a woman with freedom from unnecessary mind games and drama. Because she has a backbone, she doesn't have to worry about questions like, "Am I being used?," and is able to dismiss the men who hope to seduce her through manipulation.

The sexual revolution promised women power through their newfound sexual liberation, but promiscuity empowers nobody. It merely encourages women to think of their bodies as bargaining chips for gaining control of their relationships. But if a woman needs to resort to giving away her body in order to feel a sense of control, it shows how powerless she has become. If a notion of freedom is not based upon the truth of who a woman is, it cannot liberate her.

The results of believing a false notion of freedom are hard to ignore. In 2005, the *Washington Times* published an article entitled, "Depression: A New Sexually Transmitted Disease."[7] The author reported that according to the *American Journal of Preventive Medicine*, depression often follows early sexual activity. The study followed over 13,000 middle and high school students for two years. Of the abstinent teens, only 4 percent experienced depression. On the other hand, girls who were sexually promiscuous were eleven times as likely to report feeling depressed. What's significant about this study is that the depression did not cause the sexual activity, but vice versa. Depression did not predict behavior. The behavior predicted the depression.

Anyone who works closely with young women knows that sexually active girls often smile constantly to cover up the fact that they are confused, lonely, and frustrated. Some of them we've met are scared to cry because they're afraid that if they start they won't be able to stop. This is not to say that every sexually active single woman is miserable. But for many of them, sex is used to cover up something unhappy in their lives.

When I (Crystalina) was sexually active in high school, I would show up at school with a grand smile on my face. Although miserable, I took pride in the fact that others were jealous of my relationships. I fed off the façade. But eventually, everyone's mask comes off. Mine came off when I was alone, crying at night or flipping over a pregnancy test in the morning. Those who envied my life never knew the anguish I felt walking through the halls on Monday morning after doing something stupid with a guy over the weekend. They never saw my tears when my boyfriend hit me, insulted me, cheated on me, and walked out of my life with another girl.

All this drama ceased the day I decided to be pure and respect myself. Surely this transition to a pure life wasn't without its own set of trials. Some guys mocked me, and many of my "friends" didn't accept my new lifestyle and promptly walked out of my life. But for the first time in my life I chose to be single instead of calling on boys to rescue me from myself. I knew it was time to handle life without using a boy for a crutch. Meanwhile, the gossip took time to fade away as I established a new reputation for myself. But every trial I endured only made me stronger, as opposed to the drama of impurity that only made me weaker.

5. Chastity heightens anticipation. The Christian viewpoint of sex is often seen as nothing more than the suppression of one's passions. The commandments are seen as restrictive forces that rob people of sex and deprive them of joyful experiences that should rightfully be theirs. But is the Church trying to cheat you out of happiness and steal from you the thrill of having many partners? The Church is not robbing you of anything, but proposing to you a question: "What about the thrill of knowing only one?"

Since I (Jason) have never seen *The Notebook*, *Twilight*, *Titanic*, *Letters from Juliet*, or *Pride and Prejudice*, I can't offer you any examples of love from popular romantic movies. But from a guy's perspective, I can tell you about what I have seen. In *Braveheart*, when William Wallace weds the woman he has adored since childhood, he says, "I will love you my whole life. You and no other." When King Leonidas of the Spartans cries out before his bloody death in the movie *300*, what does he yell? "My queen! My wife. My love." When Maximus Decimus Meridius in *Gladiator* is invited by Caesar to be the next emperor of Rome, what does he prefer to such glory and power? To return home to his wife. Central to the plot of these gory, chest-thumping, testosterone-filled movies is the notion of love for a single woman.

The idea of a single love is far more exhilarating, romantic, and passionate than the idea of distributing your love to many, as if love could be divided. Love is expressed most perfectly through sacrifice, and this is why you will never find a real love story that lacks it. This is what makes them so romantic.

Today, our culture divorces sensuality from sacrifice. In the place of a vibrant love, we're shown empty lust and then promised that it will satisfy us. When the Church tells us to walk away from love's hollow counterfeit, the world wants us to believe that our freedom is being stripped away.

This bogus idea of freedom isn't merely pushed on teenagers. In her book *Girls Gone Mild*, Wendy Shalit points out that Care Bears and Hello Kitty now market thongs for grade-schoolers, and department stores feature "push-up" trainer bras. Commenting on how pervasive the pornographic culture has become, she writes, "There is no longer any mystery or power to sex—it is just expected that everything will be sexual, and so nothing is. There is nothing to wait for, or to look forward to."[8]

A young woman once e-mailed me about the decision she and her boyfriend made to begin practicing purity for the first time in their relationship. She noticed, "It's actually a whole lot more romantic." This woman was beginning to discover what is so painfully absent in the lives of the unchaste: anticipation.

When couples save sexual intimacy for marriage, they discover that chastity doesn't inhibit excitement, but heightens it. The reason they don't surrender to their temptations is because they have a goal in mind. As the philosopher Dietrich von Hildebrand explained, "Chastity means keeping the sexual secret hidden. . . . [T]he value of every gift is enhanced, if it exists solely for him to whom it is given."[9] With such an outlook on sexual intimacy, it's understandable why he said, "Purity is something wholly positive, beautiful, and attractive."[10]

6. *Chastity frees you to be yourself.*   Sexual relationships prior to marriage often stunt the personal development of the woman. Consider the case of a high school girl. If she sleeps with a guy, where does this leave her? Is it realistic to hope that a sexually active high school relationship will last through college and end in a happy marriage? Millions of girls dream that everything will end up that way, and just as many look back with broken hearts only to see how naïve they were.

Suppose the two stay together until graduation. What then? Will she go away to a college of her choice to pursue her career dreams, or will her life be determined by where he's going? If she follows him to his college or stays close to home because she's afraid of missing or losing him, what opportunities are being lost?

Years upon years of a woman's life can be spent on sexual relationships that lack a future. If such relationships are abstinent, they will typically consume a much smaller portion of the woman's emotional and mental energy. Even an adult single woman can recognize how sexual relationships often hold her back in life. How often do they help her to fulfill her potential as a woman? More often than not, they reduce her potential to what she can offer a man instead of what she can do for the world.

As a music journalist in New York, Dawn Eden lived a wild life prior to her conversion. She established a successful career and entered numerous relationships, but it wasn't until she embraced a pure life that she discovered who God was calling her to be as a woman. She remarked, "Through chastity—and only through chastity—can all the graces that are part of being a woman come to full flower in you."[11]

7. *Chastity expresses love.*   Chastity not only reveals the quality of a man, it also tests a couple's ability to love one another. As you know, men are not the only ones who experience sexual desires. All too often, the sexual desires of women are overlooked because the raging hormones of men tend to dominate any conversation regarding chastity. The struggle is a mutual one, and it is not uncommon for the woman to feel remorse for having urged the guy to make the relationship more physical.

In order for a couple to be pure, both people must deny themselves and practice self-restraint. Such a love does not throw a wet blanket on the passions. Rather, it ignites a deeper form of love. It tests a couple's love in order to see if they are willing to sacrifice. Are they willing to do what's best for each other, or do they succumb to what feels good in the moment?

Sex is often thought of as "making love." But few people consider that abstinence from sex can also be an expression of love. If love means doing what is best for your beloved, consider how many people you are loving when you practice chastity.

By respecting your body and soul, you're expressing love for yourself. You're doing what's best for you, instead of catering to men. By living in a noble way, you also bring honor and joy to your family. If you're going to get married one day, imagine the joy on your husband's face when he discovers that you've been waiting for him. If you've already made some mistakes, know that you can still give him every day from now until then. If the wait seems long, remember that you're not just waiting for a sacrament; you're waiting for a spouse. If you can put a face on your sacrifice, it becomes easier.

Through chaste living, a woman also expresses love for the men she dates. In fact, chastity and love depend on each other for their existence. A person cannot be chaste unless she is motivated by love. Although a person can be abstinent for any number of reasons, love alone fuels a passion for true purity. In the words of one young woman who decided with her boyfriend to save sex for marriage, "We both agreed that it would ruin the relationship and we're way too in love for that!"

Through living a pure life, you're also loving your future children by not conceiving them before you are able to care for them properly. For example, kids born to single mothers are far more likely to become involved in crime, live under the poverty level, have lower paying jobs, experience increased behavioral and emotional problems, become involved in drugs, do poorly in school, become divorced, be on welfare as adults, and become unwed parents, continuing the cycle of fatherlessness.[12] In response to this, some say, "We can't base our lives on statistics." These are the people who could not care any less about their children.

Most importantly, your decision to be chaste is an expression of your love for God. It brings Him joy. Have you ever considered that you—as a finite human being—are able to increase the amount of joy in heaven? It's true: The Bible speaks of how heaven rejoices over those who turn away from sin.[13] Bring joy to the heart of God and live in a way that will make Him smile upon you. Living with this desire to glorify God will help you to advance more quickly in a life of virtue than anything else. Live for Him, and love for Him.

8. Chastity expresses hope.   At the age of thirteen, Hannah received a purity ring from her parents. Through the difficult years of high school and college, she often looked at the silver band as a sign of hope—that no matter how depressing her situation might be, she was holding out for something greater. Years later, when her fiancé proposed to her, she took the ring off and gave it to him, telling him that she saved it for him, just as she had saved herself for him. He thanked her for the gift, and without her knowing, had the jeweler who was making his wedding band melt the silver of her ring into the gold of his. As her husband, he now wears the two metals blended together as one ring.

By remaining firm in her purity, Hannah showed courage in her hope. Her standards were a declaration that she chose to live for something greater that what the present moment could offer her. Because she was a woman of faith, she understood that the virtue of hope is not simply an optimistic attitude that things will eventually go her way. Hope is a theological virtue that keeps us from discouragement and sustains us in trials, reminding us that our ultimate reward is in heaven.

9. Chastity deepens faith.   A college student named Matthew once wrote to us, saying, "Jesus tells us that the pure of heart will see God. That alone is enough for me." He's right: What greater reward could we receive than God Himself?

Those who are pure in heart will not only see God in the next life, but also in this one. When a soul is pure, it could be compared to a clean window through which one can see God. Sin tarnishes the glass, and one's vision of divine things becomes obscured. This does not mean that all spiritual mysteries will be obvious to the innocent, or that God will appear to him or her. Rather, the purity of one's soul allows for a unique form of divine intimacy. In the words of Proverbs 22:11, "He who loves purity of heart, and whose speech is gracious, will have the king as his friend."

Purity also offers you a new lens through which you view life. Not only are you more able to see God with the eyes of faith, you're also more able to see Him in others. Purity unites lovers in a foretaste of heaven, because they begin to see in each other a reflection of the face of God. Wouldn't it be nice not only to see God in a boyfriend, but know that your boyfriend sees God in you?

Along with the gift of God Himself, chastity also offers us the gift of a clean conscience. If we strive for the purity of angels, we will enjoy a share of the peace and joy that they possess.

10. Chastity offers freedom from regret.   Name one person you know who regrets practicing chastity. Having trouble finding one? Now begin the litany of friends who you know who regret not having been pure. Odds are, that list is not a short one. In fact, you can add me to it. Although I (Jason) was technically a virgin when I married Crystalina, that doesn't mean that I had an angelic past. I remember the times when I went too far with girls. Afterward, it felt like a cloud hovered over the relationship. An unexpected heaviness accompanied my lust, while an air of peace seemed to surround the relationships that were pure.

When I dated Crystalina, our purity didn't ruin our ability to have fun as a couple. As anyone in love can testify, you don't need much in order to enjoy the time spent with your beloved. Some of the most mundane things in life become fun, forming the most cherished memories. When you truly love a person, sex can wait because you're so busy enjoying his or her personality. When the deeper attraction and love is absent, sex is often used as a substitute for it.

Guard the Innocence

After I gave a chastity talk at his high school, a football player approached me in his letterman jacket. More than an hour had passed since the assembly, but he returned to tell me what he had been doing in the meantime:

> During class, I couldn't hear anything the teacher was saying. All I could think about was what you said to us. You see, I've been sleeping with this girl at the university, and I really do love her. But I know we shouldn't be doing this stuff. I don't know if you're going to think I'm corny for doing this, but here's what I did during class . . .

With that, he opened his folder and showed me a piece of looseleaf paper, filled front-and-back with his handwriting. At the top, it read "100 ways to love Kelsey without having sex." I skimmed the list and noticed things like "Watch the stars," "Babysit together," and a host of other forms of innocent intimacy. A few days later, he e-mailed me about the effects of his new outlook:

> Now I don't just look past Kelsey's eyes—I look at them. I don't brush off our conversations—I hold them dear to me. We're even working

through our problems and arguments better than before, when we used sex to distract ourselves. And I've got to tell you: The list I made of 100 things to do without sex is filling up pretty fast. So I'm going to go to 1000 things we can do until our wedding date. This is going to make all the difference in the long run.

Because the chaste couple desire closeness just as much as any other couple, the practice of purity in a sense forces them to learn nonsexual ways to express intimacy. This does not stifle their love, but allows it to reach its full potential. In fact, women sometimes complain to us of their relationships, saying, "I miss when he and I used to be able to just sit around and enjoy each other's company. Nowadays it seems like all we do is get physical when we're alone."

If you've never read much of the Bible, you may be surprised to learn that it contains erotic poetry in its love story, the Song of Songs. Its author warns the newlywed couple to catch "the little foxes, that spoil the vineyards, for our vineyards are in blossom."[14] Just as these little predators could quietly destroy a vineyard, lust often undermines the simplicity of budding relationships.

To help you remain pure, remember that if God is calling you to marriage, then your future husband is somewhere out there, right now. What kind of lifestyle do you hope he's living? When it comes to the affection he shares with other women, what kind of memories do you want him to have? If you're thinking, "The fewer, the better," then why not begin to save your intimate memories for him, too? By doing so, your purity will be a gift to him, and his affection will be more unique to you. In the long run, this will bond the two of you much closer than all the "experience" the world recommends you have before marriage.

APPLY THE LOVE TEST

Have you ever noticed the difference between the way men and women give driving directions? When a man gives them, they sound like this:

> Go south on Interstate 5 for 12 miles. When you hit exit 1A, you'll turn right onto Front Street. Then hang a right on Cedar and another right onto State. At the end of the block, you'll see the building on your left.

When a woman offers her navigation services, they're filled with reassurances:

> Go down the 5, like you're heading toward Sea World. First, you'll see the bay on your right. Then you'll go past a big freeway, and then a trolley station on your left. Keep going. When you get close to downtown near where we ate at that cute little Italian restaurant last month with Nicole, you're almost there. So you need to start getting in your right-hand lane. If you start seeing signs for Mexico, you've gone too far.

When a woman is traveling to an unfamiliar area, she likes to be reminded that she's on the right track. There's nothing wrong with this. It's reassuring for her to know she's right where she should be. When a man ventures into an uncharted area of town, he isn't as concerned with being reassured about his location. If he's lost, he thinks it's some kind of game.

The point of this is that when it comes to navigating through the single years of a woman's life, she needs to be reassured when she's making the right choices. Sometimes she feels as if she's driving alone though a dark and unsafe part of town, longing to find a single landmark that will tell her that she isn't lost after all.

Take, for example, the anxiety expressed in the following e-mail from a college female:

> What my current boyfriend, and what society says, just make me feel that I am terribly wrong. Is it wrong to want your boyfriend, future husband, or husband to love you the way God loves you? Is it wrong to think that physical intimacy can get in the way? I must be so strange.

Another girl wrote, "I think the only way they would like me is if I am very sexual. Once they're done with me I think there is something wrong with me." Our book may help quell a woman's fears that she's abnormal for wanting authentic love. But God has planted within you an even more reliable tool to help you discover love: your womanly intuition.

One of the most reliable and insightful guides in the world is the heart of a woman—especially if she is a woman of prayer. For example, not long ago we met a father who was struggling with looking at online porn. He was a youth minister and a husband, and nobody knew of his secret addiction. One day in prayer he said, "God, I really want to deepen my intimacy with you." Not long after this, a woman at his church approached him and said, "I've got a word from the Lord for you. I make no judgments on this, though. If you want intimacy with God, you need to throw away your pornography. You have to make a decision between God and the porn." There is no way this woman could have known what he did in the privacy of his home. He was cut to the heart. He broke off his habit and asked forgiveness from his family.

If the intuitions of a godly woman can guide another man to overcome his vices, imagine how helpful they would be in her own daily life. Every day, your heart speaks to you. Every minute, the Holy Spirit prompts you. But just like one's conscience, a woman's intuition can be dulled if she persistently disregards it. Therefore, if you're in a relationship, don't ignore your heart if it's telling you: "Listen to me. You're being used. Get out." Have you ever noticed that we often regret ignoring our intuition but we never seem to regret listening to it?

Your heart can't lie. If you suspect you are being used, you probably are. When a woman is being loved, cherished, and led to God, she never, ever, wonders if she is being used. When that "getting used" alarm goes off in a woman's intuition, she needs to act on it before worse things happen. What should she do? Without hesitation, she should apply the love test.

The Love Test

While standing on stage before a few hundred high school students, I (Jason) rummaged through a box of their handwritten questions about dating and chastity. After opening a folded-up piece of loose-leaf, I announced an anonymous student's question. "Should I break up with my girlfriend if she won't have sex with me?"

With silent anticipation, the student body awaited my reply. "Yes!" I announced. "Absolutely." Eyes bulged and jaws dropped. For a moment, the faces of many girls looked disappointed, while pockets of male students chuckled in glee. I then added, "You should definitely break up with her. Why? Because she deserves someone infinitely better than you." Cheers followed from the girls.

If you want to scrutinize a man's motives for loving you, one of the most effective ways to do this is by applying the love test: Take the sexual element out of your relationship and see what remains. When a woman applies the love test to a man, she will get one of three reactions.

Reaction #1. Upon hearing the news of his impending sentence of abstinence, a guy may become irritated and upset. He may proceed to employ any number of manipulative tactics to get a woman to reconsider. These may include anger, guilt, or affection. He might tell her how much he loves her or remind her that she used to do it (as if she forgot).

Why is he acting like this? It's because if a man cannot control his own sexuality, he'll try to control a woman, making her think that giving him sexual favors will fulfill her need for real intimacy. If he's unable to sway her, he will leave either immediately or gradually. In his eyes, pleasure was the fuel of the relationship. When it runs out, so will he. Love is never at the center of such relationships. The boyfriend's hormones are. When things no longer revolve around him, he flees. At this point, the woman faces a painful discovery (that she probably knew all along): He wanted sex, not her.

If a girl is tempted to feel remorse for having moral standards, she should remember that it's likely that other girls have given in to him in the past. If she gives in, she'll be just like them . . . in his past. Some girls think, "If I don't sleep with him, then he'll dump me. But if I sleep with him, maybe he'll stay." If this strategy worked, he would still be dating the last girl he slept with. Have you ever noticed that the sooner a girl sleeps with a guy, the sooner he leaves? And the longer a girl waits to sleep with a guy, the longer the relationship often lasts?

Be brave and let go. There are worse things in the world than dumping a cute guy who only loves himself. And if you haven't started dating him yet, pass on the opportunity. Instead of giving a guy what he wants as a way to keep him interested—while you secretly wonder if he even loves you—apply the love test before you date him. If he fails the test, you'll know you dodged a bullet. This leaves the door open for real love.

Reaction #2. When a woman tells her boyfriend that she wants to be pure, she'll most likely receive the following reaction: Although he's not thrilled, he'll say something to the effect of, "That's okay. I'm a guy, and you know I've got my desires. But I respect you. If you want to do that, I understand." At first, she may be impressed by the fact that he didn't become angry. But before long, his desires surface. He begins to ask, "Well, can we at least do *this* or *that*?" Because he doesn't understand the point of purity, he's focused on one thing: how far he can go without making her feel guilty.

After she threw away her birth control pills as a declaration of her new purity, one woman e-mailed me to share her boyfriend's reaction. He texted her to say:

> The thought of you being happier and healthier in the long run is worth it. . . . I love you. And that's not based on how many times we get to have sex . . . it's based on the fact that you're one of my best friends, and a wonderful girl, and someone I enjoy spending tons of time with. So whether or not you want to have sex constantly or spend the rest of your days chaste, I'm here for you (small kiss on the forehead). I love you, sweetie.

Sounds pretty nice. Too bad a few weeks later he was upset because she didn't change her mind. The demands of love began to set in, and he had no idea what to do. He texted her again:

> Please don't think I want things to end. I really don't. I just keep gnashing my teeth because now I don't know what keeps you around. I feel like I don't know where we can go from here.

Trying to make sense of everything, she asked me:

> If sex isn't a factor in the relationship, what more is there? Do I just take the Pill again and go back to the way it was? Or do we try getting to know each other but not in the physical sense? I feel that with option one, we'll stay together longer, but only because it's dragged out with pleasure.

What would you recommend she do? Going on the Pill will not solve her problem. It will conceal it. The real problem is his lack of genuine, unconditional love for her.

Chastity is a real test of love, and it's sad when the guy fails the test. But the solution isn't to trash the test. That would be like preparing for medical school and thinking, "I'm going to flunk my MCAT. What am I going to do? I know! I'll rip up the test and throw it in the trash so I'll never see the grade!" The results will show up eventually, even if you try to make the test disappear. In the same way, you can't hide from what the test of purity would otherwise bring to the surface.

One woman recounted to us:

> When I told Jacob, he acted cool about it, like he kind of respected my idea, but then went into this whole lecture about safe sex and

stuff, but I'm like, "No, I don't want to have sex with you. We're not married." So he seems fine with it now, he still wants to hang out, but I'm like, "Jacob, how far is this going to go?" And he said, "As far as you're comfortable with." Like he's not pressuring me, but I feel pressured. It's weird. He seems so sweet but it just seems fake sometimes.

If a woman has dated aggressive men in the past, she'll be impressed that a guy would be willing to abide by her boundaries. The problem is that the relationship begins to resemble the dynamics between an overexcited puppy and the master who needs to keep him contained in a cardboard box: "If you stay in here, Rascal, you're being a really good boy!" The dog's master knows that if the boundaries were lifted, the animal would romp throughout the house, eat the sofa, and stain the carpets. Therefore, she sets a boundary for the pup and is grateful that the dog doesn't tear it down.

In the same way, if the idea of purity is solely the woman's, the man will think that his only obligation is to respect her morals. In his mind, he'll begin to think she owes him a treat for obeying her rules. Things might run smoothly for a time, and she'll admire the fact that he's so nice about it. And perhaps he is "nice." But face it: Almost every man on earth has the ability to be "nice." I used to have a hamster that was nice. The real question is: How many men have the maturity and courage to lead you closer to heaven? If he does not have that quality, then you have no business dating him.

One woman told me that although her boyfriend was really upset about her unwillingness to continue their sexual behavior, he was willing to stay with her. What a trooper! At first, he gave her the silent treatment as a sign of his disapproval of her purity vow. Then he questioned her faith and ethical standards and proceeded to have a tantrum about the new guidelines on their intimacy. She said, "I don't want to break up with him because he's so perfect."

If this is your idea of the perfect man, then it's time to take a break from relationships. If your boyfriend expects you to give him a doctoral defense on the virtue of chastity, something is wrong. Your feelings should be enough to earn his respect, and there's no need to apologize for having morals. All he needs to know is that he doesn't deserve the total gift of your body unless he has made the total gift of himself to you in marriage. No matter what he thinks of this, don't let any guy make you feel like he's doing you an immeasurable favor by not having sex with you. It is his duty as a gentleman, and you owe him nothing for doing what he ought to do.

If he is trying to make you feel guilty, then he's manipulating you. I remember one young woman telling me that her boyfriend complained to her, saying, "It's not fair that you just went and made this decision about chastity without even talking to me first." As if she needed a permission slip from him to take care of herself! If a guy is pouty about the fact that you have morals, so be it. It's better for a guy to be disappointed than for you to lower your standards. Women today are so timid and afraid to hurt a guy's feelings that they often end up causing themselves immeasurable harm.

Therefore, if you tell a guy you want to be pure and at first he seems to handle the news well, don't pay much attention to his words. Watch his actions. Be pure with him and see how much he really loves you. Don't be afraid that love will pass you by if you leave an impure relationship. Leaving it just may open up the door for the kind of love you've wanted all long. In the words of one British playwright, "Every exit is an entry somewhere else."[1]

Reaction #3. If Reaction #1 was immediate frustration and dissent, and Reaction #2 was feigned understanding followed by subtle manipulation, Reaction #3 is pure agreement. Upon hearing the news that you want to be pure, a guy should rejoice for having found a woman who shares his morals. Even if the two of you have made mistakes in the past, he might say, "You know, I've been thinking the same thing. Let's start over." Such a guy is not simply willing to wait *for* you. He'll wait *with* you. If you're weak, he can be strong. If he's tempted, you can hold the line. In other words, it's a partnership in which you share the goal of purity.

Of the three reactions to the love test, the third reaction is the least common. One reason it's rare is because if a girl needs to draw a line in terms of sexual behavior, it implies that the guy hasn't bothered to do it himself. You shouldn't have to beg a guy to behave.

I (Crystalina) have been in relationships in which I always felt the weight of a man's sexual expectations. But when I was dating Jason, our relationship was free of such pressure. In fact, we never had to tell each other to stop. Because we valued purity, we didn't put each other in compromising situations.

There will be times when any couple will need to say no to temptations with each other. But there's a big difference between striving for purity together and needing to shove a guy off you at the end of every date. One college student e-mailed us about the effort she and her boyfriend were making to keep their relationship focused on God. She referred to their combined "fight for purity—the joyful struggle." Her words implied a partnership with her boyfriend rather than a conflict of interests.

The love test is not something you need to give to a man repeatedly. Either he's in agreement with you or he's not. When you say "no," it doesn't mean "try later." Often, a girl finds herself asking her boyfriend to stop time and time again. Her real challenge is not learning to say no to him, but figuring out why she's so desperate for the love of a guy who doesn't respect her. Imagine how much better she would feel in a relationship if she weren't spending so much time and energy trying to teach him to behave!

Even if you and your boyfriend have made mistakes in the past, it's possible to start over. But the decision must be mutual, and not imposed. One college student told us how she and her boyfriend were able to do just this:

> I know this is bad to say, but I think that if we just kept on living the life we did, it would have ended really bad. Now, I look at him and I know that he wants to stay with me for the right reasons. It makes me happy. Over the past month, I have really felt a great bond between us and it is incredible!

Although some women forever postpone giving their boyfriends the love test (because they know he'll fail), what these girls don't realize is that applying the love test always pays off. Either it opens your eyes to a false love or brings peace of mind that your relationship is solid. Either way, you win. But the girl who never learns to say no is the one who will have the hardest time finding love. She wastes too much of her time with the counterfeit of lust.

The Satisfaction of Having Standards

Tyler and Amanda had been dating for eight months before they became sexually active. The two of them were sophomores in college, and had never been in a more serious relationship. But after a few months of sleeping together, Amanda thought she needed to tell Tyler that she wanted to stop. It wasn't that she didn't enjoy the closeness, but this wasn't the way she was raised, and she knew her parents would be crushed if they ever found out.

She was worried how Tyler would react to the news, but she trusted that he would respect her, as he always tried to do. During a long conversation, she opened up to him . . . and he agreed! She e-mailed us:

> I was kind of shocked when he said this, but I was so happy and felt more loved than I *ever* had during sex. I find myself feeling so happy and excited about our relationship. Everything we do together is just *fun*! It's less stressful and we love just holding hands and talking. I feel so blessed to have a boyfriend like this. I'm able to say no and it feels really good to see how my boyfriend respects me still. What feels even better is how I have a better respect for myself.

Yet another young woman wrote to us upon discovering chaste love after having had a string of meaningless hookups: "I can smile knowing I have found pure love. I don't think there is a feeling in the world greater than this."

As you can see, chastity doesn't necessarily sentence you to a fate of isolation and loneliness. Even if a relationship ends because a man is unable to live up to your standards, you can walk away with your dignity intact. Instead of being weighed down by remorse for how you compromised to keep him, you can hold your head high. Not only will this boost your own self-respect, severing an unhealthy relationship can also leave a lasting impression upon the guy! After leaving a man who didn't respect her, Alexis wrote:

I recently met up with my ex-boyfriend again, and he's completely different. He's gotten so much more respectful of women and he seems a lot happier. He told me after I abruptly ended our relationship (because he couldn't accept my promise to wait for marriage), that he went and thought about it a lot. Now, he's learning to respect women, and has decided to make his own promise: to wait for his bride. He may have a past, but he's letting that go in order to have a better future. I'm glad I could, ahem, put him in his place!

When you hold fast to your morals while dating, you'll also notice that relationships often end on a different note. If a guy is in agreement with your standards but things don't end up working out between you, the end doesn't taste as bitter. It's easier to let go. This is why many chaste couples who break up remain friends after their separation. How often does this happen for those who don't remain pure? Some practically need a divorce attorney to deal with the drama!

It doesn't need to be like this. Can you imagine ending a relationship and being more whole after having known the guy? Can you imagine a relationship that helps you to become yourself? This is what relationships should be. Even if things haven't gone well in the past, now's your chance to begin again. Stick to your standards, because if a woman needs to lower her morals in order to find love, then it is not love that she has found.

Saying No to Him (and to Yourself)

Even once you've entered a good relationship, you'll still need to keep your standards high. Temptations don't disappear just because you signed a purity pledge card and go to church with your boyfriend. If anything, the closer you get to a man, the more you'll want to express physically the emotional union you share. What's a woman to do with her desires?

An inadequate response to these questions would be to say, "Your body's desires are bad, but the spiritual part of you is good. Try to be as spiritual as possible." The reason why this advice would be incomplete is because God created your soul and your body. He is the author of your desires. Although this might scandalize some to read, He's also the inventor of sex. When we long for sexual union, we long for something good.

It's not shameful for a woman to desire the one-flesh union of husband and wife. However, our desires for what is good can become tainted with selfishness or impatience. Our job is to deepen our relationship with God so that we can grow in the virtues. As we progress in love, patience, and selflessness, these qualities will influence the way we seek the fulfillment of our desires. These virtues will influence our desires, helping us to want what is pure. In time, we will learn to integrate our sexual desires so that our dating relationships can become visible expressions of the love we have for God.

Temptations are bound to come, but what should you do when they happen? To cool off a steamy situation, realize that you have the power to choose between virtue and sin. If you have trouble motivating yourself to stop the pleasure, turn your heart to God and say a quick prayer for strength. Then, without delay, stop what you're doing. This will always be disappointing to one or both of you, but someone needs to do it. You're not trying to destroy the passion. You're investing the excitement instead of spending everything. You're saving it up for the place where it belongs: in marriage. As you do this, know that each time you resist lust, you strengthen your ability to love.

All temptations are easier to overcome when you're at a distance. Imagine if a robber came to your house and you saw him through the peephole. It's easiest just to lock the door. If you don't, he may try to open it. If he gets a foot in the door, it's harder to shut. But once he's in the house, it's almost impossible to get him out. In the same way, the longer you wait to reject a temptation, the more vulnerable you become and the harder it is to resist. Therefore, set guidelines that can help you to avoid temptations before they begin. For starters:

1. Stay out of situations where you know mistakes will happen.   For example, never get drunk. Also, as a couple, stay out of your bedroom. If you're in college, remember that your dorm room *is* your bedroom. Therefore, if you're hanging out in the dorm together, it's wise to be with other people. If you're alone with him, keep the door open and stay off the bed.

2. *Make clear boundaries.*   For example, no intimate touching or laying down together. Old chastity books used to recommend that couples avoid "petting." We've always been amused by the term because it makes the boyfriend sound like a labradoodle. But there's wisdom in this. Intimate touching and embraces tease your body and only serve to make purity more difficult. Keep your affections simple, because the further you go, the further you'll want to go. In other words, the more pure you are, the easier it is to be pure.

That might strike you as puritanical, but think about it. As they say, "If you're not going to Cleveland, what are you doing on the train?" Why deliberately stir up desires that will only need to be shut down? The more you do with him, the more you'll both daydream about it. When you're together, the more easily you'll slide back into the same habits. The boundaries will become more vague, and stopping will become more difficult.

3. *If you get engaged, keep it short (preferably between six to nine months).*   Hold off on accepting the ring if marriage is more than a year away. Your engagement is supposed to be an exciting time for preparing for marriage, picking out your dress, and sending out invitations. It's not supposed to feel like the forty years Moses spent wandering in the desert.

4. *Never allow a relationship to isolate you from your friends and family.*   After graduating from college, one woman shared with us the remorse she felt about immersing herself in an unbalanced relationship:

> I talk to college friends about their time at the university and they miss it so much: the fellowship, the friendship, the chaplains, the community. In the end, the only close friend I had at the university was Matt. I look back and see four years wasted on a man/boy who was absolutely unworthy of me. I thought so little of myself that I let myself become completely lost in him.

5. *Pray and fast.*   Your life will always be a reflection of the depth of your prayer life. The greater your union with God, the more this will transform your daily life. One lost form of prayer is fasting. This means to abstain from something you like. It can be anything from skipping the ketchup, or snacks between meals, or a strict fast of bread and water for one meal or one day, if you are able.

In the eyes of the world, this advice sounds silly. You want to know how to avoid making sexual mistakes with your boyfriend and we tell you to cut down on the ketchup. But fasting does several things. It trains you in self-mastery, whereby you gain control over your body's desires. It teaches your body to be subject to your will. In other words, you teach your body that it won't die if it doesn't get everything it wants. Have you ever seen a spoiled kid at a toy store throwing a tantrum? Sometimes when we spoil our bodies with pleasure, they become like brats who can't take no for an answer. Fasting helps you become the master of your body.

When you make a deliberate fast, it's also as if your body is praying. It lifts your heart and mind to God and praying becomes easier. You can also offer your fast as a prayer for purity or you could offer it up for your boyfriend or future husband.

6. *Create strategies to stay pure.*   Talk to each other about ways to guard the simplicity of your love. For example, if you and your boyfriend are going too far, give him a kiss on the forehead. This can be a loving signal between the two of you that you need to cool off. Keep the affection simple, and you'll discover a new peace in the relationship. After trying this, one young woman discovered, "I feel proud of my relationship instead of ashamed of it."

Frequent Faller

One of the most common e-mails we receive is: "Even though my boyfriend and I have talked about our boundaries, we often mess up and go too far. I feel really bad about it, but it keeps happening. What should we do?"

Just because you've done it before doesn't mean you need to do it again. When a couple has already crossed certain lines of sexual intimacy, it becomes especially difficult to avoid making the same mistakes in the future. This is partly because God designed our sexual desires to be all-consuming. In other words, when we light that flame of sexual passion, it can become like a forest fire that is not quenched until it devours everything in its path. If the blaze cannot be contained, it can burn a relationship to the ground.

How tragic it is when a couple deeply loves one another and yet allows lust to erode their love. How do you guard against this? If you feel you've already gone too far with your boyfriend, you could say:

> You know I love being with you, and I've been wanting to talk to you about this for a while. But I've been kind of afraid to say it. I know you want me to be open and honest with you, so here goes: When we're getting physical, and things start moving too fast, part of me wants to move forward but my heart is telling me to stop. I don't want to say anything at the time because I don't want to hurt you or make things awkward. And sometimes I don't want to stop. It's like a tug-of-war in my mind, and I'm not at peace. I'm not blaming you for this, but I want to tell you that I really need you to help us not to go there. Please don't wait for me to stop. That's the key. By keeping things pure, I know our love will only grow stronger.

Tell him that you feel weak in this area and that you want him to help lead the two of you toward purity. Let him know that you want to be able to trust him with your soul. Men work best when they have a task to fulfill. This is not about getting you off the hook, but making him feel more accountable for keeping things pure. He'll be better at drawing the line if he is not waiting for you to do it. Meanwhile, take on the same role that you've asked him to fulfill. Don't wait for him to say no, because his soul is in your hands, too.

In the future, you'll know when you are going too far when your conscience begins to nag you. You think, "We'll stop in just one more minute," or "We've done it before. What's one more time?" or "He'll stop soon." Afterward, you beat yourself up: "I wished we stopped sooner. Why did we end up doing that again?" Then you end up having "The Talk" with him:

"We need to try better."

"Yeah. I'm sorry that happened."

"Me too."

One young woman told us that she knew she went too far with her boyfriend because "I felt so awful and still feel so bad about it, but *I know* my intention was good. So why do I feel so ashamed?"

To prevent this drama, find someone to whom you can be accountable. Both of you need this. You cannot expect to win this battle for purity if you're fighting alone. You need a solid married couple, pastor, role model, or youth minister whom you can meet with on a regular basis. Be open and honest with them about where you are at and when you fall. Without this, we do not know how much success you will have. That's how important it is.

Although an accountability partner will help to make purity more possible, each person's purity is ultimately in his or her own hands. But by striving together toward chastity, you'll always see each other as a gift.

The Gift of Love

On our wedding way, as I (Jason) stood before the altar, I saw Crystalina's silhouette through the stained glass windows on the back door of the church. The doors swung open, the violin and organ music played, and tears fell down her cheeks and mine. As she began to walk toward me, gazing at me through her veil, I had an overwhelming thought of God the Father's hands behind her, giving her to me as a gift. I realized that through our struggle for purity, we were blessing God by leaving the gift of each other in His hands until His time.

While we were dating, I could feel His constant calling in my heart for a deeper kind of purity. It was not that God was never satisfied with us, but that He was always gently inviting us to live a deeper commitment to Him in the way we expressed affection to each other. He was always calling us to be more and more generous with Him, in response to His generosity to us. It seemed like the more we gave Him, the more we were able to receive from Him. It was as if He wanted us to be more generous with Him for our sakes more than for His sake.

If you feel that you and your boyfriend repetitively fall into sin, you need to change the behavior or take a break from the relationship. If the two of you are incapable of living a chaste courtship, it may be a sign that neither of you are ready to be dating. This doesn't only apply to fifteen-year-old girls, but also to those who are thirty-five. If you don't know what to do, I always believe that the answer to all our questions is to love. Love your body. Love your future husband. Love God. Do these things, and your path will become clear in time.

QUIT RATIONALIZING

(Crystalina) As women, when our dating relationships turn physical, our natural tendency is to preserve them. If we give ourselves in an intimate way, we don't want to lose the guy. For Christian women, tensions begin to rise in our consciences. We'll begin to reason with ourselves as to why certain sexual behaviors are acceptable, why our love is more important than the moral laws. We mistakenly think we're the exception because our love is so unique. This is a temptation for all couples: to place ourselves above the law of God, as if our emotions elevate our behavior beyond reproach.

When it comes to knowing how far is too far, some people recommend that you take the time to discover your own values, what you feel "ready" to do with a guy. In other words, how far is too far, for you? The problem with this is that it's all relative. In other words:

> My values may be different than your values, and what's right for me may not be right for you. If my boyfriend and I feel strongly enough about each other, and our relationship has lasted long enough, shouldn't we be able to express that in any way we want?

The problem with this approach is that the ultimate authority becomes one's feelings. It turns our opinions into our god, making us the author of right and wrong. This is the core issue when it comes to making choices about our bodies and our sexuality. Does each couple determine their own set of moral laws?

Because of our stubborn pride, we may assume that God created moral laws to make us miserable. Especially in the realm of sexual morality—when the gratification is most immediate—we tend to push Him away. As for the rest of the commandments, we aren't as annoyed by His laws: "Don't kill? Okay. Don't steal? That's fair. Don't covet my neighbor's ox? I can do that. Don't lust? WHAT!"

God's laws are not burdens to those who wish to love. Rather, they free us to love. Unfortunately, many people see the rules and wrongly assume that they are the heart of the Christian life. They may think, "If I want to please God, I need to follow His laws. Then I'll go to heaven when I die." This isn't Christianity. It's hedging your bets: "I'll give God this, and He'll keep me from going to hell." Such a minimalist idea of the Christian life hardly has the power to motivate a person to give up everything and follow Christ.

There can only be one God. Either we call the shots, or we trust in what He has revealed to us. According to God, you'll know you're ready for sex when you have a ring on your finger. In other words, you should unveil your body to a man only after he has lifted your wedding veil.

Purity is about having the humility to open ourselves to the will of God. Instead of asking how far we can go toward sin, we begin to ask how far we can go toward love. This does not mean that we are freed from temptations. It just means that when they occur, we don't turn inward and ask ourselves, "Am I ready for this? Do I feel comfortable doing this with him?" Rather, we turn our hearts to God, asking Him a very daring question: "What is pure in your eyes, and how do you want me to live?" Instead of seeing purity in the negative—as if it's merely the absence of sexual sin—take a positive approach. See it as the freedom to express God's love through your body. Instead of seeing purity as a list of no's, see purity for what it is: a yes to love.

Some girls may hear this, and say, "I'm not really into the churchy thing, so I don't know if this really applies to me. Besides, I have too many desires." But who placed those desires on your heart and in your body? Your sexual desire was created by God, and it's a sign that you have been created to make a gift of yourself. God just wants to make sure you don't reduce that gift to a loan. You desire love, and God wants nothing different for you. He wants to make sure you don't settle for anything less.

While I was in my bad relationships, my intuition made me feel twinges of doubt. But my fear of losing God faded as I became more focused on keeping my boyfriend and our mutual friends. Justifications formed in my mind like clouds blocking out the light of my conscience. I knew that God would always be there for me, so I put Him off to the side. In an effort to quell the disturbance in my soul and to quiet my friends and family who might oppose my relationship, I began to rationalize.

It takes humility and honesty to admit these rationalizations, because they become a security blanket for us. They protect us from admitting that something is not right in our relationships. If we let go of our justifications, we wonder what would be left of our love. All that would be left is the truth, but we should not be afraid of this. Love, as Scripture says, "rejoices with the truth."[1]

Rather than face the truth, we often justify lust (and bad relationships in general), thereby weakening our ability to give and receive love. Here are the top ten ways we do this:

1. "He's really sweet."

When we find ourselves in bad relationships, what do we do? We zone in on his positive qualities in order to distract ourselves from the negative aspects of the relationship. Perhaps the most common excuse we offer ourselves and others is that the boyfriend is thoughtful and sweet. What we often forget is that being sweet is easy. The real question is: Why is he sweet?

Sometimes a guy will be sweet because he needs to make up for the times he's been bad. When he turns on the charm, we temporarily forget about all the hurt he's caused. But it won't be long before the cycle continues. I once heard it said that when a guy often acts disrespectfully to you, his bad behavior is not a piece of the puzzle. It solves the whole mystery. It tells you who he is. So don't get wrapped up in the bliss of his candy-coated personality when he's trying to make it up to you.

In other cases, some men will act sweet as a ploy to gain sexual closeness. One young woman wrote to us, saying:

> I lost my virginity to a certain boy who I find the most beautiful person I'll ever meet and I truly feel I will love him forever and no one will ever make me feel the same.

A few sentences later, she added:

> But we never officially dated, and even though I hate to admit it I think he only used me for sex and it hurts that he didn't see anything more in me. So perhaps I wasn't ready. But I don't regret it because I do care deeply about him and that's what I think sex is: it is the deepest, most passionate, and complete surrendering of yourself to someone you care about.

It's mind-boggling to think that a guy who used her for sex and then discarded her was the most beautiful person she thinks she'll ever meet. This is the blinding power of physical intimacy, and it has blinded people for ages. In her book *The Privilege of Being a Woman*, Dr. Alice von Hildebrand, a noted philosopher, mentions a nineteenth-century German drama, in which the storyline is all too familiar:

> [W]omen are usually brought to their fall, not so much because of lust, but because of the promise of eternal love, or because they are told that their lover will kill himself if she does not yield to his wishes, or because of sheer vanity, or because they desperately want "to be wanted" and protected. How sweet it is to hear, "I have never seen a woman as beautiful as you are." "You are the only one who has ever touched my heart." The drama of Faust and Margarete comes to mind. It is so terribly tragic that when Margarete finds herself pregnant, abandoned, and in a desperate situation, she utters the words: "it was so good; it was so beautiful." She nurtured the illusion that the "great" man who conquered her actually loved her and, when her eyes were opened, she was threatened by despair.[2]

If a woman is sexually active and convinced that her boyfriend is sweet, she should introduce the practice of abstinence until marriage in order to make sure he can maintain his sweetness while being pure.

2. *"We're not always doing it. There's more to our relationship than sex."*

The easiest thing in the world is to condemn the sins we're not tempted to commit. For example, a sexually active woman who has genuine feelings for her boyfriend may look down upon girls who engage in meaningless hookups. Since she has no desire to settle for one-night stands, she convinces herself that she's superior to those who do. But by doing so, she is diverting her attention away from her own behavior.

She may think to herself:

> It's not like I'm having a string of meaningless flings. My boyfriend and I are committed, we have plenty of other common interests besides sex, and our relationship is balanced. It's not like that's all our relationship is about.

This idea that they're "not always doing it" distracts her from the fact that they shouldn't be doing it at all. In other words, the frequency of premarital sex does not determine its morality. Also, just because their relationship goes beyond physical intimacy does not mean that the physical intimacy is justified. In fact, emotional intimacy is not a justification for sex outside of marriage, but another reason to save it.

When a couple says, "Our dating relationship is more than sex," they overlook the fact that the sexual act expresses more than a dating relationship. It expresses a complete gift of one person to the other —marriage. Even though a dating couple shares a deep emotional bond, sexual intimacy speaks something more. It speaks the language of permanence.

Women know in their hearts that sex should mean something. This is why so many women say that they don't want to sleep with a man "unless I know he loves me." Alice von Hildebrand also noted, "It is love alone that gives sex its true meaning."[3] But if a woman doesn't know the truth about love, she won't understand the meaning of sex.

You decide: Should love be temporary, or forever? Should it be coerced, or freely given? Is it uncommitted, or faithful? Is it lifeless, or life-giving? Is it hidden, or announced to the world? If you believe that romantic love should ultimately be a life-giving public declaration of freely given faithful love that lasts forever, then you've just described the wedding vows.

When a bride and groom stand at the altar, they promise that their love will be free, total, faithful, and open to life. When they leave the church and enter the sanctuary of their bedroom, they will exchange those vows with their bodies. In other words, sex is the wedding vows made flesh!

However, consider how unmarried sex contradicts each of these promises: Instead of being free, the sexual union is often driven by lust. They might be monogamous, but they haven't made vows of fidelity. Instead of being a total gift, they have made no binding promises to belong to one another until death do them part. Finally, their love is not open to life. They're probably terrified at the idea of pregnancy. In other words, their actions are speaking the opposite of love—even if their intentions are good.

Therefore, the question is not: "Should a dating relationship require more than sex?" but rather, "Should sexual intimacy require more than a dating relationship?"

3. "We've been together so long."

I'm willing to bet that you know at least one dating couple who should have broken up eons ago. They've been together for so long it seems like they can't deal with life apart from each other. No matter how bad things get, they always seem to make up, get back together, and drag it on. There's so much drama in the relationship that you could base a reality show on it. Looking at their relationship from the outside, it's easy to see how they both would have been better off if they stayed apart the first time they broke up.

Although it's easy to judge them from the outside, it can feel impossible to let go when you're the one involved in such a relationship. The more a woman invests herself in a guy, the more she'll cling to him. She'll come to believe that the duration of her relationship is somehow a testimony to its value. But the length of a relationship does not determine its worth. This is a difficult principle to accept when you feel like a breakup would require you to admit that the last few years of your life were a total loss. But this is no reason to stay.

The person who clings to a bad relationship is like the person who says, "I know I'm driving in the wrong direction, but we've already gone ten miles. I don't want to go back and admit I made a wrong turn. So I'll just keep driving until we circle the globe." This person obviously needs to turn around if she wants to reach her destination. In the same way, the longer you remain in a bad relationship, the longer it will take you to heal from it.

Just as the length of a relationship cannot be used to measure its value, neither does it justify sexual intimacy outside of marriage. If a woman does not understand this, she'll live under the presumption that she should not have sex until she's "ready," or until she's found the "right one."

I (Jason) recall meeting one such woman who didn't want to lose her virginity until she felt this way. On Valentine's Day, thinking that she was ready and that she had found the one, she gave her virginity to her boyfriend. He broke up with her before he left the room. She may have felt ready for sex, but she was hardly ready for its consequences.

Sex is not a way to keep a guy, or even a way to express how much you like him. The act of sex says, "I am your wife, and I would be happy to bear your children in nine months." But odds are, you're not ready to say that. What you probably mean to say is, "I really like you and I hope we'll end up married several years from now." But this is not the language spoken by sex, regardless of how long a couple has been dating. If love demands that you give everything, making love should be no different.

4. "I already gave myself to him."

Especially when a girl loses her virginity, she struggles to let go of the guy. She probably never wanted to sleep with more than one guy, and she doesn't want to admit she made a mistake. I (Crystalina) lost my virginity at the age of fifteen. Letting go of that relationship seemed impossible at the time. I couldn't bear the thought of being so close to a person and then becoming less than friends with him. The relationship—which never should have begun in the first place—ended up lasting far too long. After a drawn-out breakup, I eventually had the courage to let go. But imagine I didn't. I would not be married to Jason today, and our children would not exist. So much depends on having the courage to let go of what was never meant to be.

If you've slept with a guy, this is no reason to stay in a relationship. It's just a reason why you find it difficult to leave. Neurologists have discovered that intense bonding deactivates the circuits in the brain that are supposed to make judgments about another person.[4] This explains why some girls remain in terrible relationships despite the fact that everyone keeps begging them to get out.

If you know in your heart that the relationship isn't right, have the courage to let go. Otherwise you'll only prolong your suffering. If you find it difficult to break things off, at least begin by being pure with your boyfriend. Without the clouding of your judgment caused by sexual intimacy, you'll see more clearly and will be more able to make the right decision. If you're meant to be with this guy, then you'll have the rest of your life to enjoy sexual intimacy in marriage. But if he's not the one, what's the point of giving him any more of your heart, your body, and your life?

5. "My family really likes him."

To test how much your parents like your boyfriend, imagine the look on their faces if you disclosed the full truth about your relationship. Imagine if they could see every action done in private, read every text message, and hear every conversation. If the image of your dad running to find his baseball bat comes to mind, odds are your parents only like who they think he is. Therefore, don't delude yourself into thinking you should stay with a guy because your parents have fallen in love with a guy who exists only in their imaginations.

6. *"But we really love each other."*

It has been said that the Sanskrit language has ninety-six words for love and that ancient Persian had eighty. Each word had a distinct meaning. In the English language, our lack of linguistic precision is painfully obvious when it comes to the word "love." For example, a husband might "love" his wife and "love" beer nuts. Because of the ambiguity of the word, it's difficult to know what a person means when he or she claims to love another. For the sake of clarity, we'll offer one definition of human love: to do what is best for your beloved.

When I was sexually active, I never thought to myself, "How can I use my boyfriend today for the sake of my selfish gratification?" Such a thought never crossed my mind. But was I really loving him? Was I doing what was best for him?

In every love, the couple will feel a desire for union and a desire for the good of the other. We can know the difference between love and lust based upon which of these desires takes precedence over the other. Lust is when the desire for physical union becomes more important than the desire to do what's best for the other. Love is when a couple can hold off on the heaven of physical intimacy for the sake of leading each other to heaven itself.

In the end, when a relationship is based on a false notion of love, the truth will always surface. A man with decades of experience in counseling couples noted, "The rickety-ness of the structure must show itself in time. It is one of the greatest of sorrows when love proves to be not what it was thought to be, but its diagonal opposite."[5]

He also noted, "Love as experience should be subordinated to love as virtue, so much so that without love as virtue there can be no full-ness in the experience of love."[6] This is a dense quote, but re-read it if necessary and unpack its meaning. He's saying that the emotions of love must be placed under the virtue of love. When a couple is able to do this, they discover the richest form of intimacy.

If we can agree that love is the act of doing what is best for the other, then it's impossible to love a boyfriend through sex. Aside from the statistics and studies regarding STDs and pregnancy rates, what are the effects of sex on the soul? Consider the words of St. Paul:

> Do not be deceived; neither fornicators nor idolaters nor adulterers . . . will inherit the kingdom of God. . . . Avoid immorality. Every other sin a person commits is outside the body, but the immoral person sins against his own body.[7]

Elsewhere, in his letter to the Christians in Thessalonica, he writes:

> This is the will of God, your holiness: that you refrain from immoral-ity, that each of you know how to acquire a wife for himself in holi-ness and honor, not in lustful passion as do the Gentiles who do not know God. . . . For God did not call us to impurity but to holiness. Therefore, whoever disregards this, disregards not a human being but God, who [also] gives his holy Spirit to you.[8]

By caring for your boyfriend's soul, you prove your love for him in the most profound way. If two people claim to love one another and yet have no concern for each other's eternal salvation, how can this be considered love? The chaste couple knows that purity is not about following a list of rules in order to avoid hell. It's about want-ing heaven for the person you love.

Love is eternal. This is why a friend of ours proposed to his wife with the following quote from a fourth-century Christian writer:

> I have taken you in my arms, and I love you, and I prefer you to my life itself. For the present life is nothing, and my most ardent dream is to spend it with you in such a way that we may be assured of not being separated in the life reserved for us [heaven]. . . . I place your love above all things, and nothing would be more bitter or painful to me than to be of a different mind than you.[9]

By means of this quote, my friend demonstrated to his bride-to-be that the only thing he desired more than being with her in this life was making sure that they'd spend eternity in heaven as well. He knew that sacrifices made out of love for one another bring a couple closer than any pleasure on earth. Therefore, if you truly wish to express your love for a man, prove your love through purity.

When purity is understood in this way, you can see its connection to love. As a result, it becomes more appealing. We'll grant that the idea of abstinence is boring. It means "no sex." Purity is different, because it goes beyond the mere absence of something. It is a participation in the very love of God. Instead of allowing emotions to fuel your love, the source of your love is God Himself. After all, any animal can have sex. But only a creature made in the image and likeness of God can express pure love.

For the sexually active unmarried couple, the problem is not that they love each other too much, but that they love one another too little. Their love is pleasurable, but is it patient? It may be fun, but is it sacrificial? In their hearts, they feel close to one another through sexual intimacy, but what they're missing out on is the closeness that comes when two people do what's best for one another. They lack the intimacy that comes only through sacrificial love.

7. "He doesn't pressure me to have sex."

Because so many men today are crude and sexually suggestive, some women think that any guy who refrains from making perverted innuendos is practically chivalrous. Especially if a woman had previously been in a relationship where the guy couldn't keep his hands to himself, she'll be amazed to find a man who doesn't pressure her. What she may not realize is that she may be dating the smooth criminal we discussed earlier: Although he might not pressure her to have sex, he won't pressure her to be innocent, either.

Even when a woman consents to sexual intimacy, this is no guarantee that she'll look back at her decision with pride. After finishing college, a woman e-mailed us about her previous relationship. The couple dated for years and were certain that they were meant for one another. They had become rather physical, but didn't think much of it because the decision was mutual. In her e-mail, she reflected upon her decisions and said:

> Over a year out of this relationship, I shudder with disgust at myself and what we did. But at the time, I would have sworn to your face that it was out of love. . . . I suppressed my doubts and proceeded to keep him and me secure the only way I knew how.

Even though this young woman could not see it at the time, the sexual intimacy she shared with her boyfriend created a deep insecurity within her. She had offered him everything a woman can physically offer and had given her heart away in the process. Because she didn't possess the security that a wife enjoys, she used sex to keep him committed.

When sex becomes the soul of a dating relationship, the couple misses the opportunity to work on the qualities that make for lasting love. Things such as friendship, family time, spirituality, trust, patience, and purity get less attention. As a result, the overall health of the relationship can wither. A sense of uneasiness begins to settle upon the heart of the woman. Because the foundation of love is weak and the life of the relationship is resting on lust, she feels an increasing threat that the end is inevitable. She knows it, and the truth scares her. But she usually just keeps having sex because without it the relationship would stand on nothing.

8. "He'd be devastated if we broke up."

When the topic of relationships is discussed in a Christian context, the focus often rests solely on chastity and boundaries of physical intimacy. But there are boundaries of emotional intimacy as well. When a couple shares every hidden secret, memory, and fear with one another, they create between them a bond that isn't easy to separate. If signs of trouble arise in the relationship later on, one partner often feels trapped. This person then stays because of pity. But this is no reason to remain in a relationship.

A man who cannot stand on his own two feet without you is not the man you want to marry. Such a needy guy will not make a good husband and father, but it isn't your job to help him overcome this. His dependency is not a reason to remain, but proof that you should leave. If your relationship is unhealthy, then you may be the one to end up devastated if you stay.

9. "He'll change."

A mother approached me (Crystalina) after I spoke at a women's conference and explained that she wished she had heard my talk fifteen years sooner. Back in college, she dated a man who had some personal problems, but she always hoped he would change. Now, a decade into their marriage, she's seeking a divorce because things only grew worse with time. Not surprisingly, she said her children were "devastated."

The phenomenon of dating troubled guys is rampant among women, partly because women are blessed with a motherly tenderness that seeks to heal others. But this gift of the feminine genius becomes dangerous when it mingles with romantic interests. The woman begins to commit herself to the rehabilitation of a man instead of enjoying a relationship with a gentleman who has his act together.

Girls often romanticize about tomorrow because they don't want to focus on today. They're so busy dreaming about their future that they forget to prepare for it. As a result, their dreams never materialize. If you find yourself in a relationship in which you aren't content with your guy, ask yourself the following questions: "Would I be happy twenty years into marriage if his habits never change?" "Am I happy with such a guy raising my children?" "Would I mind if my kids turned out to be just like him?" Give yourself and your kids the best, and don't ever date a guy hoping he'll change. It's unfair to him and to you.

10. "We're going to get married anyway."

In high school, I (Jason) knew I had met my soulmate. We went to a few dances together and I could envision myself with her forever.

Today, she's married to a friend of mine. In college, I met a girl and never felt so strongly about a woman before. We dated . . . until she broke up with me and later married a friend of mine. Then, I met the girl I *knew* I was going to marry. We *knew* we were soulmates. We dated for years, talked about marriage, and even tried on wedding rings. But I broke up with her, and she—you guessed it—married a friend of mine. Then, I met another girl and *absolutely knew* in my heart that she was the one. We dated for years, and talked to her parents about marriage. But we didn't end up marrying. In case you're wondering, she also married a friend of mine.

Except for the initial high school crush, these were not passing infatuations but serious relationships. However, it was not until I was twenty-four years old that I met Crystalina. By then, it seemed as if all my friends had already married my ex-girlfriends, so I suppose she didn't have much of an option! The reason I give this litany of relationships is to prove that you can't judge the future of a relationship by the intensity of your emotions.

I might sound like a hopeless romantic because I fell in love so many times. But while I was with these girls, you never could have convinced me that I could find anyone more amazing than each of them. Because I had never experienced such intense emotions and attractions before, I confused infatuation with destiny. Regardless of how intense a person's emotions may be, no one except God knows the future. Therefore, it is wise to reserve for marriage the forms of affection that belong within it. Think about it: How much more special will it be on the wedding night when you've waited, or at least started over!

There's nothing wrong with looking forward to marriage, but when you begin plotting wedding dates years into the future, you are playing games with your heart. You become emotionally engaged, and that often leads to greater temptations because you begin to assume that you will become husband and wife based upon how close you feel.

Don't assume that the closer you get to marriage the more justification you have for becoming sexually intimate. Being married is a lot like being pregnant. You either are or you are not. In fact, sleeping together when you are so close to the sacrament of marriage is even more of a problem, because two people who love each other enough to marry ought to have more concern for each other's soul. Even if you have saved sex for the guy you hope to marry, this does not make your actions moral. It just means you're optimistic.

As you can see, behind every sin or bad relationship is a justification, and behind every justification is a fear. Consider the ten you just read, and look at the fear that lurks behind each one:

1. He's really sweet . . . but why?
2. There's more to our relationship than sex, and we're not always doing it . . . but how long would we last without it, and should we be doing it at all?
3. We've been together so long . . . but what if it ends?
4. I already gave myself to him . . . but what if that was a mistake?
5. My family loves him . . . but would they even like him if they knew the truth?
6. We really love each other . . . but what if it's lust?
7. He doesn't pressure me for sex . . . but shouldn't I expect more from a guy?
8. He'd be devastated if we broke up . . . but is that a reason to stay?
9. He'll change . . . but what if he's just changing me?
10. We'll get married . . . but what if we don't?

I've heard it said that when you truly love a man, you don't just love him for who he is. You love who you become when you're with him. When a relationship is healthy, pure, and godly, there will be no need for rationalizations and fear. Peace and gratitude will exist instead. Therefore, never move forward in a relationship unless your conscience is at rest. This may require a painful amount of honesty on your part, but do not be afraid to listen to your heart. If you can't be honest with yourself, are you really being honest with anyone?

Grow a Backbone

"I am not a fruit."

With these words, a Muslim woman began her comments to a room of teenagers. As you would expect, the teens responded with a puzzled look. She repeated herself:

I am not a fruit. I grew up near a marketplace, and the men would walk down the aisles of fruit. The men picked up and examined everything before they bought one. They would touch them, smell them, handle them, and toss them back into the pile. After rummaging through the batch, they would pick one, buy it, and leave. I am not a fruit.

The students got her point. Unfortunately, many women today settle for being treated like produce. With a helpless shrug, they slough off the irreverent things men say and do to them by assuming "Boys will be boys. What can I do about it?" If a woman wants to receive a more dignified response from men, she needs one quality above all: a backbone.

Spinelessness Is a Choice

When a woman chooses to settle for poor relationships and poor treatment from men, it's not simply because she lacks self-esteem or self-love. Although this plays a role in her refusal to assert her rights, there's another reason why she tolerates being treated badly. There's something in it for her.

At first, that may sound absurd. But think about it: The woman who stays in a bad relationship is there because she would rather not be elsewhere. She fears that she will lose something (or someone) if she stands up for herself. So she stands quietly in the shadows and hopes that her life will change for the better by itself. Even in the midst of an insecure and abusive relationship, many women find security. In order for such women to be liberated from the confines of their dead-end relationships, they must see the empty lies behind their fears. Here are the top five.

1. Fear of disappointment   There is no limit to the number of women today who settle for nothing in life because they are afraid to hope for anything. In their eyes, the best way to prevent disappointment is never to hope.

Indeed, a woman is safer without taking risks. This is true in all human endeavors. If you don't want to lose in a sport, the surest way to achieve that is not to play at all. Don't even try out and you'll be undefeated. The only way to win is to risk losing. It is much the same with love. One seventh-century monk remarked, "Hope is the power behind love. . . . When hope fails, so does love."[1] A woman might prevent certain disappointments by refusing to set high standards, but she will eventually have to face the greatest of disappointments: She was created for love, but she never had the courage to pursue it.

2. Fear of loss   A seventeen-year-old high school girl e-mailed me (Jason), anxious about the fact that her boyfriend was heading off to an out-of-state college in a few weeks. She was considering sleeping with him for the first time, in an effort to keep his attention away from the rowdy college girls that would soon be coming his way. I suppose she thought of her virginity as some kind of vaccination for his hormones—as if an inoculation of lust would prevent him from desiring anyone else.

I can understand what she was thinking: "If I don't give it to him now, he'll find another girl who will!" And maybe she was right. Maybe he is that type of guy. If so, he's worth losing.

But what if she slept with him, employing her sexual tactic to win his attention? Her attempt would have been futile. She just would have put herself on par with the girls whose competition she fears. If she wanted to keep a decent guy, she could do that by showing how different she is from the college girls she's so worried about. The strength of her allure should rest in the fact that she is unlike other women. If she wants him to remember her when he leaves for college, the last thing she needs to do is conform to the mold of a buzzed and flirty sorority girl, bereft of any moral compass.

The bottom line is this: Guys don't fall in love with girls by getting physical with them. We may fall into lust that way, but love is a different matter. Pleasure may be nice, but it doesn't increase love in the heart of a boyfriend. The world tells you that such behavior will help you to win a man, but as one woman mused, "If you have to ask someone if he'll still love you tomorrow, then he doesn't love you tonight."[2] If you want a guy to love you, live in such a way that makes him in awe of you.

One wife told me that when her husband proposed to her, she asked him, "Why me? You have so much going for you, with your career and everything. You could do anything with your life. Why is it that you want to marry me? Why now?" Without hesitation, he replied, "Because I'm afraid if I don't, I'll never find anyone like you." Like her, become what you are: unrepeatable.

3. *Fear of abstinence*   It may sound strange to be afraid of abstinence, but some women are terrified to stop having sex. Although the thought of catching an STD or getting pregnant might cross their minds, they're far more concerned with the consequences of abstinence.

Throughout history, women have been tempted to use the intoxicating power of their sexuality for the wrong reasons, including the desire to gain control, execute vengeance, or obtain security. As one woman mentioned to me, "I would pressure him to have sex with me because that's the only way I knew how to feel secure about my-self." When women debase the gift of their sexuality in this way, they debase themselves. It could be said that sex for security is like pros-titution, with emotional gratification being offered instead of money. While the man uses her for one thing, she uses him for another.

Usually her intentions are anything but malicious. Her behavior is more of an act of desperation than of spite. As one college woman confessed, "I figured if he was happy then maybe, just maybe, I was one step closer to getting him back." To such a woman, purity is frightening. But what she should fear is what will happen if she's not pure. Without purity, a woman will not possess assurance as to why she is being loved. How secure can a woman feel in the arms of a man whose love she doubts?

4. Fear of the unknown Although unchaste relationships tend to be unpredictable and turbulent, such an environment may be all a woman knows. For the girl who routinely shuts down her conscience in order to say yes to a boyfriend or potential hookup, the idea of finally saying no might make her feel as if she's losing control in her relationship.

Many women notice that they began fighting with their boyfriends more after they became sexually active, and then they fought even more when the women took the sex away. To avoid confrontation, many choose to remain silent and sexually available. If she decides to turn him down, what will he say? How will he react? All of a sudden, because she's choosing not to appease him, she surrenders the ability to control his response. Just the thought of having to deal with this uncertainty is enough to make many girls keep their stan-dards below the radar. They don't want to make a fuss. They may think, "What if this guy leaves me? Will I find someone else willing to love me?"

Never settle for less than you deserve because you're afraid that nothing better will come along. What you really should be afraid of is how much of your life is passing you by because you're too busy doing things that are beneath your dignity.

5. Fear of rejection The most common reason why women don't set higher standards is because they are afraid of being rejected for daring to have them. When a girl allows these fears to dictate her choices, she'll begin to tolerate just about anything in a relationship. One high school girl shared:

> He would come over, and though I'd try to talk or to watch a movie, all he ever wanted to do was physical activity. I was somewhat uncomfortable with this, but rather than lose a friend, I shut my mouth. I knew I was being used, but I kept making excuses so that I wouldn't feel as horrible as I did. However, feeling so bad was inevitable.

Another told us:

> My boyfriend broke up with me because he says he is confused. I miss him soooo much and I really want to date him, like so bad, and not because I just want a boyfriend, but I really do love him. I'd do anything to make him happy, or anything that would benefit him, even if I'm not happy. I lost my virginity to him, I gave him everything.

If you are currently in a relationship in which you are also willing to "do anything to make him happy," even at your own expense, I want you to stop reading our book. Mark this page, close the book, and hit yourself over the head with it. Then continue reading.

If a woman is willing to be unhappy for the sake of a man, this is not a sign of how much she loves him. It's a sign of how desperate she is to feel accepted. She forgets what she really wants in life because she's so busy trying to conform to what he wants. Such an unhealthy obsession shows that she's not even ready to be in a relationship. Why would a girl put herself through this? Stasi Eldredge explains:

> The reason we fear to step out is because we know that it might not go well (is that an understatement?). We have a history of wounds screaming at us to play it safe. We feel so deeply that if it doesn't go well, if we are not received well, their reaction becomes the verdict on our lives, on our very beings, on our hearts. We fear that our deepest doubts about ourselves as women will be confirmed. Again.[3]

What is this deepest fear? It's that you're just too much. Or that you're just not enough. Letting go of this fear isn't easy. As incoming freshmen at high school or college, the girls learn that they don't want to be too assertive, too prudish, too serious, or too anything.

Because they're not sure of their own identity, they settle for the next best thing—trying to be who they think others want them to be.

If a woman raises her standards, will she find herself alone? Initially, she probably will. Although it may sound counterproductive, a woman must deliberately decrease her odds of finding a guy in order to increase her odds of finding a soulmate. Things such as modest dress and high moral standards will diminish the number of men willing to pursue her. However, it will also increase her appeal to those who are worthy of her. Nonetheless, there's no way around it: Standards will cause you to feel lonely at times. But put things in perspective: One woman discovered after quitting her cycle of sexual relationships that "though I felt lonely, I'd felt lonelier in the past with a lover by my side."[4]

The lower a woman's standards, the larger the crowd of men she'll have to choose from. Initially, she may feel enthused that so many men are interested in her. However, it becomes disheartening when she realizes that they're more interested in their own gratification. One woman said in her e-mail, "I don't know how I keep finding the guys that just want to use me. But I'm really starting to think that there is no guy that will like me for me. And you have no idea how depressing that is."

The wait to find a decent man may feel excruciating at times, but why not hold out for a guy who loves you for who you are, not for what you give him? As you wait, know that your interior struggle is normal. It's a necessary part of the journey as you become the woman God created you to be. But in the midst of the storm, make the choice to stay true to your hopes and values. Don't toss them aside. By doing so, you would be giving up on your very self. Stay true to your standards, because it's a far better thing to be disappointed in men than to be disappointed in yourself.

What's Your Alternative?

Before explaining how you can grow a backbone, it's helpful to reflect on the consequences of choosing not to have one. The story of

Jessica shows the radical outcome of a girl who never learned to say no:

Anyways, he was three years older than me at the time. We had really only seen each other twice (and only for a brief ten minutes each time) before we had sex. I was drunk and stoned when I lost my virginity. I remember *making* myself get that way so that I wouldn't have time to say no to him, and thus possibly lose him. I did it with him in one of his friend's houses—a strange place I had never been to before—and I remember that after he was done, I asked him to stay with me for just a few minutes so my mind could catch up to what my body had just done, and he said no. He looked away from me, and walked out of the room. I went out to him and wrapped my arms around him and he said, "What are you doing?" I was confused. He then walked me back to the convenience store where my friend was picking me up, and he kissed me goodbye, and that was the last time I saw him. I tried calling him for about two weeks, but he always turned off his phone, or wouldn't pick up—and finally his friend picked up one day and told me that he was done with me and if I didn't stop calling she would "break my face." That was the end of that.

Afterward, she went through a cycle of guys and eventually met one who seemed the sweetest of all. He pursued her for months, and she finally gave in and slept with him as well. Then he stopped returning her calls and text messages. She concluded, "Now it's more than obvious that he is bored with me." She continued:

I don't wanna be the easy girl anymore, I don't want to be the slut, and I don't want to have STDs. I don't want to be tossed aside. But I'm too weak to say no. I don't know how to. I barely get any hugs ever. I get NO physical affection from anyone anymore and when I do get it from people I know in my life, I pull away to avoid to being hurt—and when I have strangers who show me affection and wanna sleep with me . . . I say yes and I do it because I want to feel safe and in someone's arms for once, even if it's only for a few minutes. But afterward, it hurts more.

It has often been said that the definition of insanity is doing the same thing over and over, hoping to get a different result. But this is what Jessica was doing. None of the men in her life could have given her the love she desired. They surely told her what she wanted to hear so that she would give them what they wanted to feel. Their embraces were only a mirage that left her feeling stranded in a desert. The consolations she sought from them turned out to be nothing more than a form of self-torture.

Yet another woman e-mailed me and confessed, "My stupidity coupled with my effort to be nice to everybody makes it hard to stand up for what I believe in." If you can relate, then it's time to get a backbone. If you don't, then you'll give more and more of yourself away while feeling that you have less and less to offer. Before long, many girls end up thinking that sex is the only thing they have to gain the interest of men.

To prevent this, understand that rare things are worth more. Girls (and guys) without standards are easy to find. And they're also easy to get bored with. On the other hand, the more pure you are, the more desirable you become. At times the standard of purity can bring about times of loneliness. But don't feel too depressed about that. Even the most popular and attractive people sometimes feel lonely—and perhaps more than you would ever imagine. What's important is that you don't use sexual intimacy to avoid feeling lonely. Instead, find healthy ways to surround yourself with those who do care about you.

From now on, don't be afraid that guys will leave you unless you give them something sexual. Turn the tables for once. Let the guys be afraid they're going to lose *you* unless they know how to respect you! Besides, the men who leave you because of your standards would have left you anyway, once they got what they wanted. Do the smart thing and get rid of them now, without losing any of your time or dignity.

Sprouting Your Backbone

After giving a presentation at a junior high in Washington, D.C., three seventh-grade girls approached me. They explained:

> Jason, here's the problem: We don't know how to say no to boys. We do things with them that make us feel uncomfortable. Even if a dork or a jerk asks us out, we say yes. Then, when we don't have a boy, we get sad and cry and eat ice cream and get overweight. What should we do, because right now we're sad because we aren't dating anyone?

No kidding. This was their question. In the most loving tone possible, I replied:

> Get over it. The last thing this world needs is a couple of women who can't stand on their own two feet because they need to cling to a boy to be secure and happy. You're in seventh grade and it's not like you would want to end up with these guys anyway, would you? Cheer up!

They laughed, gave me a quick hug, and bounced away, smiling without a concern. Now, it's not always that easy, but I think sometimes we need a loving kick in the pants more than anything.

It has often been said that the only thing more expensive than education is ignorance. In the same respect, the only thing more costly than having a backbone is living without one. It may seem difficult to be strong and to say no to passing pleasures and dumb relationships, but a more difficult life awaits you if you're weak. In fact, if you want love, the most important word in your vocabulary must be "no." As one man said, at some point in your life you have to "decide that you want it more than you are afraid of it."[5] After all, if you really want love, you can't spend your life cowering in fear that you'll never find it.

In order for a woman to grow her backbone, she sometimes needs to be reminded that it's okay to have one. It also helps to see women whose backbones are firmly in place. Take, for example, Lakita Garth, who is an abstinence speaker and former Miss Black California. She states:

> I'm president and CEO of my own company. All of my employees are men, and you know what? Pretty soon, hopefully, I'm going to have my own little office, maybe a little office building strip mall off somewhere, and I have to hire a janitor, you know, to service my building, and you know what I'm going to do? I'm going to have to have some applications before you can even see my face. And then there's the interview process, when you sit across from my table in my office and my building. I want you to fill in an application with your full name, not "Mooky" or whatever alias you're going by this week; and I want all your telephone numbers, not just a cell or a pager. I want to see some previous work experience, I want to see if you have a criminal record, and, as a matter of fact, I want some character

references. I want you to write that all down, and that's just to clean my toilet, and most women don't have that much sense, to get a last name from guys who will take off all their clothes and have sex with them.[6]

What are the chances that a woman like this would allow herself to be taken advantage of? In Lakita's case, she didn't. She held fast to her morals, praying that in God's time, He would send her Mr. Right. She eventually met her husband, and appreciated God's sense of humor when she learned his last name was Wright!

It's comforting to see when a person's hopes are fulfilled. But what's a girl to do when her quest for a loving relationship seems bleak? What should she do when she's tempted to fall back into the pleasures of an empty life in an effort to drown out her fears of uncertainty?

This is a serious time of training, when a woman must cling to the promises of God as revealed in His Word. To St. Paul, God said, "My grace is sufficient for you, for my power is made perfect in weakness."[7] Elsewhere, in Paul's first letter to the Corinthians, he reminds us:

> No temptation has overtaken you that is not common to man. God is faithful, and he will not let you be tempted beyond your strength, but with the temptation will also provide the way of escape, that you may be able to endure it.[8]

When you feel that you don't have the strength, bring these verses to mind and turn your heart to God, asking Him to fulfill His promises in you.

Don't be disturbed if there is a struggle within you. At times, it seems so easy to do what is wrong yet so difficult to do what is right. You feel as if you're always fighting the current, and at times you'd rather let go and float downstream. You might feel weak, but resistance is the only way to build endurance and strength.

To boost your spirits, take to heart the following things that young women have told me. I would put these girls in my Backbone Hall of Fame:

A teenager in Los Angeles shared with me one of the criteria she uses for screening out the wrong type of guys. In her words, "I don't mean to sound cocky, but I don't want to marry a guy unless he's worthy of my body." By this, she didn't mean that she had a perfect figure. She just knew her dignity.

Other girls who share her outlook on relationships have said to me such things as:

I view my body as a shrine that only one man will ever see, my husband.

If I am good enough for God, then I am good enough for everyone, and I don't need to make myself any less of a woman to do that.

I don't need to be someone's toy in order to be accepted. I just need to be the best person I can.

I've decided to look at myself as a gem hidden in a treasure box and my future husband will be the first and only one to open it.

I know that God made me in His image and likeness and as such I am a beautiful daughter of God. If someone can't see that, it is their loss.

When you bring such confidence into your relationships, it raises the bar for men. In her book *Modestly Yours*, Camille De Blasi recalls a memorable date from college:

It was our first date. We were going to a dance, and I was all dressed up in a long, pink gown. He parked right in the middle of a mud puddle, got out of the car, and started walking toward the building. He didn't even notice that I was still in the car, and was talking to me as if I were right behind him. I knew he was still talking to me because the back of his head was bobbing up and down. So I just sat there in the car and waited. After a while, he must've figured out something was wrong, because he turned around. When he saw me still in the car, he gestured as if to say, "Git yourself on down here, girl!" I just sat there and blinked a couple of times. He cupped his hands around his mouth and yelled, "What are you doing? C'mon!" So I smiled. He walked to the side of the car, leaned over the puddle, right up to my window, and shouted, "Are you okay? Let's go!" So I locked the door. Okay, maybe I overdid it a little, but he ended up opening the door for me. Of course, it also ended up being our last date. But that's alright. I didn't make him open the door for me because I'm stuck up and think I'm extra special and deserve to have doors opened for me. It was because I have a very serious and important job, too. It's my job, as a woman, to inspire men to be noble, brave, honorable, and to protect and defend the loveliness and beauty of every woman.[9]

Another young woman, when breaking things off with a boyfriend who didn't treat her with honor, said, "Not only do you not deserve my body, you don't deserve my time!" Still another said about her ex, "I told him that if he can't deal with my decisions, to walk out of my life until he can treat me like a human."

No girl wants to hurt a guy's feelings, but you sometimes need to do this in order to teach him how to act like a man. I know one girl who simply tells guys, "I don't hook up. I have morals. If you don't respect that, then go home." One of my favorite quotes came from another young woman, who wrote to me, "Sure, attention from boys feels good. But knowing that I'm too good for half of them feels even better!" All I could say in return is, "You go, girl."

If you take on such an attitude, you'll discover that it feels much better to love yourself than to feel lusted after by unworthy men. It's not easy to end bad relationships, but the following woman put things in perspective:

My ex-boyfriend could not have been my future husband. Why? Because if he was, he would have wanted me for my mind and heart as well. But it didn't seem that way. My future husband has standards he will need to live up to. They're nothing big, but to me, they're important. He'll have to earn my body by first loving my mind, my personality, my heart, and my soul. If a guy truly loves me, he'll love the rest of me first, before seeing my body.

Not only does a woman display her courage through her standards, she also displays her intelligence. A Harvard student named Janie Fredell wrote in her college newspaper about her choice to be pure:

The woman who succeeds in resisting this temptation is she whose sex appeal transcends her sexual aptitude. Such women boast the intelligence necessary to make healthy life decisions, the charm to win the attention of men without promise of physical compensation, the maturity to acknowledge the difference between love and lust, and the confidence to demand the former in situations where they are pressured to compromise themselves for the latter.[10]

Janie went on to note that the "mysterious allure of virginity" is ultimately rooted in "the notion of strength: the ability to withstand temptation even in the face of societal norms and expectations." When a woman possesses such strength, she'll begin to look at men and relationships in a new light. After breaking off a relationship with her friend with benefits, one woman shared, "I actually pitied him. I realized that I wanted pure total self-giving love. I want a guy who's willing to give me a second chance to be pure, not a guy who takes my second chance away."

You will notice a common thread in all of these quotes. None of the girls derive the value of their lives from the opinions of men. Their sense of worth comes from what they believe and how they live. It comes from within them, not from without. None of these girls saw any logic in losing themselves for the sake of winning a guy. They knew that you have to be yourself in a relationship. If you're not, eventually the truth will come to the surface. If you're not being loved for who you are, then it isn't love at all.

It may feel awkward to practice the confidence that these women exude. Your first steps might feel wobbly as you follow their lead. But the more often you stand up for your dignity, the easier and more automatic it will become. Don't doubt yourself. Courage is not a genetic trait that some have inherited and others have not. People do not persevere because they are strong. They become strong because they persevere. The path is not an easy one, but take courage: The harder the climb, the greater the view will be when you get to the top.

How do you begin the ascent? Step one is to ask God to help you. Talk to Him—heart to heart—about all of this. If you've been far from Him, know that He isn't mad at you because of the past. It has been said that God is more eager to help you out of a bad lifestyle than a mother would be to snatch her baby out of a fire. He's there for you, and will give you every grace you need to conquer your fears. Tell Him, "God, I don't have the strength. Give me yours."

He'll answer such prayers, but He waits for you to ask.

A popular spiritual maxim is that you ought to "pray as if everything depended on God and work as if everything depended on you."[11] To begin your part of the work, remember that the only way to gain the respect of others is by respecting yourself and refusing to live in fear of what others think. You might not be able to dismiss your fears in an instant, but you can choose to live as if those fears no longer have the power to control your fate. Your fears may linger for a time, but that doesn't mean you need to obey them.

Animal experts say that dogs have an innate ability to sense fear in people. When Crystalina and I were engaged, I bought her an adorable Chihuahua puppy—that turned out in my humble opinion to be more of a nippy, spoiled cat. If you attempted to move him from his bed—which, by the way, Crystalina adorned with black and gold satin sheets—he'd lunge toward you, attempting to tear off one of your fingers. But if you approached him with confidence, he was docile as a lamb.

I don't want to compare men to dogs, but the analogy works here. Guys can sense when you don't have a strong will, and many of them will take advantage of you because of it. But when players sense strength, they often don't bother to try. Therefore, even if you don't feel you have a backbone, "fake it 'til you make it." Just be who you hope to be.

Having a backbone is not always about being harsh and blunt, though. At times, such an approach may be required. But more often than not, you can be both soft and strong, graceful yet uncompromising. Imagine if a cute guy asks you out but you know he's probably not who you want to end up marrying. Instead of shooting him down and proclaiming your higher standards, you can simply say, "You know, I really enjoy your friendship and I've liked getting to know you. But I'm not really interested in a relationship. So would you mind if we just got to know each other better as friends?" This way, it sounds more like an invitation than a rejection.

Your need for a backbone doesn't merely apply to your relationships with men. You especially need one in your interaction with other females. Out of a desire to fit in, how many millions of young women do regretful things and become who they know they're not? How much of our lives are wasted pretending to be who we think others want us to be?

Set Your Standards and Don't Settle for Less

(Crystalina) In order to defend our standards as women, we first need to establish them. While some girls know exactly what they want in a relationship, others don't seem very picky. Just as some women focus more on getting married than on who they're marrying, many young women pay more attention to landing a date than to who they're dating. They may think, "Well, he's mostly good. Why complicate things?" It doesn't take long for such relationships to implode.

For example, one single woman asked:

> My boyfriend has slept with girls before, and he said he can't imagine marrying a girl with whom he was "unfamiliar." Sometimes, he gives me a hard time because I don't initiate physical stuff with him. Am I being a prude by not sleeping with him?

It's interesting that her ex said that he couldn't marry someone with whom he was "unfamiliar." If that's his litmus test for a bride, then why didn't he marry the rest of the girls with whom he was so familiar? If you're with a guy who thinks sex is a tryout, don't go out for the team.

This woman is not a prude. She's just dating a walking hormone. One reason why she never initiates physical activity is because a woman does not desire to give of herself when she senses the man is only interested in taking. She's more concerned with guarding herself than giving herself. Her intuition to pull away from her boyfriend is her built-in defense system. Women naturally recoil from a user. They guard the treasure—not just of their body, but of their very selves. By establishing non-negotiable standards for future relationships, a woman builds a castle around her heart. Unless a guy is man enough to ascend the wall, he has no chance of being with her.

After I broke off my bad relationships in high school, I took a few years off from the dating scene to re-evaluate my priorities in life. During this time, I created a list of sixty things that I hoped for in a husband. I decided that I had spent enough time in my life compromising on the guys I dated. For once, why not set the bar as high as I wanted?

It didn't take long before the smooth-talking and sweet-smelling guys came into my life. But this time I knew there was no point in wasting my time with a guy I didn't want to spend the next seventy years of my life with. So I refused to date them. As the days and months turned into years, there were times when I questioned if my list had made me too picky.

Some items on the list were just for fun, such as the fact that I was hoping he was a world traveler and that he wasn't too tall. Others were non-negotiable, such as the fact that I wanted him to be a man of God who believed in chastity. What's amusing is that I met Jason (who is 5'7") while at a chastity conference in the Bahamas, after his plane had just arrived from his previous trip to Israel! God knew the desires of my heart.

If you hope to get married one day, make your own list. Feel free to daydream, but make a mature distinction between what's essential and what is not. This is not a list requiring perfection. But it should at least contain the essentials of a healthy relationship. The purpose of the list is not for you to tell God that you want a man who is a saintly 6'4" millionaire model who cooks, has a foreign accent, owns a chocolate company, gives great foot rubs, and rescues abandoned puppies from the animal shelter. If you're not willing to date a person unless he's perfect, then the fault is not in him. It's in you. Every person has his faults. If you think you've found the perfect man, you're setting yourself up for disappointment.

What essentials should be on your list? Here are some thoughts:

- I want him to be my best friend.
- He needs to love God more than he loves me.
- Instead of bringing out my weaknesses, he brings out my dignity.
- He's kind and gentle with me.
- He builds me up and does not wear me down.

- He treats his mom with love.
- Besides respecting me, he respects himself.
- I want him to have strong morals so I don't need to convince him of mine.

It's wise to set these standards before you enter a relationship instead of springing them on a boyfriend who barely meets half of them. But the sooner you develop your own personal list, the better. Then you can begin the important work of being the kind of woman who deserves such a man. Become your own list, because he deserves nothing less in you. Just imagine the kind of guy you hope to find. What kind of girl do you think he's looking for?

Pure Persecution

Suppose that you decide to raise your standards after having made poor decisions in the past. Expect resistance. If a girl who used to flirt with every boy on campus suddenly shows deep respect for herself, guys will give her a hard time. But this is only because their pride is hurt. They miss having around the spineless girl who giggled at their perverted jokes. At first, they may not take her seriously. They might joke about her change of heart, saying they know it won't last. But if she stands firm, they'll grow to respect her.

Any wise woman will understand that no matter how she lives, she'll pay a price. One girl asked us, "How do you deal with all the pressure in college to have sex? I've got a reputation as being the 'Virgin Mary' and guys are taking bets out on who can get me in bed first." First, she should realize that there are far worse insults than being called the "Virgin Mary." Actually, it's quite a compliment to be equated with the greatest woman ever to exist.

As every girl knows, if you practice purity, you'll be called a prude or a tease. But if you don't, you'll be called a litany of less pleasant names. Therefore, if everyone needs to pay a price for the way they live, why not choose a lifestyle that will pay off? If you have received insults for your decision to follow God's plan, count them all as blessings. In his epistle, the apostle St. James wrote:

Consider it all joy, my brothers, when you encounter various trials, for you know that the testing of your faith produces perseverance. And let perseverance be perfect, so that you may be perfect and complete, lacking in nothing.[12]

Although it's difficult to hear the insults of those close to you, know that all of heaven is applauding you. Perhaps some people in your life have given up hope in you. Prove them all wrong. Your friends may not see strength in you. Your own family may not see it. You might not even see it! But if you draw near to God, in time you will see it and joy will be yours.

If guys mock you, put bets on you, or try to wear you down with their worn-out lines, we want you to remember it all. If girls try to tear you down for holding a higher standard for yourself, don't forget their words. If you want, write them down. Make a list of them. Let them laugh about it now, and then when you stand at the altar on your wedding day in your luminous white dress, we want you to listen closely: Where is the laughter? Where is the mockery? They're silent, and every one of them would love to be in your place on that day. You waited, and you won. You've been freed from the baggage of the past and you've prepared yourself to begin the rest of your life. With a clean heart and a pure body, you can stand at that altar and give yourself to the one who is man enough to be worthy of such a bride.

Now what were those names they called you? I'll bet you already forgot them!

Waiting with Wisdom

While this romantic image of the perfect wedding day sounds blissful to most single women, the fact is that it hasn't arrived. Some of you wonder if it ever will. What are you to do in the meantime? Give yourself permission to hope. Allow yourself to experience the ache within you for something beautiful. It's not childish to dream about finding a love that helps you become the woman you want to be. However, no one can give you this kind of love. You have to work for it.

The love you desire can be found. But the process begins by loving yourself enough to avoid the guys who don't. Throughout your single years, you'll be offered the opposite of love far more often than the real thing. Anticipate that this will be the case, and don't be discouraged by the reality of it. If you can begin this new life with realistic expectations, you'll be more prepared to live it.

All girls grow up hearing about fairy-tale romances. But many of them are raised in families that are quite the opposite. Because of divorce, infidelity, and abuse, countless young women have never seen a man properly love a woman. How is a girl to hope for something she's never seen? Even if she does have a vague notion of how love should be, she might refuse to hope for it, assuming that such dreams will only end in disappointment. For this reason, many women no longer expect to find a good man. As they read the pages of this book, a shadow of cynical skepticism is cast over their hearts. Who can blame them?

What these women have not taken into consideration is the providence of God. He can accomplish what you cannot.

Recently, while on a speaking tour in New Zealand, I (Jason) met a man who reminded me how God always provides for those who trust in Him. He said that in Christchurch, New Zealand, a group of religious women wanted to put on a Christmas play for their church. Because they wanted to make it as authentic as possible, they decided to include a real donkey. Apparently there weren't many donkeys around, and the ones that could be found were far too expensive. So they decided to pray for a donkey.

Each of the women drew a picture of the animal and put it under her pillow, as a reminder to pray for this intention when going to bed and waking up. Before long, an unfamiliar man showed up with a donkey and offered to loan it to them for the upcoming play. They were elated. However, the donkey had one strange feature: It had no tail. Nobody thought much of this until the women looked at the pictures each of them had drawn. Sure enough, every one of them forgot to draw a tail on her donkey! The moral of the story is that it helps to be specific when you ask God for something.

God can take care of even the smallest details if we remain faithful to Him. Even if you've never seen authentic love between a husband and wife or between a boyfriend and girlfriend, it isn't a figment of your imagination. God placed that desire for unconditional love in your heart. You have been created for love. Don't settle for less. As St. Paul says, "Let us not grow tired of doing good, for in due time we shall reap our harvest, if we do not give up."[13] The harvest he speaks of is not finding the guy of your dreams. Specifically, he's talking about your eternal reward from God. But even in this life, our joy can only be found in His will.

HANG UP ON HOOKUPS

Have you ever gone to the grocery store on an empty stomach and passed by an employee offering free food samples? Because you're surrounded by food—but not actually eating any of it—any bite tastes heavenly. You walk away thinking, "That was the best taquito I've ever tasted." It was probably pure lard, but because you had nothing else in your stomach, it seemed infinitely satisfying. If you're like us, you probably make a few more laps to swipe more samples in hopes that the taquito lady won't remember you.

However, if you spend too much time gorging yourself on the appetizers, you lose your appetite for the real meal. When a woman settles for a hookup, she does the same thing in terms of love. She stuffs herself with guys, who, for lack of a better description, are the cheap taquitos, when her stomach is made for the seven-course meal. If the real thing ever comes along, she'll be too stuffed to accept it.

Although this comparison might be amusing, the reality of hookups is anything but. Why would a woman loan her affections to men who are obviously interested in only one thing?

The Psychology of a Hookup

After studying the sexual lifestyles of students at numerous colleges across the country, Donna Freitas summed up the motives behind hooking up when she wrote:

Within hookup culture, many students perform sexual acts because that's "just what people do," because they are bored, because they've done it once before so why not again and again, because they're too trashed to summon any self-control, because it helps them climb the social ladder, and because how else is a person supposed to snag a significant other in a community where nobody ever dates? Living within hook-up culture means putting up an "I don't care" front about behavior, submitting to unwanted experiences, and, in many cases, slowly chipping away at personal standards, expectations, sense of self, and respect for others, until these are sublimated so fully that students almost can't remember what they were in the first place.[1]

Women hook up for a myriad of reasons. But if they are daring enough to examine their motives, they can uncover the core issues that fuel their behavior. Only then will they be prepared to set out for the love that satisfies.

Why would a girl hook up? Here's a deeper look at a few of the most common reasons.

1. "Maybe he'll commit." A young woman e-mailed me (Jason), saying:

> I've been seeing this guy on and off for a few years, and we hooked up the other night even though we're not really together now. He goes a little too far sometimes, but I'm afraid to lose him because he's all I have. What should I do?

This girl was so afraid to lose him that she was blind to the fact that she didn't have him to begin with. It's difficult to imagine how many young women like this have assured their potential love interest that they were content with a hookup, despite the fact that they wanted a relationship. Why do they settle? It's because they've bought into the myth that hooking up with a guy will make him more likely to commit.

As a guy, allow me to explain how we work: When a hookup does lead to more, it usually leads only to more hooking up. That's it. What little you have in terms of a relationship will come to a swift end as soon as he gets bored or finds someone else more desirable. Think about it: How many loving relationships and happy marriages do you know of that began with a desperate girl hooking up with an uncommitted guy? If you can't think of one, what are your odds of becoming the exception?

Some girls discover this the hard way. After hooking up, one fifteen-year-old said, "I didn't expect the guy to marry me, but I never expected him to avoid me in school."[2] When a girl gives away her body or her kisses as if they are boy bait, the guy will lose all desire to pursue her. After all, what's left for him to desire when she has already fulfilled his basest wishes within a week of knowing him? What else will he care to discover about her? Her musical talent or witty personality? Her emotions, spirituality, or political viewpoints?

In the mind of any man who is willing to hook up with a girl, it's all downhill after the physical. A male student from Duke University commented, "If a girl offers, I'm not going to turn her down. But I'm also not going to call her up and ask her for a date afterward."[3] Although drawn to her in the pleasure of the moment, he'll secretly resent the fact that she's so accessible. She isn't a challenge for him.

If you want a guy to cherish you, you must understand that your kisses are rare and your body is a treasure. Neither is given away freely. When a woman has this mentality, she becomes more alluring. When she loves and respects her own body, she invites men to follow her example. Her lifestyle of purity says, "I only give myself fully to the one man who has given himself fully to me." As you can see, this message is a challenge of love, not an invitation to use. Certainly, most men will not rise to the challenge. But that's not a loss, because you don't want to end up with such guys anyway!

2. *"It's just for fun."* One journalist, who interviewed many college students in order to assess their attitudes toward hooking up, reported that the dissatisfaction seemed almost universal. One young woman said that the entire scene left her feeling unhappy and depressed, but:

> She embraced it as if it were "the best ever," just a normal part of the college experience. She thought she was supposed to like it, but to be honest, she actually hated it. Her fellow classmates nodded their heads

in silent agreement. . . . We're not happy with the hookup culture, they said. We feel a constant pressure to do things that make us feel unsettled.[4]

A confused brand of feminism promotes the idea that women have the right to be just as sexually aggressive as some men—as if the vice were worthy of emulation. Such individuals would consider chastity an unfair burden to impose upon free-spirited individuals who want to express their sexuality in whatever way feels best to them. But those who hook up for fun should pause to ask themselves one question: "Is this really fun?"

A radio show host offered:

I remember the challenge from one female teen on my radio program who demanded to know, "Why can't I have sex in a casual way with a number of people if it feels good? My mother couldn't give me any good reason." . . . "But," I asked, "can you feel really good if you know that ultimately nobody cares about you, nor you about them, much at all? Isn't that a lonely thought—a lonely feeling?" She quietly said, "Yes."[5]

When a woman habitually hooks up, she might claim to feel no remorse. But shamelessness will not cure the problem of shame. When tempted to reduce your sexuality to "fun," realize that the gift of your body is worth so much more.

Women resent players because they use women for the sake of fun. But when a girl settles for hooking up, she becomes what she despises. As a result, she often ends up loathing herself. Not only will she begin to lose respect for herself, she'll also come to respect guys less. She may argue that she doesn't feel guilty about it, but her lack of guilt is not a sign that she's happy. It's just an indication that she's numb.

3. "I don't want a committed relationship anyway."   When a woman claims not to desire commitment, it's safe to assume that she has been burned in the past and has lost all desire to become vulnerable again. It's not that she finds the idea of unconditional love to be bland. In her eyes, it's captivating but unrealistic. Therefore, she keeps her expectations low so that they won't be dashed. But when a woman becomes so fearful of hurt that she renders herself unlovable, she becomes her own worst enemy. In the words of Dawn Eden, "It is the fear of disappointment that disappoints."[6]

Emotional detachment doesn't prevent disappointment. For evidence of this, a journalist from the *New York Times* interviewed a number of high school students to assess their attitudes about casual physical relationships. She noted:

> You just keep it purely sexual, and that way people don't have mixed expectations, and no one gets hurt. But, invariably, people do. Many teenagers told me they were hurt by hookups—usually because they expected or hoped for more. But they often blamed themselves for letting their emotions get the best of them. The hookups weren't the problem. They were the problem.[7]

College students feel the same. After sleeping with her boyfriend, a university student instant-messaged her friend about the fact that she was comfortable sleeping with him but fearful of loving him:

> I want to be independent and I think that it is important for women of our generation but saying I love someone and need him it's like contradictory. . . hypocritical . . . but I also don't want to give into love because I am scared he won't call me . . . and I will be heartbroken and then feel like a stupid girl that should have known better.[8]

A woman may assert that she's too busy to settle down in a serious relationship, and this may be true. But if she's hooking up in the meantime, it shows that she's attempting to divorce her heart from her body. As one teenage girl said, "I've become really good at keeping my emotions in check. . . . I can hook up with a guy and not fall for him."[9] Such a woman may feel as if she's acquired a useful skill by her lack of vulnerability. But when you remove the risk that comes with vulnerability, you also remove the opportunity to be loved.

In her book *Captivating*, Stasi Eldredge outlines the core issue when a woman closes herself to the possibility of love:

> If she cannot secure her relationships, then she kills her heart's longing for intimacy so that she will be safe and in control. She becomes a woman "who doesn't need anyone—especially a man." How this plays

out over the course of her life, and how the wounds of her childhood shape her heart's convictions are often a complex story, one worth knowing. But beneath it all, behind it all, is a simple truth: women dominate and control because they fear their vulnerability. . . . We hide because we are afraid. We have been wounded and wounded deeply. People have sinned against us and we have sinned as well. To hide means to remain safe, to hurt less. At least that is what we think. And so by hiding, we take matters into our own hands. We don't return to our God with our broken and desperate hearts. And it has never occurred to us that in all our hiding, something precious is also lost—something the world needs from us so very, very much.[10]

What the world needs is for women to climb out of their shells of fear and become who God created them to be. When they do this, they'll become more powerful than they could have imagined. Just look at the power one pure girl had upon the following player, who e-mailed me:

In the past I have been a huge flirt and even a player, hooking up with different girls just for fun. I saw relationships as something that would only lock me down; hooking up was much easier. I got what I wanted from it and never had to worry about seeing them again. But after a while, that got old. As I matured, I realized that these girls meant nothing to me. I remember going to a club and grinding with a bunch of different girls, including hooking up with a girl I met that night. As I drove home, I was not happy or pleased with myself. In fact, I felt an urge to go shower and pray to God for forgiveness. It was the lowest point in my life. While my friends were cheering me on for getting some, I was unhappy and disgusted with both myself and the different girls. It was through that event that I realized that hooking up would give me pleasure, but that was not the pleasure I really wanted.

That was my life, until my new girlfriend came around. She is a girl I started off wanting to hook up with only, never considering anything more. But she told me she wouldn't hook up with me or any guy. She respected herself too much for that, and she refused to be used. And for some reason, when I heard that, I respected her more than any other girl I ever met. We began talking and I began to like her a lot. I have finally found a girl that I care about. I have thrown my past aside and I am completely loyal to this girl. I have made a commitment to care for her and protect her. She makes me happier than anything else in the world.

It's hard to imagine any woman would prefer his previous relationships to his current one. All women want to be romanced, but some settle for being seduced. They're so busy convincing themselves that nobody is getting hurt that they fail to see that nobody is getting loved either.

4. *"It makes me feel wanted."*   As a woman, I (Crystalina) would argue that most girls who hook up are looking for intimacy, not sex. There's an enormous difference between the two, but girls often learn this the hard way. For example, girls often imagine during uncommitted physical intimacy that the guy wants her. But he doesn't want her. He wants pleasure . . . at her expense. One girl said:

> I used to hook up with guys and think that if I gave them what they wanted, they would like me more, and if I said "no" to them, that they would think that I'm a prude, or hate me for some dumb reason. But I realized that that's exactly what they want me to think so I will give them what they want.

Sometimes we become so hypnotized by the attention given to us by men that we never see what we're doing to ourselves. We've all played the same denial game. When we're falling from God, we always try to justify it. We think to ourselves, "Well, it's not like I'm doing *this*, or *that*." Sometimes we get so focused on what we're not doing that we don't realize what we are doing.

If you're making out with a guy you just met at a party, a voice in the back of your mind will say things like, "This isn't that bad. We're just having fun. After all, there are drunk people having sex down the hall." Instead of comparing yourselves to a real relationship—where a kiss actually means something—you settle for less and compare yourself to those who have no morals. Don't be fooled. You deserve to be wanted . . . but for what?

When a woman settles for being wanted for the wrong thing, her heart will be restless. Victoria, a high school student from the Midwest, confessed, "In his arms, it feels like love, but in my heart it feels like emptiness." When looking back at his own hookup habit, one man came to the same conclusion, saying:

I hadn't found love. I'd found casual sex with all kinds of strings attached. Acceptance? No one really cared. They were too worried about getting burned themselves.[11]

If you desire to feel wanted, realize that hookups are not rejection prevention. If anything, although a hookup may feel like acceptance, it's always a dismissal.

5. *"I'm just a spontaneous person."*   No doubt spontaneity is a fun quality for a girl to possess. But pure spontaneity is very different than hooking up. For example, while I was dating Jason, I called him up to come help me with something at my apartment. Before he arrived, I scattered rose petals over the carpet. I had soft music playing, and strawberries and sparkling cider waiting for him on the table. Then I took him to his favorite restaurant, and he expected none of it. It was spontaneous—and innocent.

Many people think that they are being "spontaneous" by giving in to their hormones and emotional needs at the drop of a hat. This is often lust, impatience, or dependency (or all three) under the guise of romance. Spontaneity is not the issue. The real question is how the impulses of a person have been trained. Most girls are never taught how to relate to guys in nonsexual ways. You'll find advice in teen magazines such as, "If you meet a cute guy, try surprising him with a long kiss to see if there's a spark between you." This is insane. Physical intimacy is not a way to see if a guy is potential dating material. The physical intimacy is the icing on the cake, not part of the foundation. If we use it to measure the potential in a relationship, we're misusing our kisses and misguiding ourselves. When we settle for meaningless "spontaneity," we forget the intoxicating excitement of simple acts of meaningful affection.

6. *"What's the big deal?"*   When a woman claims that a hookup isn't a big deal, I wonder what isn't the big deal. Is her body not a big deal? Her affections? Her kisses? What's so insignificant about these things? The dignity of women is related to the love they give and receive. Love alone will fulfill them. If this is true, what happens to a woman's dignity when she settles for the "love" of a hookup?

If it's wrong for one person to use another, then if two people are using each other, it's twice as wrong. But this isn't easy to admit. If a teenage girl believes that casual sexual encounters aren't something to fuss over, it may show a lack of intellectual maturity. Psychologists often say that most young people are in the concrete operational stage of thinking. What this means is that most of them have no idea how the decisions they make now will affect them in the future. All they see are present rewards, not future consequences. By failing to look into the future, they often make life-altering decisions.

After maturing beyond this stage of mental development, women find other ways to ignore their troubled consciences. The "not a big deal" cover-up is wishful thinking on the part of those who have given away too much. Part of them hopes that what they have done isn't anything to be concerned about. But this denial only leads to a greater need for more coping mechanisms. Every lie requires a bigger one to cover it.

Hanging Out, Hooking Up, and Hoping for Love?

(Crystalina) In high school, a female friend of mine was obsessed with a guy who was still in love with his ex-girlfriend. Occasionally, my friend would hang out with him, hoping to take the place of his lost love. On one occasion when she and I were over at his house, I watched the two of them flirting while playing video games. He had so many pictures of his ex-girlfriend above his bed that I remember thinking that he might as well have built a shrine to her! All the memorabilia only served to deepen my friend's ambition to become his woman. In an effort to win her place, she hooked up with him a few days later. And then again a few days later. She realized that her efforts were in vain later that week when she saw him driving into the parking lot of school with his ex beside him.

Women often make the mistake of confusing a hookup with the hopeful beginning of a loving relationship. In order to understand why such encounters fail to spark a man's lasting interest, it's helpful to consider what men think about the women with whom they hook up.

One college male evaluated his hookups this way:

> If she's attractive and there's evidence that I used protection I feel extremely positive about my actions. . . . If she decides to hang out too long, wanting breakfast or cuddle time, this begins to make me angry and I feel less positive. If she is not good looking and/or friends of acquaintances with someone that knows I have a girlfriend, I regret my actions and wish I had shown more self-control the night before.[12]

One man poured out his frustration about some women's post-hookup expectations by gasping, "They want you to call back and to call them up and to hang out, and it's not just after a party and that sort of thing. Like, *during the day!*"[13] High maintenance, indeed!

When a guy hooks up with a girl, he may not remember her number, or even her name. He won't remember her because he doesn't respect her. How could he? If her kisses were just for fun, so was she. Yet another college male said, regarding his own hookups:

> Of course, these "relationships" lack substance or a future, which makes the sex actually worse. I do not feel that remorseful however. I am still respectful of the opposite sex.[14]

One woman e-mailed us to say that she hooked up with a number of guys because she "wanted to be respected." I'm sure the guys appreciated her efforts, but not a single one gained respect for her. Thinking you'll gain respect through a hookup is like thinking you'll have more cash if you put your money in a paper shredder.

Some might think that hookups have become the norm on college campuses because dating is nearly extinct. But the opposite is true. Hookups are contributing to the extinction. One reason why the idea of courting a woman in college is rare is because if a man can receive all the physical benefits of marriage without even knowing a girl's last name, he's not likely to pop the question anytime soon (much less woo her with real romance). One teenage boy explained, "Now that it's easy to get sex outside of relationships, guys don't need relationships."[15]

Every woman agrees that most guys are pansies when it comes to initiating love because they fear commitment or rejection. When a woman tries to solve the dilemma through sexual aggressiveness, she only harms her own chances. This is because guys won't cherish the woman who throws herself at him. Because she appears desperate, she's less attractive. As one woman noted, "The same armor that enabled me to tolerate casual sex made me less attractive to the kind of man I most desired."[16] Furthermore, what you win a man with is what you'll keep him with. If you win a guy with passion, then the relationship will depend upon that for its existence. When it fades away, so will he. If you want to find a man who will stay with you for the long-term, then your sexual value should not be your first selling point.

So where does this leave us women? If we're passive, we may be ignored. If we're pure, we might intimidate guys or be written off as frigid prudes. But if we're aggressive and impure, we'll get used.

What's the solution? In order to alter the culture, fears must be faced. The reason why hooking up has become so prevalent is because it preys upon the weakness and fear of both men and women. Men often fear commitment, and women often fear that having high standards will lead to loneliness. Where do these fears collide? Hooking up. The man does not give of himself, and the woman is afraid to expect more.

Following such encounters, the sense of disappointment seems most acute in the females. One mentioned to us, "When you see people kissing in movies, you're like 'awww.' But when you hook up, you're not saying 'awww.' " Another teen described her hookup by saying, "Everything we did together just seemed so hollow and robotic." Such women will be the first to tell you that a hookup isn't a prelude to a real relationship. It's a pacifier for one.

Hooked on Hooking Up

If a woman engages in serial hookups in search of fun, love, power, or social acceptance, she may begin to form more than a habit. She may form a biological addiction. This is caused through a chain of chemical reactions in her brain. Through sexual intimacy, the human mind experiences a surge of dopamine that rewards the brain for the pleasurable activity. Drs. Joe McIlhaney and Freda McKissic Bush explain:

> Dopamine makes us feel good because of the intense energy, exhilaration, and focused attention it produces when we do something important or stimulating. It makes us feel the need or desire to repeat pleasurable, exciting, and rewarding acts.[17]

Scientists have discovered that sexual arousal and intimacy also causes a woman's brain to be "flooded with oxytocin, causing her to desire this same kind of contact again and again with this man she has bonded to, producing even stronger bonding."[18] This neurochemical creates an immense emotional connection in the woman that only grows stronger according to how physically intimate she becomes with the man. The closer she becomes, the more difficult it seems to pull away.

However, should a woman bond and break many sexual relationships, she damages her ability to create a committed relationship. Scientists have noted:

> Each person actually changes the very structure of the brain with the choices he or she makes and the behavior he or she is involved in. . . . [Through casual sex], the synapses that govern decisions about sex in both the male and the female brains are strengthened in ways that make it easier to choose to have sex in the future, while synapses that govern sexual restraint are weakened and deteriorate.[19]

This not only keeps a person coming back to the same source of stimulation (the current relationship and its pattern of behavior), but will drive her to become sexually intimate more quickly in future relationships.

This damage is not irreparable, but re-wiring the brain's circuitry will take time and effort, in proportion to the extent of the previous behavior. It could be compared to a person who has learned to play the violin right-handed now needing to learn how to play it left-handed.

Many people assume that our desires shape our choices. What they fail to recognize is that, over time, our choices begin to shape our desires. You begin to crave what you choose. One woman confessed, "I've been in a cycle of physical relationships with guys and I just don't know how to stop. I'm not even sure I want to stop."

If a woman who feels addicted to sexual encounters can free herself for a time of abstinence, new insights will dawn upon her. She'll probably see that although the pleasure was desirable, she was not simply addicted to that part of it. She was hooked on the feeling of assurance it granted her, temporarily quelling her fear that she was not wanted. Her true longing was not merely for pleasure but for companionship.

Addictions are not merely biological. They can also be emotional. Sometimes it is difficult to distinguish one from the other. One young woman confessed:

> I started to talk to more guys and I led them on, eventually leading to me doing sexual activities with them. I hooked up with a total of five guys this summer. Even though I didn't go all the way, I still feel ashamed. After the first guy I got addicted and started craving it. I'll admit that I never got a relationship, I just got used repetitively.

What was she craving? Was it the physical pleasure, the feeling of being wanted, or the passing thrill of both? For most females, it's more about acceptance than pleasure. Do women enjoy sex? Most would assume so, but one woman responded, "Most teenage girls don't. They find it rushed, unromantic, and awkward."[20]

This shouldn't be a surprise, considering how a woman is made. One expert on the female brain noted that a woman's sexual pleasure is greatest "only if the amygdala—the fear and anxiety center of the brain—has been deactivated."[21] How is a single woman to shut down the looming worry of being caught, impregnated, used, or infected? Most can't, and this partly explains why alcohol often plays a role in casual sex, making it more palatable. But if a woman is doing something she hopes to forget in the morning, she's better off not doing it at all.

It has often been said that the best way to ruin pleasure is to make it your goal. Across the globe sociological studies have found this to be true, by assessing levels of sexual satisfaction among singles and married couples. Not only do married couples experience higher levels of sexual satisfaction, but a senior researcher with the National Institutes of Health added:

> Couples not involved before marriage and faithful during marriage are more satisfied with their current sex life and also with their marriages compared to those who were involved sexually before marriage.[22]

In Norway, sociologists studied more than two thousand people in their twenties in order to assess how sexual satisfaction relates to one's relationship type. In their words, "Among both males and females, the sexually active unattached were the least satisfied with their sex lives."[23] Therefore, if it is pleasure that a woman seeks, why look for it in its least satisfactory form?

Sexual intimacy ought to be blissful. Although this may shock some, it's a foretaste of the eternal union we will experience with God. This is not to say that heaven is sexual, but that heaven is a blissful eternal consummation of love. Sex on earth is a mere shadow. It's just an imperfect analogy. Christopher West explains:

> The passionate union of man and woman in God's plan is meant to be an *icon*, an earthly sign that points us beyond itself to our eternal destiny of union with God. But when we lose sight of our destiny, when we lose sight of union with God as our ultimate fulfillment, we begin to pin all hopes for happiness on the earthly image. The icon then degenerates into an idol. We come to worship sex itself.[24]

This isn't a poetic exaggeration, as West elsewhere points out: "We worship that which we think will satisfy our deepest hunger."[25] But if we gorge ourselves on what cannot satisfy, our souls begin to starve.

The Cost of a Hookup

Guilt is to our souls what the nervous system is to our bodies. When a person suffers a first degree burn, the skin is red and the injury may be quite painful. A second degree burn is more severe in terms of pain and physical damage, which involves blistering. A third degree burn involves the greatest trauma; the skin becomes so blackened and charred that the nerve endings are destroyed. Because of this damage to the nervous system, the victim is unable to feel the pain in the areas where the burn is most severe.

The same could be said of a woman who has been burned by sexual sin. When she experiences an initial wound of having been taken advantage of, she recoils in pain and requires time to heal. She knows the significance of the violation she has experienced. However, should this injury become a pattern of behavior, she will lose her ability to perceive the loss.

Without nerves, you would never know when you were damaging your body. You could sit on a flaming stove and tell everyone that it's a painless experience. But the damage is being done to your body. If anything, more harm would be done because your brain would not be notified of the danger. Just as a third degree burn kills one's nerves, emotional numbness sets in once a conscience becomes dead.

When a woman smothers the voice of her conscience and claims that her casual sexual behavior is harmless, this does not mean that she is free of injury. She's losing her ability to bond, but she's afraid to assess the damage. Not only does she lose her sense of healthy shame, she weakens her ability to express and experience love. Take, for example, a female university student who remarked, "To say that I have to care about every person I have sex with is an unrealistic expectation."[26]

Love is a task that seems daunting to the person ingrained in lust. In her book, *The Privilege of Being a Woman*, Dr. Alice von Hildebrand explains:

> Every sin brings with it its own punishment. Apart from the possibility of serious infections, lewd people will never taste the true beauty of a sexual union based on mutual love and lived in reverence. . . . They will experience lust, but their punishment is that they will never taste the sweetness of true love.[27]

When a woman's vocation to love becomes warped through the habit of hooking up, she loses the desire and ability to trust and to give of herself. It becomes a vicious cycle, because in order to have intimacy, she must emotionally reveal herself. But such a thought terrifies her. Plagued by doubt, she thinks, "If a good and loving man really knew me, he wouldn't want me." So she wears a mask, although that same mask prevents what she seeks: to be loved without it.

It's one thing to lose the ability to give love, but it's a whole other matter to lose the ability to receive it. In order to find love, women must accept that they are lovable. This creates a challenge for those who doubt that they are. For example, a friend of ours began dating a beautiful woman at San Diego State University. Once he fell in love with her, she abruptly ended the relationship, telling him, "Chad, I don't know how to tell you this, but I don't date good guys. I can't. I only hook up. I'm sorry." And with that, she left him. She knew she had encountered a genuinely good man, and she panicked. He was crushed because he wanted to offer her what she deserved all along. But she had trained herself only to offer men what they'd be least likely to reject: her body.

Even gorgeous women often believe that they have no true beauty to offer. Many hide behind the beauty of their bodies. They direct all male attention to what is physical so as to distract them from seeing the woman herself. As strange as it may sound, she removes her clothing so that she can cover herself up. As one woman noted, "If you hunger for intimacy but fear rejection, it is much, much easier to let a man touch your body than to let him touch your heart."[28]

A woman does not arrive at this kind of emotional frigidity overnight. It is a process that begins with a fear, usually of loneliness. Should she harbor this fear, she often lowers her morals in an attempt to find love. A spirit of discouragement soon settles in because her efforts will fail. After a time of discouragement, she may begin to settle for the habit of using men and allowing herself to be used by them. Meanwhile, a sense of despair seeps into her personality. She not only settles for what is not love, she justifies her actions and begins making rationalizations for why she has abandoned her quest for it. In the end, she reaches a state of total resignation. When she arrives at this place, she has become so accustomed to wearing a mask of carefree happiness that she might even begin to think she has become liberated. Enslaved is more like it.

A rabbi noted, "At first, sin is like an occasional visitor, then like a guest who stays for a while, and finally like the master of the house."[29] He added that sin is not merely a temporary lapse in the strength of the will, but actually weakens the will until it is crippled. All along, we tell ourselves that we're free not to make these choices, but our freedom slowly dwindles as we become servants to our vices.

Unraveling the Lie

Sin always offers empty promises. In the case of sexual sin, one of the many false promises is that it will offer the woman a sense of control. Women's magazines attempt to make women feel more powerful for knowing how to seduce a man. But nearly all the advice revolves around one thing: how she can better please *him*. If such advice is so empowering, why does it imply that the value of a woman rests in the level of her desirability to men?

Should a woman take to heart the miserable advice of such magazines, she'll discover that she can temporarily catch a man's attention through sex. However, the security offered by lust is a mirage. If the devil promises that a sin will offer you power and control, the opposite is typically true: Through the sin, you will fall under *its* power and control. For this reason, Raïssa Maritain referred to Satan as "Author of despair! Prince forever of illusory independence!"[30]

His empty promises are just as pernicious for men as for women. One young man wrote to me:

> I began to notice that the more sex I had, the more I wanted. I had always heard that having sex was a way to get rid of sexual tension, but the opposite was true. Having sex increased my desire. It was like a drug. I couldn't stop myself, yet at the same time, I wasn't satisfied at all.

An astute evangelical pastor explained why this cycle occurs:

> Lust is never satisfied. Lust would like us to believe that it can make us happy. If we just give it what it wants, it will stop pestering us and be satisfied. Don't buy it. Lust is never satisfied. You can't bargain

with it and come out a winner. Lust hijacks sex. It wants to train your desires to delight in the thrill of the forbidden so that you lose your godly appetite for what is good.[31]

If it is power you seek, try holding back. As one woman noted, "[Purity] is not a matter of asserting power in order to manipulate. It is a refusal to exploit or be exploited. That is real, and responsible, power."[32]

Making Love or Mocking Love?

Some people assume that the problem with hooking up is that the couple is going too far. But if you think about it, they aren't going far enough. In fact, they aren't going anywhere. They're just using each other and then going their separate ways.

Especially in college, women are immersed in a culture in which it is extremely difficult to hold fast to any values or spirituality. The typical campus is such a godless and hedonistic place that a girl feels like an outcast if she longs for something more meaningful than an alcohol-induced hookup. She may be branded as a naïve prude who needs to quit setting her standards unrealistically high and just learn to let go for once and have a good time. It may even sound appealing, until it happens.

For every woman who wavers in her hopes of finding a lasting love, remember that your attitude toward hooking up will impact far more than your upcoming weekend. Christopher West poses the question:

> Are men and women willing to pay the price of renunciation, sacrifice, and discipline required to find and live the love that *does* satisfy? The answer to this question will determine the entire course of a person's life.[33]

Chastity is not merely about restraint, but about preparing to make a total gift of yourself. But if you choose to give up this quest for godly love, where will this leave you? As you can imagine, a hookup doesn't exactly prepare you for the sacrament of marriage. It does the opposite. By means of the hookup, a woman trains herself to avoid what is essential to love. Consider some of the things that love requires: sacrifice, patience, trust, and exclusivity. If hookups disregard all these things, how is a woman who has focused merely on the physical excitement of a fling supposed to make the transition to the real thing?

Contrast the mentality behind hooking up with the idea of intimacy expressed by this newlywed couple. The husband noted, "Sex isn't about what you get out of it. It's really about the gift of self to another person. It's more about the gift of self and less about satisfying your urges." His wife, Nicki, added that when it comes to married love, "It isn't about give and take. It's about give and give."[34] How does one transition from hooking up to this kind of selfless love?

Your single years are a training ground to learn the meaning of sacrifice. Learn it now and you will gain for yourself a key to love that you will use throughout your life. As you've probably discovered by now, the goal of our book is not to help you hunt down a husband and capture a ring, but to progress in the virtues that can sustain a life-long love. Besides, when you find your soulmate, this doesn't mean that you've crossed the finish line. Marriage is filled with constant challenges that require you to die to yourself. But if you practice sacrificial love now, it will come naturally to you when you need it the most.

Hookups and the Meaning of Life

While I (Jason) was driving past a "gentlemen's" strip club, a neon sign caught my attention: "$10 cover charge!" Just the sight of it made me want to want slam on the brakes and pull over—not to see the girls, but to tell them that they were getting ripped off. A guy can find ten dollars in between the cushions of his car seats! It should cost a man the commitment of a lifetime to see the treasure of a woman's body. But while these strippers settled for a $10 admission fee, women who hook up are waiving the cover charge.

This is why prostitutes don't prowl around college campuses. They would go out of business, because sex is free at the parties. You just give a girl a beer, tell her she's pretty, and the hookup begins. As one person said, "When a guy goes to a hooker, he's not paying her for sex. He's paying her to leave." But when she's a hookup, you don't even need to pay her for that!

Our words have been harsh against hooking up because humans have been created to participate in a much greater love. If God is love, and men and women are made in His image and likeness, this means we're made in the image and likeness of love. When a man loves a woman, he can see in her a glimpse of what Adam originally saw in Eve. He sees something divine in her. Although this might sound strange, the expression of their sexual love is meant to reflect God's love. His love—although not sexual—is a love that is free, total, faithful, and life-giving. Therefore, when couples truly love each other, they unveil the love of God to the world—and to each other!

Odds are, you aren't going to hear this vision of sex and love from MTV. But it's stamped into your heart and even into your body. There's a desire in all of us to find ourselves through a total gift of ourselves. But when it comes to hooking up, it's the opposite of what we're made for. Instead of a total gift, it's a partial loan. Neither partner is satisfied because it's a negation of love. They aren't giving themselves. They're losing themselves.

If a girl never learns how to say no to lust, the day will come for real love and she won't know how to say yes. This is one of the gravest consequences of lust, because humans cannot live without love. While this may sound drastic to some, in the case of a hookup, nothing less than the very meaning of life is at stake. If we have been created for love, then a hookup is the complete inversion of the meaning of our existence! No wonder it leaves us feeling so empty afterward.

How to Stop Hooking Up

When a woman realizes that she needs to quit hooking up, it's often not a simple fix. The behavior is usually a facet of a broader lifestyle that involves who she hangs out with, where she goes, what she thinks of herself, and how little she prays. In order to uproot the habit, begin by seeking the grace of God.

When I (Crystalina) was trying to break away from an impure life, my decision to change never seemed to last. It wasn't until I chose to do it with God by my side that I was able to succeed. Leaving a bad habit in the past is not simply a matter of pulling yourself up through your own determination and willpower. You are free to try it on your own, but you'll fail. Don't think for a moment that you're unworthy of God's unconditional love. It is precisely the weight of our sins that entitles us to His fathomless mercy.

With Him by your side, courageously look at why you have made the choices you have. Is it because you fear rejection? Have you lost hope in love? Do you doubt that you are lovable? Are you depressed and seeking out affection as a drug? When we feel most vulnerable and lonely, it's easy to turn to the empty pleasures of the world.

Some women keep things sexual, superficial, and flirty with men in order to avoid the emotional entanglement of real love. However, when we use superficial, aggressive, and flirty efforts to win a guy's attention, these behavior patterns continue into the relationship. We turn into man-pleasers and become so concerned with making guys happy that we end up feeling like garbage.

Resist the temptation to think, "Oh, it was just for fun, and I was drunk anyway." This doesn't answer the deeper issue regarding why you think it's tolerable to be left alone in the morning. Without knowing what motivates you to hook up, you'll continue the pattern of behavior.

Hooking up often feels as if it is filling a need. However, bad habits such as cutting, eating disorders, and hooking up always involve false needs. Psychologist Jeffrey Satinover explains:

The filling of a false need leads to a temporary experience of pleasure which, for a time, overrides the genuine need it is hiding. *But the genuine need is not being met.* After an invariably short time, then, the original distress returns, stronger than ever for having remained wholly unaddressed. The transient experience of pleasure provides but the illusion of fulfillment; the disillusionment only sharpens the true need. Immediately the craving returns, again and again, and soon a habit has been established: the habit of turning to the fulfillment of the false need whenever the true, underlying distress is aroused. And it's always aroused because it's never filled.[35]

The woman who hooks up must learn how to address her true needs properly. Until she does this, she'll find it nearly impossible to break away from her bad habits and addictions.

Once you find the root cause, examine your motivation to stop it. If you're trying to quit a behavior simply because it makes you feel guilty, elevate your motives. Do it for the sake of love. You not only deserve to be loved. You also have an obligation to learn how to love. Take this seriously, and consider what is at stake. As a woman, you don't seek out relationships simply to feel loved by another. You also seek to share your love. You have something to offer beyond the physical. Do you believe this? You're not just yearning to have a man by your side, but to be there for him as well. God plants within all of us an ache to give and receive. However, a hookup thwarts all of this.

It's not enough to avoid casual sex. God calls you to more. In the words of St. Paul, "glorify God in your body."[36] He's not inviting you simply to avoid hookups, but to possess a deep and radiant purity. You might object that your past is anything but radiant. But perhaps you've become so absorbed by the past that you're forgetting to look toward the future.

ADMIT IT: FRIENDS WITH BENEFITS ARE NEITHER

"The day we met in person, Melissa was in a foul mood," described a newspaper reporter:

> Her "friend with benefits" had just broken up with her. "How is that even possible?" she said, sitting, shoulders slumped, in a booth at a diner. "The point of having a friend with benefits is that you won't get broken up with, you won't get hurt. He told me online that he met a girl that he really likes, so now, of course, we can't hook up anymore. . . . I have my friends for my emotional needs, so I don't need that from the guy I'm having sex with. . . . It's really stupid, I know," she said, shaking her head. "It's kind of ironic, isn't it? I try to set up a situation where I won't get hurt, and I still manage to get hurt."[1]

For the sake of defining our terms, being "friends with benefits" is similar to hooking up, except for the fact that a friendship precedes it and the physical encounters continue for an indefinite amount of time. Hookups, on the other hand, tend to be more spontaneous and short-lived. Despite the differences, one is not much better than the other. As Melissa—and countless other women—have realized, the problem with being friends with benefits is that you aren't being a friend, and you aren't getting the benefits you might imagine.

Yet if women tend to be so dissatisfied with the arrangement, why has it become so common? One reason is that men no longer feel the need to ask women out. One young man observed:

> Being in a real relationship just complicates everything. You feel obligated to be all, like, couply. And that gets really boring after a while. When you're friends with benefits, you go over, hook up, then play video games or something. It rocks.[2]

One has to wonder if the girl went home after the video game thinking that her quasi-relationship "rocks." Odds are, she probably wishes he'd drop the video game controller, take her for a walk around the neighborhood, and ask her to be his girlfriend. But she'd better not hold her breath if she hopes this will happen. She's already violated an unspoken code of female courtship that every woman prior to the 1960's seems to have taken for granted: The more physical you become with a guy prior to a relationship, the less likely your relationship will last—or even exist. Why?

Consider the message it sends to a single man when you hook up or become his "benefit." You're saying, "I am willing to sleep with a man who is not my husband. I'll even dole out physical favors without demanding the respectability of a relationship, let alone a marriage." This is not the message you want to give to a potential mate. He knows that such a woman is not the type that he'll want as a spouse, so he'll see no point in committing to her in the first place. It's a harsh reality, but until men consider such women honorable, the unwritten rules aren't likely to change.

Violating this natural law of relationships will bring inevitable frustration, especially for the woman. This is because friends with benefits rarely evolve into stable and meaningful relationships. Despite this obvious fact, how many women harbor the hope that it will? Sometimes the situation feels almost like a relationship, but it always lacks the commitment and stability of true love. One young woman recalled:

> I always thought: Jeff and I are each other's back burners. When we didn't have a significant other, we were acting like a couple together. I think that's what has made it so hard to let go.

Another woman shared with me the pain she experienced from being friends with benefits:

> Every time we were together, we ended up having sex or doing other stuff. He started referring to us as "friends with benefits" and always

asked me if "having casual sex" was okay with me. Of course, it wasn't, but I always said yes because I didn't want to lose him. He claims we have the best type of "friendship" because we can just hang out like friends do, but we can have sex, too. He says we have all the good parts of a relationship without actually having one. Now that I'm typing those words on the page, I can't believe how stupid I am for falling for all of it. When my friends are in similar situations involving guys, I am quick to tell them that they are worth more and to get out of the situation. I wish I would listen to my own advice.

For many women, the semblance of a relationship becomes a source of consolation. They think: "I know it's not ideal, but even if I don't have a real relationship, at least I have something. I guess that's better than nothing." What such women do not realize is that those are not her only two options (having nothing or being friends with benefits). If you refuse to be used, you're not left with "nothing." You're free to enjoy life without the drama of an unpredictable quasi-relationship and free to focus on more important matters—like yourself.

What is essential is that you not define yourself by the absence (or presence) of a boy in your life. As Dawn Eden remarked, "Once you allow yourself to be defined by your loneliness, it's a small step to violating your most deeply held beliefs."[3]

What's the Point?

A popular men's magazine interviewed a player, asking him what he thought about women who are friends with benefits. Among other things, he said that he considered them to be "somewhere between a girlfriend and a hooker." Every woman knows that he's right. So why would a girl settle for that?

The motives behind being a friend with benefits are similar to the reasons why a girl hooks up. It's not because she's a fun, wild, and spontaneous girl. Often behind the friends with benefits label is a girl hoping to win over the heart of a guy by giving him sexual favors. Girls may act as if they're detached and satisfied, but that's called denial. No matter what she says or how big she pretends to smile, every woman knows that she is not designed to be disposable. As a college woman said, "I'm confused, because it seems like I don't get the 'friend' part, but he still gets the 'benefits.' "[4]

Such relationships don't leave only the women feeling hollow. Men sometimes express the same emptiness and ache that inevitably follows the misuse of one's sexuality. One teenage boy explained, "We'd hang out and mess around some and I'd leave. Afterward I'd feel dumb, like it wasn't needed. But before you do it, you feel like it's definitely needed."[5]

We all know uncommitted sexual intimacy is anything but intimate. However, when a woman feels used, she often tries all the more to keep the relationship and rehabilitate it so that she'll never have to admit that it was unhealthy. If she can cling to the guy long enough for him to stay, then she assumes that no big mistakes were really made. If he leaves, then she is faced with her greatest fear: that she gave away both her heart and her body to a man who only loved her for what she gave him. If you're currently in such a "relationship," be clear with your "friend" that the benefits are over.

If he mocks you for respecting yourself, do not internalize his words. One fifteen-year-old shared with us how difficult it was to pull away from her previous life:

> I told one of my "friends with benefits" that I'm not doing that anymore and you know what he said? "Don't worry about it, I have lots of other women. Besides, you'll come around eventually. Girls like you can't stay innocent." And he's right. Another one told me that it was too late for me anyways, and the guys who I'm going to go after deserve more than some slut. And he's right, too. A friend of a guy I used to date sent me a message today, told me that he heard I was an easy slut, and that he wanted to have some "fun." I explained that I believed in purity now. His reaction? "Why would you do something like that when you've screwed up this much? Don't you realize that you're virginity is *looooonnnngggg* gone?" And he's right, too. I deserve my life. It was my choice in the first place.

Thankfully, although she was tempted to despair that their words were true, this brave young woman rose above the low estimations others had of her. She declared, "I won't be someone's opinion, someone's game to play. I refuse to let my past become my future." Follow her lead, and never allow yourself to be defined by those who do not love you. If a guy lacks confidence in your ability to be pure, it's just a reflection of how little confidence he has in himself.

The Science of Sex

"Whenever I date a guy, it seems like sex becomes inevitable," a college student shared with us. "The relationships never last because I either get bored with them, or they get bored and cheat on me. Is something wrong with me?"

Nothing was wrong with her. She, like you, has been perfectly made. Her problem is that no one ever explained to her how a woman is made. When a female experiences physical affection and especially sexual arousal, her brain releases a neurochemical called oxytocin.[6] Women also experience a surge of oxytocin during childbirth and breastfeeding. Often called "human superglue" because of its role in human bonding, this chemical can play tricks on a woman's mind.

Beyond mere bonding, oxytocin dulls your critical thinking abilities and your memory.[7] It causes an inability to remember disturbing things such as labor pains or the negative traits of a sexual partner. It also helps with the positive recall of good memories. All of this is great in marriage, because it helps couples stick together through tough times. But it's a recipe for disaster outside of marriage, because you lose your ability to see clearly the value of a relationship. It binds you and blinds you. You downplay the negative . . . until it's too late to ignore.

One might consider it a memory airbrush, and this partly explains why girls have such a hard time convincing their friends to leave harmful sexual relationships.[8] In her book on the female brain, Dr. Louann Brizendine recommends not getting too close too soon with a guy: "If high levels of oxytocin and dopamine are circulating, your judgment is toast. These hormones shut the skeptical mind down."[9]

Nowadays, a woman needs her brain to be functioning at full capacity in order to successfully navigate the dating scene. She can't afford to miss the warning signs of a potentially bad relationship because she's in a hormonally-altered state of mind. Therefore, be careful with any guy who seems too affectionate. Affection can make you feel things for a guy that you wouldn't feel otherwise. It can make you fall in love with the feeling of being touched instead of with the person himself. Let your brain make up its mind about a guy before allowing it to be fogged over by physical intimacy.

Without knowing the scientific facts about oxytocin, a pair of men wrote a manual on how to seduce women. In it, the two Casanovas recommended sleeping with a woman as soon as possible. Why?

> Once a woman has had sex with you, the rules change. Now instead of trying to justify getting rid of you, she's trying to justify why you were worth having sex with in the first place. Instead of being on the hunt for your bad points, she's more likely to be on the lookout for the good.[10]

It has often been said that the most important sexual organ is the brain. This is not merely true for women. Men also release oxytocin during intimacy, but the levels are not as high as in women. However, men's brains release a chemical called vasopressin. This hormone is associated with an increase in the sense of responsibility. After sex, it will make a man step back and think to himself, "Wait a minute. Am I ready for all this? What if she gets pregnant? Am I ready to be a dad? Do I see myself marrying her? I don't even know what I want, so I better not be doing this stuff." This partly explains why some guys run away from women soon after sleeping with them, while husbands typically don't fear adult responsibilities. The same neurochemical that causes a single man to be haunted by fear will drive a husband deeper in his devotion to his wife and family.

One young man e-mailed us the following. As you read his comments, watch how the effects of oxytocin and vasopressin played out in the male/female relationship after they became sexually active:

> I felt tied down because all we'd ever do on weekends is she would come to my house or I'd go to her house and we'd do whatever and that was it. Also, she started talking about marriage plans and how many kids we were going to have. I know that she meant in the future but it still made me feel very uncomfortable. During our breakup, she cried constantly and told me she loved me and that I'm always in her future. I'm only seventeen and don't want that kind of commitment

right now. I want to go out on the weekends and have fun with my friends. Every time we do this or that, I get scared that she's pregnant. I live in constant fear. I like her a lot but don't think that I love her because I'm too young. I know she told me she loves me, but sometimes I feel she's being sabotaged by herself and she just likes the stuff we do together. I think those feelings are getting in the way of her true ones. Please help me, and let me know what I can do.

Women who find themselves disappointed by lust need not despair. If a woman can understand the way her body and soul have been created, she'll understand that there is nothing defective in her. If she acts in a way that is contrary to the way she is designed, she'll naturally feel broken and discontent. But if she musters up the courage to hope for something better, she has taken the biggest step toward finding it.

Your Body Is Not a Benefit

Have you ever noticed that women rarely, if ever, initiate the idea of becoming friends with benefits? The suggestion typically comes from the male. This is not to say that men are the guilty aggressors and women are the helpless victims. After all, both parties agree to the lack of meaning in their partnership. As one young woman said, "It's equal. Everyone is using each other. That's fair."[11]

To steer clear of such "relationships," begin by avoiding brain pollution caused by things like impure television shows and smutty magazines such as *Cosmopolitan* and *Seventeen*. Such programs and periodicals offer advice that borders on the miraculously stupid. Take, for example, the July 2005 issue of *Seventeen* magazine, which explained that a woman can know she's ready for sex if she can handle the idea of the guy leaving her afterward.[12] In other words, players and prostitutes are ready for sex, but husbands and wives are not. Or consider the wisdom of the *Cosmopolitan* relationship expert who responded to a woman who asked the following question:

I've been hooking up with this guy for months, but he said he doesn't have time for a relationship. Then he saw me flirting with another guy and told me that he doesn't want me hooking up with other people. Does he have feelings for me?

The relationship expert begins on the right track by saying:

I hate to be the bearer of bad news, but this dude is t-r-o-u-b-le. He's selfish and possessive—a heartbreaking combo. Not only that, but he doesn't want to be your boyfriend. It couldn't be any clearer if he said it right to your face. Oh wait, he did say it to your face. Clearly, this guy wants all the perks of hooking up with you, minus the responsibility.

Then he adds:

Jerks like this are often incapable of having a real relationship, regardless of who the girl is. If you can handle that reality, booty-call away. But if there's even the smallest chance that you're developing feelings for him, I suggest you get the hell out now.[13]

So if she has no feelings for him, she should give away her body, but if she likes him, she should run? Reading such ridiculous advice should serve as a potent reminder to women why they should not settle for being friends with benefits—or waste a moment of their lives reading *Cosmo*. But even if a woman rejects such magazines, she will not be able to escape the world's confused notion of love.

You may have noticed that our modern culture has invented a vast array of names for those who settle for a lack of commitment. Some consider themselves to be in "open relationships," which is a nice way of saying that neither partner has enough self-respect to consider cheating to be a problem. Others get fancy with the terminology and consider themselves to be in relationships that are "polyamorous" (meaning "many loves"). This is the most ironic label, because if the person truly loved any one of his partners, he wouldn't feel any need for the others. The problem is not that the person loves too many people, but that he or she does not love any of them.

What are the essential qualities of romantic love? For starters, consider permanence and exclusivity. How many times have you seen the initials of two lovers carved into a tree, or a notebook doodle of a heart that contains two initials within it? If the guy is extra romantic and perhaps a little tipsy, he'll use spray paint to declare his love on a freeway overpass. You'll notice that such twitterpated vandals never use chalk or pencil. The mark is permanent and bold because they want everyone—especially the girl—to know they are in love. The declaration of love is public knowledge, and the relationship is exclusive. This explains why you never see graffiti that reads, "Brandon loves Ashley, Taylor, Samantha, and Alexis." While a person may have a crush on a number of people at the same time, love always requires a decision to choose one individual above every other person on earth.

If you have ever settled for reducing your body to a "benefit," you know that it's the opposite of what you long for. No one dreams of meeting her knight in shining armor and becoming his friend with benefits. Has there ever been a romantic movie based on such a concept? Despite the fact that most Hollywood love stories hardly portray anything close to authentic love, why is it that there has never been a love story based on the concept of the booty call? Bring to mind your favorite romantic scene from any movie. Now, allow us to alter the words. The man stares into the eyes of his beloved and says to her, "You're so beautiful. You mean more to me than life itself. But I really don't feel like dating you. Instead, I'd appreciate it we could have a meaningless and uncommitted physical relationship." Can you imagine college girls watching such a movie in their dormitory TV lounge, sharing their tissues as they sobbed in envy over such a rare and priceless love?

Every true love story has a common theme: total self-giving. Love is not complicated. It demands total commitment because it could not exist with anything less.

Learning a New Love Language

"I decided to give up sex and dating because I don't know how to date without sex anymore."[14] The college senior who admitted this must have felt as if she had walked miles down a road, only to discover that it was a dead end. Another woman e-mailed us to say:

> I have just never known a relationship without sex. Expressing myself and my feelings in a sexual way has become a big part of who I am as a person. . . . Or who I thought I was. . . . I always thought if I took away that ability to sexually express myself I wouldn't know how else to grow in a relationship or what else to give.

What both of these women need is to become proficient in a new love language. Without realizing or intending it, they have both grown accustomed to communicating falsehoods with their bodies. Think of it: If you sleep with a man you are not married to, you are speaking a lie to him with your body. Your body says, "I am totally yours. I give myself entirely to you!" But offering a man your body is not the same as giving him yourself. Only within marriage does the language of sex speak the truth. "I am yours." The total gift of the body accompanies the total gift of self.

If love is a total gift of self, then uncommitted sex is the inversion of love. It's a temporary loan. Some might think the Church is imposing its moral rules on people when it demands a permanent and faithful love between two lovers, but isn't this what the human heart longs for?

If we are willing to allow God to heal us, He can transform our appetites and teach us the language of true love. No longer will we look upon God as a rule giver who wants to extinguish our passions. We'll begin to see Him as a lover whose desire is to enflame us with His love so that we'll be capable of illuminating the world with it. Your desires don't need to disappear. They need to be set ablaze!

The idea of pure desires might sound contradictory to you, but chastity means being sexually attracted, but choosing the greater good for the other. It means you allow God's love to permeate your affections. In order for this to happen, we must first throw aside the false notion that religion and sexuality are at enmity with one another. Could it be possible that erotic love could be pure? Could sexual intimacy be sanctifying? In God's plan for sex, the answer to both questions can be an emphatic yes!

Although in the past you may have used your body in a way that drove you and others further from God, you are still made in His image and likeness. Your body is still capable of expressing the love of the Blessed Trinity. This is quite a calling. But you're worthy of nothing less.

9

Remember the Meaning of a Kiss

I (Jason) was in second grade the first time a girl kissed me. She happened to be my friend's older sister, and I was infatuated with her for as long as my seven-year-old mind could remember. Because she was a sophisticated older woman (in sixth grade), she always seemed out of my league. But one summer day I was given the task of feeding her goldfish while she was on vacation. When she returned to discover that I hadn't killed it, she thanked me and gave me a peck on the cheek. Even though she was kissing me like she would have kissed a cute guinea pig, I was ecstatic. I walked back to my house, and I doubt that my feet even touched the sidewalk.

A decade later in high school, I found myself in the TV lounge of a college dorm, making out with a girl I had met forty-eight hours earlier. We met, hooked up, and went our separate ways in the course of a one-week summer camp. When the week was over, she said, "You're not going to leave me like the other guys . . . are you?" Feeling bad for her, I told her we'd be in touch. Then I proceeded to leave the camp an hour later without even bothering to ask for her number.

I felt pretty low, but I never planned for it to happen like it did. At the moment, we probably thought we were spontaneously romantic. But all the excitement happened so effortlessly that it left me bored. As the camp was drawing to a close, I knew what would happen if I dragged on the "relationship." Each time we got together, we'd end up doing the same stuff, and eventually more. Although some guys would have seen this as an open door, I knew the door was leading somewhere I shouldn't go. I knew I didn't treasure her, and that bothered me. I had also lost respect for who I became when I was with her.

So what happened in the span of those ten years between these two kisses? Why did I get bored so quickly with kisses that should have been so captivating? The answer is that the kiss had lost its meaning.

The Gift of a Kiss

Ten years after my meaningless summer camp hookup, I stood at the altar, and amid the cheers of my family and friends, kissed my bride. During our courtship and engagement, Crystalina and I aimed to keep the relationship pure and the kisses simple. As the months progressed, I realized that I treasured her more each day. She became more captivating to me because our relationship retained a sense of mystery.

My hope for you, should you choose to enter the sacrament of marriage, is that you will experience the interior peace of being looked at—and kissed by—a man who values your soul even more than your body. One young man e-mailed me about the change of heart he had experienced after leaving behind an unchaste life. Looking forward to the allure of a pure love, he mentioned in his letter that all the physical stuff with other girls "won't even start to start to match the intensity, passion and love that just a peck on the lips and a smile will from my future wife."

If this is your heart's desire, ask yourself, "What are my kisses worth?" Our goal in encouraging you to ask this question is not to wag a finger at you for the kisses you've squandered. Our hope is that you will come to discover the worth of a kiss.

Have you ever considered why so many people enjoy watching daytime talk shows? My theory is this: No matter how bad your life may seem, you feel like you're doing fine after seeing how chaotic and disordered the lives of the guests on the show are. The same thing happens in our daily lives when it comes to purity. After hearing the Monday morning gossip about who did what with whom over the weekend, it's easy to think of yourself as being immaculate. Because we are immersed in a sexually saturated society, it's rare that we pause to consider the meaning of a simple kiss.

Teenage girls often debate with their religion teachers, saying such things as, "What's the big deal with just making out with a guy?" When I hear this, I want to ask these girls, "Isn't there something in you that wants it to be a big deal? Isn't there something in you that wishes it meant so much more than it typically does?" We often get so hung up on rules and boundaries that we miss the point. We fiercely defend our freedom to reduce physical intimacy to entertainment.

Because so many people give away kisses as if they were handshakes, the more innocent souls tend to think of themselves as outcasts. I've had young men whisper to me, "I'm sixteen, and I've never even kissed a girl. Is that bad? Are girls going to think I'm boring?" If they weren't so afraid of their own innocence, they might realize how attractive women find it. I tell them:

> Trust me, if God calls you to marriage, your bride will not find your innocence boring! If anything, girls get bored with guys who only have one thing on their minds. Guard that first kiss, because it is a gift that you can only give once.

You may be thinking, "That's cute advice for someone who's never kissed someone, but what about those of us who have given away more than just a few kisses?" First, don't let yourself be defined by the past. It's done. All you have is now and the future. When it comes to future relationships, look at things in a new light. Instead of living in the moment, begin to think of the future. After all, what's the point of kissing people who you probably won't know a year from now?

If you are having a difficult time knowing where to draw the line, ask yourself the following three questions:

- How much would you want some other woman kissing your future husband?

- How would you kiss a guy in front of your dad?
- How much kissing would you do with Jesus Christ present in the room?

To the first question, you may have thought, "Back off, girl!"

To the second, you were probably thinking, "That's just gross."

To the third, you may have thought, "What's Jesus doing in my room?"

But in each case, you know in your heart what is pure. When an action is pure, you never ask if it's wrong. However, when an action is tempting, we often find ourselves asking if it's okay. If you sincerely want to know if a particular form of affection is "going too far," don't ask yourself, "Is this bad?" Ask yourself, "Is this pure?" If you want to know the will of God as it relates to purity, go to Him in prayer. He's not waiting to take something away from you. He's waiting to teach you to love.

What He's *Thinking*

When it comes to sexuality, girls are wired differently than guys. Typically, a woman is aroused more gradually than a man. This is not to imply that females lack sexual desire. Quite the contrary. A woman's desires can be stronger than a man's at times. However, a good way to understand the difference between the curve of arousal in a woman and a man is to compare how long it takes an iron to warm up as compared to a light bulb. The light emitted by a bulb occurs instantly. Similarly, the sexual appetite of a man can be triggered immediately through sight, imagination, or touch. However, while a woman's sexual desires can be kindled by these things, they typically do not occur in an instant.

When a couple is kissing, the woman may be thinking about how cute the guy is, how nice he smells, or how close she feels to him. For her, the kiss is often an end in itself. Meanwhile, the guy is almost certainly thinking about what's going to happen next. For him, the kiss is often the means to an end. The reason why kissing is known as "first base" is because the goal is to get home. This does not mean that a guy will only kiss a girl for the sake of going further. But it does mean that once he's passionately kissing her, that is where his body wants him to go.

If your goal is to remain pure, reserve passionate and prolonged kissing for marriage. Instead of igniting desires and constantly trying to quench them, you're saving the fire for the day you won't have to put it out.

Pure Desire

Some people who mock the idea of chastity assume that the longer a woman goes without indulging in her sexual desires, the more repressed and neurotic she becomes. If this is the case, it shows that she is not free. Freedom is not the ability to release your inhibitions and indulge in lustful behavior. The person enslaved to lust is only as "free" as an alcoholic who celebrates the fact he can get drunk whenever he wishes.

Young women may wonder, "Why does God give us such powerful hormones now if we aren't supposed to get married for ten more years? What am I supposed do with all my desires in the meantime?" Perhaps the first thing to remember is that it's normal and healthy to have sexual desires. This is the way God made you, and you should be more concerned if these desires aren't present.

One reason God allows us to experience such desires before marriage is because we first must learn to control them. By learning to control their passions, couples acquire two important skills.

First, the couple becomes free to love. Unless a person learns sexual self-control before marriage, he or she will be incapable of loving a spouse properly inside of marriage. The world often claims that men and women need sexual experience prior to marriage in order to be sexually competent. But as one husband pointed out, "If you can't say no to sex, what does your 'yes' mean?"[1] The chaste person who knows how to love will have an easier time learning to express sexual love than the person who has become engrained in the habit of lust.

Second, the couple train themselves in faithfulness. If a dating couple can't resist the allure of forbidden fruit now, what will they do when temptations arise within marriage? How assuring it will be for the bride who marries a man who has self-control! Prior to marriage, if he is able to resist temptations with the woman he loves more than life itself, then he should have no trouble staying true to her in marriage. Because he has developed self-mastery, he is able to bless his wife with the peaceful assurance of his fidelity. Such a gift is certainly worth more to her than any sexual "experience" he could have acquired prior to marriage. Because their vows are more likely to endure, they can enjoy a lifetime of learning how to express intimacy within marriage.

To begin growing in this self-mastery, keep your imagination in check. Many Christians feel discouraged by such a challenge because they mistakenly assume that sexual desires are the same thing as lust. The desire for sexual intimacy is not the enemy. Lust is, because it involves using another for one's selfish gratification.

At times, you feel torn between two loves. You may think: I want to be close to God, but I also want to be close to my boyfriend. How can I express my physical desires to be close to him without drifting from God? Is this even possible, or do I need to choose between them?

Thankfully, you can integrate your desires with your faith, without having to annihilate either. Our sexual desires are not supposed to be eliminated. But they do need to be ordered according to authentic love. If purity required people to eliminate their sexual urges, we'd have to assume that married couples would either be incapable of purity or incapable of passion. God's design is for us to have both—to wed passion and purity.

How do we do that? For starters, learn to distinguish between a lustful thought and a temptation to lust. A temptation is the sudden thought of a forbidden act. To the extent that this thought is beyond your control, you are not morally responsible that it came to mind. However, what you do with that thought determines whether you gain merit or guilt as a result of it.

If your thoughts are beginning to drift toward lustful things, try to draw them back as soon as you recognize what you're doing. If you're tempted while you're alone, trace the shape of the cross on your forehead. Say the name of Jesus. Announce to heaven and hell with your words and your body that you belong to God. But don't just pray *against* the temptation. If you're tempted toward a particular person, pray *for* him. Turn your temptation into an act of intercession.

Where do you draw the line when it comes to your thoughts? One rule of thumb is to remember that if the particular action is not moral for you to act upon, then do not allow your mind to linger on the subject. For example, if you're not married, don't fantasize about marital intimacies. It's not wrong to desire such intimacy, but you would do well to wait on God, allowing Him at the appropriate time in your life to lift the veil from that mystery.

What do you do when sexual desires come to mind? Saying to yourself "I'm not going to think about it" isn't likely to be very effective. In order to overcome any desire, you need a stronger one. You do this numerous times every day. You desire to sleep in, but you overcome that desire in order to get to school or work on time. You might want to eat a particular food, yet deny yourself the indulgence for the sake of your health.

In a similar way, in order to overcome the temptation to lust, you need a broader vision and a more powerful desire . . . to love. Sexual desire is a source of energy, and it cannot be repressed. It must be directed somewhere. In order to do this, remind yourself that purity expresses love. If you do not understand this, you'll always feel like you're having to turn down chances to love. You are not. You're turning down lust so that you can be free to love.

Without this positive motivation, one may succeed in saying no to individual temptations and in scolding one's desires, but the motive is often based in shame or guilt. Without a bigger picture of God's plan for human sexuality, one may resort to sweeping one's desires under the rug. *That* is what leads to repression. When a sexual desire arises, the person thinks, "That's bad. I shouldn't think about that." A tension exists inside, because he or she knows something good is there.

In order to develop a healthy sexuality, we must acknowledge the goodness of how we have been created, without losing sight of the fact that the effects of original sin still exist. When we open our minds to the beauty of God's plan for sexuality, not only will we see the goodness of it, we'll discover the joy of living it.

Living It and Loving It

Growing in purity is a day-by-day process that continues throughout your life. But we warn you, the more you start to practice purity, the more you'll fall in love with the peace that comes with it! That's why girls are only able to dismiss the idea of purity until they discover how fulfilling it is to be loved for the right reasons.

When you meet guys who possess the virtue, you'll see a spark in them that is missing in the average guy. One young man e-mailed me to say how proud he was to discover that his new girlfriend appreciated his purity. He said:

> All the guys she dated, she secretly was disgusted by, because they were whiny and petulant into coaxing her into sex; but she wrote that she finds my (challenging!) self-restraint and respect of her person to be very masculine and it makes her love me more.

If you wish to find such a guy, don't kiss anyone you are not dating. Some guys will be turned off by the fact you take your kisses so seriously. But that's a good thing! Many men don't deserve you, and you need to know how to identify them. Without pleasure, a lustful man quickly loses interest. Like a duck that turns its tail and swims away when a bag of bread crumbs is empty, the man whose goal is pleasure finds no need to wait around for a girl who thinks her kisses are priceless. Meanwhile, the man in love experiences the opposite reaction. You'll capture his attention by the very fact that you're not readily available.

Without question, purity is beautiful. We're not talking about repression or prudishness, but about having a confident and serene sense of your dignity and worth. Therefore, hold on to your kisses.

The more you save, the less you regret. How often do you hear of a woman who regrets having too little sexual experience before marriage? What woman stands at the altar on her wedding day, wishing she had smooched a few more guys?

WEAR SOMETHING REVEALING—BE MODEST

The woman is the most beautiful sight on earth. Nothing comes close. Sunsets and rainbows are lovely, but no man gets addicted to looking at pictures of them on the Internet. If a company wants people to stare at their advertisement, they don't put a butterfly on it, they put a woman on it.

Although I (Jason) am not in favor of advertisements that show bikini-clad women lying on cars in order to sell them, I think we'd all appreciate the absurdity of seeing a similar ad with a man draped over the hood. Such a sight would make most people laugh out loud. We would feel an urge to say to the man, "Get off the car. You're going to dent it! Put on a shirt and change the oil." Men aren't as alluring as women. Because women have been gifted with the ability to captivate others without saying a word, they possess a unique power. The question is, how will you use that power? In other words, who will you be for men?

Everything in the world tells women, "If you've got it, flaunt it. There's no harm in showing a little skin." What the world doesn't seem to realize is that a woman reveals more of herself when she dresses modestly. Through modesty, a woman tells the world that she has more to offer than her body. It is an unspoken invitation for others to consider where her true value lies.

Could it be, then, that the immodest styles that are force-fed to young women today are actually telling women to hide behind their bodies? Could it be that the women who pride themselves on how confident they are about their bodies are less than confident about their actual worth? In a surprisingly honest e-mail, one young woman explained to me why she had such difficulty with the idea of opting for modest outfits:

> As for the way I dress, I just can't really stop because I like making guys happy. I kinda feel like it's my purpose in life. They like the way I dress and I like the way I look when I dress this way, and so do they. It feels like they kinda like me more even though they might just want me for my body, which I don't even really have a problem with. It's been like that my whole life and that usually leads to them caring about me for a short while or just us breaking up because I won't give him any. I don't mind it because I feel really good when they care for me even if it's just for a little while.

This young woman found herself in a predicament. In her heart, she longed for more than the temporary thrill of being someone's eye candy. She yearned for a love that seemed so alien to her everyday experiences with men. Odds are, she had surrounded herself with guys who didn't value her intelligence or personality. Yet their stares and comments were proof to her that she possessed something of value. Perhaps it even gave her a sense of power because she had something they wanted. Most of the time, she probably wasn't interested in the guys. She just wanted them to be interested in her. One could imagine her thinking, "If I dress modestly, I'll lose their attention and be left with no one to desire me. Why would I want to do that?"

This illuminates the core issue. In our culture, girls are rarely affirmed for anything other than their looks. Women are rarely touched in a loving, nonsexual way. Few experience the freedom and joy of being loved by a man whose motives are pure. Because of this vacuum of authentic affirmation, many women resort to immodesty as an act of desperation to be noticed. It's an act of impatience that cries, "I'm sick of waiting around for guys. This outfit will get their attention." The problem with this approach is not that it fails, but that it often succeeds. The woman gets a guy who desires her for the wrong reasons.

While there's nothing wrong with opting for outfits that make you feel confident, a problem arises when this is done at the expense of others. People often say that immodest women fail to respect themselves. But the point is rarely made that immodest women also fail to respect men. One woman remarked that "respecting a man makes it unthinkable to seduce him to win his affection."[1] While some women dress to be noticed, others hardly think of men when they pick their outfits. They're more interested in being attracted to themselves.

If a woman understood male psychology and realized our weakness in the area of keeping a pure imagination, she would opt for modest clothing as an act of charity toward us. If you don't think of men when you choose your outfits, begin doing so. Don't be afraid to be modest. Besides, if you knew what was going on inside the minds of many guys, you'd be afraid not to be modest.

Bikinis, Tools, and Brain Scans

Male college students at Princeton University were invited to participate in research projects to measure how the male brain reacts to seeing women in bikinis. I'm sure there was no shortage of guys who volunteered their noggins to broaden the frontiers of scientific progress. Anyway, the test subjects were placed in a brain scanner and for a fraction of a second were shown photographs of women in bikinis, as well as of men and women dressed modestly.

When the young men viewed the scantily clad women, the part of their brain associated with tool use lit up. Even though some of the images were shown for as little as two-tenths of a second, the most easily remembered photographs were of bikini-clad women whose heads were cropped off the photos! The purpose of the research, according to Susan Fiske, a professor of psychology at Princeton University, was to examine ways in which people view others as a means to an end.

The researchers discovered that when some of the men viewed scantily clad females, their medial prefrontal cortex was deactivated.

This is the region of the brain associated with analyzing a person's thoughts, intentions, and feelings. Fiske remarked, "It is as if they are reacting to these women as if they are not fully human."[2] She added, "It is a preliminary study but it is consistent with the idea that they are responding to these photographs as if they were responding to objects rather than people."

She considered this discovery to be shocking, because, "The lack of activation in this social cognition area is really odd, because it hardly ever happens." Researchers had witnessed such a dehumanizing absence of brain activity only once before, during a study in which people were shown images of drug addicts and homeless people.

Another study performed on undergraduate students at Princeton found that when men are shown images of women in bikinis, their brains associate the women with first-person verbs, such as "I push," "I handle," and "I grab." When shown images of modestly dressed women, the men associated the images with the third-person forms of the verbs, such as "she pushes," "she handles," and "she grabs." In other words, the fully-clothed women were seen as being in control of their own actions, whereas the immodest ones were to be acted upon.

Although scientists were surprised by these findings, they won't come as a shock to those who know the origins of the bikini. Its inventor was a French automobile engineer named Louis Reard, who worked at his mother's lingerie business. When he created the first two-piece bathing suit in 1946, he hired a stripper to debut the outfit, because no model was willing to wear it on the runway![3] The nude dancer, Micheline Bernardini, worked at the Casino de Paris and apparently didn't have any qualms about wearing underwear in public. The runway models felt quite differently. Over half a century ago, these French models took for granted what today's scientists from Princeton find surprising.

Pure Allure

While the effect of immodesty on men is well documented, the impact of modesty is rarely explored. Just as bikinis cause some men's brains to overlook a woman's intentions and thoughts, modesty does just the opposite. It invites men to consider how much more a woman has to offer. If bikinis objectify women, modesty personalizes them.

Women who wish to be taken seriously by men may want to reconsider the power of modesty. In the words of Wendy Shalit, "Modesty, on the other hand, instead of treating men like dogs, invites them to consider an idea."[4] The virtuous woman does not veil her body because she thinks that it is bad. Nor is she hiding herself from men. Rather, she is revealing her dignity to them.

A similar comparison could be made of how God revealed His glory to us through the Incarnation. While writing about the miracle of God becoming man in the person of Christ, an eighth-century monk said that Jesus was telling us:

> I am covered by a cloud of flesh not that I may be hidden from those seeking me, but that I may be less bright for the sake of the weak. Let them heal the eyes of their minds, let them purify their ears, with faith, so that they may be worthy to look upon me. For "Blessed are the pure of heart since they will see God."[5]

Something similar could be said by the woman who dresses modestly:

> I am covered by a cloud of modesty not that I may be hidden from the men seeking me, but that I may be less bright for the sake of the weak. Let them heal the eyes of their minds, let them purify their hearts, with faith, so that they may be worthy to look upon me. For "Blessed are the pure of heart since they will see God."

It is not arrogant for a woman to think of herself in such terms, believing that her body is a window of heaven. It's humble. Humility is nothing more than the truth, and the truth is that there's glory in the way a woman has been created. Perhaps this is why one brilliant medieval philosopher called the sensitivity to shame "a healthy fear of being inglorious."[6] If that's true, one could argue that modesty is a healthy confidence of being glorious.

From a male perspective I can say that a modest woman appears more confident than those who wear less. It's as if she doesn't feel the need to rely on her figure to announce her value. The modest woman is saying, "You can't just have me. You have to win me over. I do not give myself away to those who simply want me. You must be worthy of my heart . . . and of my body." She doesn't look like a prude. She looks like a woman who lets her dignity speak for itself.

Such confidence serves as a repellent to superficial guys. It may even intimidate them because they intuit the fact that a cheesy sexual pickup line won't win them any points. At the same time, her honorable attire serves as invitation to honorable men.

This is not to say that a modest outfit will guarantee you love. But it opens the door for it. When you dress in a classy way, it shows that you anticipate that you will be treated with dignity. Your external appearance reveals your interior disposition. Although it's a crude comparison, this is how men in search of prostitutes know how to find them. They'll cruise the streets of a shady part of town keeping their eyes open for the woman whose attire reveals her intentions. Not every guy will stop for the prostitute, and not every guy will treat a modest girl with respect. But they know exactly where she stands.

Obviously, not all women who wear suggestive outfits behave accordingly. But this is beside the point. The fact remains that it's counterproductive to dress in a provocative way while expecting reverent behavior from men. A woman should be given respect regardless of how she dresses. But when a woman hopes for manners while dressing like a dancer from a rap video, she's not helping her cause. It would be like the CEO of a company hoping to be taken seriously when she shows up to a board meeting wearing sandals and shorts. A true executive would use her attire to advertise her professionalism.

A woman well aware of this principle is Kim Alexis. As a supermodel, she appeared on the covers of more than five hundred magazines, including *Glamour*, *Vogue*, and *Sports Illustrated*'s swimsuit issue. Looking back, she regretted having posed for some of the images and explained:

> Dressing like a floozy tells the world, "Look at me, want me, lust after me. I'm easy and you can have me." Displaying intimate parts of the body is a form of advertising for sex—so if you dress to attract sexual

attention, you can hardly blame anyone else if that kind of attention comes your way.[7]

This helps to explain why girls who dress immodestly while expecting respect often wonder why real love is so hard to find.

The Advantages of Modesty

Regardless of how a woman dresses, love is not an easy thing to find in today's culture. Even the most modest women will attest to this. But consider the advantages that modesty affords you.

1. You have more to reveal.   In the words of one perceptive woman, "Someone who is almost naked in front of strangers, on the other hand, has little left to reveal to her lover."[8] Because you're not exposing yourself to the general public, you're telling men that your sexuality is yours, not theirs. You assert control over a commodity that is made cheap by the modern world. It's as if you're saying, "Why should other guys be permitted to gawk at the gift of my body that is reserved for the one man who will love me above all others?"

2. Femininity inspires authentic masculinity.   By feminine, I do not mean weak or passive. Authentic femininity is a combination of class, tenderness, and virtue. When a woman possesses these traits, a man will naturally want to be more of a gentleman around her.

In my travels, I cannot count how many young men I have encountered who were won over by the modesty of their girlfriends. I've seen slobs, thugs, and players become chivalrous gentlemen because they finally found a woman who demanded more from them. I'm still not sure why the women dated them in the first place, but in each of their cases, it was the modesty of a woman that caused a spark in them. This ignited a blaze that drove out the darkness in their hearts and opened their eyes to the fact that women are worth being courteous to. This may sound too good to be true, but I've seen it too many times to write it off as a rare miracle. Modesty has power.

While immodesty triggers impatient lust, modesty sends out an invitation and a challenge to love. After realizing this, one woman wrote:

> I made some subtle changes to my wardrobe, banishing the flimsy in favor of skirts that fell to my knee and tops that fitted, rather than clung to, my figure. Though these changes weren't drastic, they had an instant effect on men's responses to me. Where a social peck on the cheek would have been customary, they now shook my hand, or, in the case of one charmer, kissed it.[9]

Without question, modesty impacts men. A young man e-mailed me about the girl whose modesty opened his eyes:

> She was the most beautiful girl I had ever laid eyes upon, not in the sense of her physical appearance but because of the aura that she gave off. The only way I can relate it is in comparison to how you spoke of modesty. Because she was smart and talented she was more appealing to me, and a much greater challenge. But this wasn't a challenge to win her sexually, but her whole being.

This man noticed that a beauty exists in woman that surpasses the physical. When one catches a glimpse of it, all her other beauties are put into perspective. Through modesty, a man can learn to appreciate a woman as a gift to be received, not some goal to be conquered.

3. Modesty sets the tone of a relationship. It tells the man that the woman doesn't have any plans to throw herself at him or beg for his attention. While some girls become sultry to help guys overcome shyness, such attempts are futile. Immodesty does not inspire courage in a man, but lust. If a guy wants you enough, he'll pursue you. We don't need to see your belly button to know if we're interested in you.

Therefore, do us a favor by dressing in a way that reminds us that you are worth more than the sum of your parts. When a woman dresses with dignity, she's announcing to the world that she'd rather not be called "hot," "sexy," or "bootylicious." Instead, "pretty" and "beautiful" would be just fine, thank you.

4. Modesty shows that you understand — and respect — the opposite sex.
Men are visually stimulated far more than are women. Part of this
is because of the way our brains are wired, and the other factor is
the beauty of women. It's an intoxicating combination.

When a woman becomes aware of how easily men are visually
stimulated, she must choose how she will use this information. Just
as some men take advantage of a woman's desire for love in order
to acquire pleasure at her expense, women sometimes prey upon the
male desire for visual stimulation for the sake of feeling desirable.
We're both guilty of using each other's weakness to our advantage.
And we're both called to something greater.

In the beginning, our motives and desires weren't so muddled. At
the dawn of creation, when Adam first saw Eve, her body revealed
to him that they were meant to become one. Their bodies revealed
their call to love and to give themselves to each other. That call to
love is stamped into our bodies. This is why tight clothing captures
a man's attention so easily. It captivates him, and it should. It's a
glimpse of the one God created for us to love. You may have noticed when guys stare at a woman in public, their facial expressions
almost look as if they've never seen a woman before. With each experience of feminine beauty, I believe that men unconsciously feel an
echo of Adam's original awe at the creative work of God.

Because of original sin, we have fallen away from our original innocence. Typically, when a man views a woman's body, he doesn't
simply appreciate her womanhood. Our disordered lust gets in the
way of our call to love. The beauty of the body, instead of reminding
us of the beauty of the person, often distracts us from it. Every man
longs to behold beauty. Likewise, every woman longs to be looked
at with awe and reverence, as Eve first thrilled the heart of Adam.
However, there is a time and place for both of our desires to be
fulfilled: within the security and sanctity of marriage.

When a woman reveals too much before then, she may see excitement in the face of a man, but she'll know that his eyes lack
reverence. Therefore, don't give in to the temptation to be gawked
at. By choosing modesty, you use your knowledge of a man's desires
to help him see his call to love.

5. *Modesty reminds you of your worth.* Even though modesty is usually spoken of as a means to educate men about the dignity of women, it's equally effective in reminding women of their own value. We have lost count of how many high school and college women have expressed to us their frustration over the treatment they receive from guys on campus. The basic problem is that young men feel comfortable grabbing, groping, slapping, or pinching women as they pass by in the hallways. After this less than cordial greeting, crude jokes are often broadcasted. What do the women offer in retaliation? Usually nothing more than a flirty stare of semi-disapproval.

Why the silence? At what point did these young women give men such power over them? If a girl wishes to reclaim the authority to speak against dishonorable men, she'll have more confidence in her speech if she's modest in her dress. Her words will have greater effect because they won't be speaking a different message than her outfit.

When a woman chooses to dress modestly, it's deliberate. Usually, it begins when she decides to throw away a portion of her current wardrobe. Then she'll begin the arduous process of looking for modest clothing. Not much thought goes into buying sexy clothes. A girl will say to herself, "Oh, that is so cute. It goes perfectly with my shoes," and the sale is complete. When selecting a modest outfit, the process is more involved. The woman is conscious of how her clothing reflects her standards. Every time she puts on the outfit, it will be an unconscious reminder of what lifestyle she is choosing to lead.

6. *Men don't get bored with modest women.* If a guy leaves you because you wish to be pure, it's not because he's bored. It's because lust is impatient. Although most men will be drawn more quickly to women who are immodest, notice how rapidly the interest burns out. One woman observed, "Modesty is really much more exciting than promiscuity. Without any obstacles in the way of desire, what is there to desire?"[10] The answer to her question is: someone else. Perhaps the best example of this is the man addicted to pornography. He sees everything a woman can physically offer him, but he won't commit to her photo for more than a few seconds.

When a man falls in love with a woman who veils herself, he will be drawn to her in an enduring way. Modesty inspires an allure that lasts because she retains the element of mystery and directs his attention to more than the external. By your very nature as a woman, you are mysterious to men. Guys may be a mystery to you, but it's just because we're pathetic at communicating. You're mysterious because you are a woman. Retain that mystery by considering your body to be a secret, spoken only to the one who deserves to know it.

No Man-Begging

Women often flirt in a sensual manner for the same reasons they dress seductively. They understand how to grab a man's attention. Perhaps they're frustrated that guys aren't pursuing them and they feel the need to drop some hints. However, when a girl is flirty and looking for love, she's undermining herself. To understand why, consider what goes on in the mind of a guy.

If a girl is flirty toward a man, he may presume that she's the same way around other guys. Strike one. If she's forward and suggestive toward him, it may be flattering at first, but he won't feel any deep awe for the woman. He'll almost feel sorry for her. It looks like she's man-begging. Strike two. Finally, if she's pursuing him, she's taken away the thrill of pursuing her. Strike three. She's out.

The following may sound politically incorrect, but it's true: A girl is out of place when she pursues. Likewise, the guy is out of place when he's the one who has to be swept off his feet. Just imagine a guy leaning over his balcony at night, blushing as he listens to a young lady serenading him from the garden below. In her stilettos, she carefully ascends the lattice outside his room to bring him flowers and a kiss. There's a reason you've never dreamt of doing this. It's messed up.

Some women may find all this talk to be detestable, outdated gender stereotyping. If that's the case and you want to be liberated to pursue the guy, go for it. As a male, I assure you that guys will happily let you fawn over them. Do yourself a favor and don't make it so easy. We need the adventure, the challenge, and the thrill of winning you. When you look desperate for our attention, you take this all away. We may be afraid of approaching a girl, but any man worth your time will take the risk.

The man should initiate the relationship. It's romantic, it honors the woman, and ultimately it's a sign of Christ's love for His bride, the Church. People are free to do otherwise, but I don't think many girls grow up dreaming of how they are going to pop the question to Mr. Wonderful. If he wants you, let him come and pursue you. You're the prize, not the pursuer.

Modest in All Things

The virtue of modesty is not something that guides your decisions only when picking out a skirt. It's more than what you wear. It's a complete affirmation of the respect owed to a woman. It's a lifestyle that permeates your conversations, your text messages, your posture, your mannerisms, and even your dancing.

Speaking of which, unless a woman carries pepper spray, she'll have a challenging time preserving her modesty at the typical dance club or prom. Whether it's called "freaking," "bumping and grinding," "booty dancing," or "juking," the concept is the same. For most women, the idea of dirty dancing with three hundred people in a darkened musty room doesn't have much appeal. One teenage girl e-mailed me to say:

> Before I went to one of the dances, I said all the girls who danced like that were hoes. Next thing you know I'm doing it. The first time a guy tried to freak dance with me, I said no. The second time, it seemed like the inevitable, so I danced a little, but the third time, I was just like out of control.

She went on to explain that she felt desensitized by the environment, all the while feeling like her external actions were the opposite of her internal emotions. She added, "I allowed myself to be degraded."

Yet another girl e-mailed me after she broke the habit of booty dancing, and said, "Why someone would want to do something even

mildly sexual with a big disgustingly sweaty guy she met ten minutes ago and doesn't even know the name of is *beyond* me!" Her
assessment probably rings true for many. However, until women can
agree that bumping and grinding isn't the best way to convince men
of their dignity, you can be sure that the boys aren't going to point
this out to them.

Practical Pointers

If you are determined to use your womanhood to invite boys to be
men, it helps to have some practical pointers for how to live the virtue
of modesty. When picking out an outfit from the store or from your
closet, ask yourself the following questions:

- Does this outfit fit me or cling to me?
- If I lean over, will my outfit show too much from the front or back?
- Does this wardrobe complement my personality or distract from it?
- Does this outfit draw a guy's attention to my face or to my body
  parts?
- By the way I dress, am I inviting guys to act like gentlemen?
- What is my outfit asking for?
- If I wanted to be used by a guy, how would I dress?

Aside from these pointers, remember that modesty is not merely
an attitude. It's one of the twelve fruits of the Holy Spirit.[11] If you
wish to radiate your God-given beauty, you need to live in union
with Him. Ask for the virtue of modesty. It is a grace from heaven,
given so that you will be a reflection of heaven.

If you've read the book of Genesis, you may have noticed in the
second chapter that the woman is portrayed as the crescendo of creation. God's creative work began with the lower forms of life such
as vegetation, progressed up toward the wild animals, and then, after the creation of Adam, reached its highest point in Eve. Without
question, God has blessed women with a share of His own infinite
beauty. In a sense, she could be thought of as a mirror of the beauty
of God. Because of the goodness of her body and soul, she reflects
His likeness in a unique way.

All beauty comes from God, and should point our hearts back toward Him. As a woman, your task is to use this gift to draw the hearts of men toward God, while avoiding the temptation to distract them from Him. Your modesty is a "ministry of beauty."[12] Or, in the words of one teenager, "A woman should be so hidden in Christ that a man has to see Christ just to see her."

Change the Culture

It's noble for you to wear modest clothing. But don't stop there. Change the fashion industry while you're at it. Sound impossible?

In Seattle, an eleven-year-old girl decided she was tired of the fashions being offered to her at a department store. Her mother noted:

> You see girls doing a lot of tugging. They want to be covered, but they are not having the clothes cooperate. . . . The girls want to look feminine and they want to look pretty, but the only look the stores offer is sexy.[13]

Therefore, the daughter did what any reasonable sixth grader would do: She contacted their corporate offices and requested that some changes be made. In her letter, she wrote:

> I am an eleven-year-old girl who has tried shopping at your store for clothes (in particular jeans), but all of them ride way under my hips, and the next size up is too big and falls down. I see all of these girls who walk around with pants that show their belly button and underwear. Your clearks sugjest that there is only one look. If that is true, then girls are suppost to walk around half naked. I think that you should change that.[14]

The girl's letter found its way to Pete Nordstrom executive VP of the company. Executives returned her letter, letting her know that they would be working to educate their purchasing managers and salespeople about the need to offer a greater range of fashion choices for youth. There's nothing better than a sixth grader shaping the decisions of corporate America!

Meanwhile, consider the teenage girls who took on Abercrombie & Filth (um, Fitch). A&F has a well-earned reputation for trying to outdo themselves in crudeness. In one of their catalogues, an A&F "sexpert" recommended to young men that they sleep with young schoolgirls, as opposed to older ones. He compared the "fruits" of biting into "fresh apple right off the tree" versus the "store-bought variety that sit on the shelf wrinkled and bruised from the handling."[15] If this wasn't enough to infuriate women, A&F began selling women's T-shirts with the following slogan emblazoned on the chest: "Who needs brains when you have these?"

Twenty-four young women from Pennsylvania had seen enough, so they initiated a "girlcott" of Abercrombie. The protests made local headlines, and eventually landed them an appearance on NBC's *Today Show*. In total, the girlcott story appeared in 21 cable news segments, 312 local TV news markets, 6 national and international radio spots, 67 regional newspapers, 4 national newspapers, 8 international newspapers, and 23,000 mentions on the Web.[16] Within five days of the *Today Show* appearance, Abercrombie & Fitch released a statement, agreed to discontinue the shirt, and arranged a meeting with the young women. A&F was probably surprised when the young women arrived at the meeting in business attire with a power point presentation on how Abercrombie could change for the better.

As one final example, high school girls in Tucson, Arizona, rallied to gather four thousand signatures to encourage a local department store to carry more modest clothing. A high school sophomore who helped with the petition drive explained that she was frustrated that the "skirts keep getting higher, and the pants keep getting lower."[17] The store responded, hosted a modesty fashion show, and altered its inventory by supplying more modest jeans, prom dresses, and formal attire.

Other women have launched modest swimwear lines. Modesty fashion shows are beginning to sweep the country, and countless web sites have been created to sell classy and cute modest attire. Women aren't helpless when it comes to changing their culture for the better. What's needed is courage. After all, brave individuals are the only ones who have ever improved society.

What Will You Offer the World?

"Leah? . . . Leah? What's going on? What's going on?" The photographer lowered his camera and watched the color drain from the model's face.

Leah Darrow had spent years of her life in the fashion industry and had been a contestant on the television show *America's Next Top Model*. But nothing prepared her for what she saw in New York City during a risqué photo shoot for an international men's magazine. The last thing she recalled was the voice of the photographer, reacting to her ghostly white appearance.

While still conscious, Leah recalls zoning out:

> I had died, and I was standing before God, with my hands open. And I was in my outfit that I was wearing for my photo shoot. I was offering Him my last action on earth. And I was saying, "Here: This is what I have to offer you. This is the last thing I have done to love you, to serve you, to praise you."

Nothing else was said. God's head bowed, and Leah came back to the photo shoot:

> And I just knew that I couldn't do this any more. I knew God had given me talents and gifts, but I had become some type of fashion prostitute, selling the gifts God had given me for the world. I walked out of that photo shoot, I walked out of New York City, and I chose to give my life back to Christ.

Upon receiving a $16,000 check for the photo shoot, she tore the payment to pieces, preferring the wealth of her dignity to the poverty of her former affluence. Today, Leah travels around the country speaking to young women about how to dress with style without compromising their class.

Her remarkable conversion offers a useful examination of conscience for all women. If you really want to know if your attire is fitting for a Christian woman, ask yourself: If Jesus Christ returned to earth, would I want to meet Him while wearing this outfit? Although it may sound a bit apocalyptic, dress like you're ready for the Second Coming. It's not just about preparing to meet your judge. It's about preparing to meet your groom. Dress accordingly.

LOVE YOUR BODY

When a woman's body appears on the cover of a tabloid magazine, only one of three headlines will accompany it. Either the magazine will praise her perfection, lament her obesity, or announce her anorexia. Not surprisingly, the average American girl begins dieting when she is eight years old.[1] More than half of teenage girls are, or think they should be, on diets.[2]

They're not the only ones struggling to stay thin. Revlon decided that Cindy Crawford was too fat for them, and decided to give her a digital diet—by using computers to make her arms appear skinnier in their advertisements.[3] When supermodels can't even live up to today's standard of beauty, how is any woman supposed to like what she sees in the mirror? Because we live in such a superficial culture, most girls develop a dislike—and sometimes hatred—of their bodies before they finish elementary school. As hard as the media may be in critiquing the quality of a woman's figure, no one is more demanding on the woman than herself.

In a quest to receive love and acceptance, many women unknowingly pay homage to a certain cult of the body. They begin to idolize the perfect figure and sacrifice themselves in order to obtain it. This is usually not a deliberate choice. For most girls, it feels like more of an obligation. But the end result is always the same: Because the worship of anything other than God will always leave a person unfulfilled, these women are never satisfied.

The process may begin with the normal physical comparisons that play out in a girl's mind when she begins to recognize that looks matter to guys (and other girls). On the bus ride to school at the age of eleven, she sees billboards of airbrushed women zoom past her window. At home, she turns on the television and sees unblemished models offering advice on how she can become just as desirable as they are if she says and does the right things for boys. The seeds of untruth are sown in her impressionable young mind. She goes to a movie and sees people with flawless figures living happily ever after with other beautiful people. An impossible standard of perfection is erected without her noticing. As she listens to gossip around school, she learns how the body of a woman can be used as bait to catch the attention of men.

In her longing for the perfect look, she may starve herself or begin to binge and purge. In her desire for acceptance, she may allow boys to become too physical with her. Because she fears her own fertility, she may begin using birth control to avoid the natural consequence of sexual intimacy. Sexually transmitted diseases and abortion sometimes follow. Feelings of depression cloud her life, and her heart is weighed down with an inescapable feeling of loss. She can hardly recognize herself, and may begin to blame and hate herself. To numb the emotional pain, she may even cut herself or contemplate taking her life. One lie feeds upon another, yet every one of them promises relief along the way. She wanted none of this, yet ended up with all of it.

Where did she go wrong? How could such an avalanche of suffering have been prevented? Each lie must be untwisted so the truth can begin to heal her. Here's the truth.

Love Your Body

Angelina Jolie, Jennifer Aniston, Nelly Furtado, Oprah, and Martha Stewart. What do all these women have in common? Each of their bodies was digitally altered in photographs in order for them to appear more perfect to the public. Martha and Oprah were digitally decapitated and their bodies replaced with those of younger models when they appeared on the covers of *Newsweek* and *TV Guide*.[4] *Us Weekly* paid a half-million dollars for the publishing rights to a picture of Brad Pitt and Angelina Jolie taking a stroll on the beach when their affair began. *Star* magazine didn't have the same image so they created a composite photo of Brad and Angelina, noting in a small caption on the contents page that the image was not real. What's worse is that an Australian tabloid took an old photo of Jennifer Aniston with Brad and replaced her head with Angelina's![5]

If that's not low enough, *FHM* men's magazine obtained a picture of Nelly Furtado and digitally disrobed half her clothing to make a racier magazine cover. The cover blasted "Nelly Furtado! Canada's Sexiest Export in Her Hottest Ever Shoot!" She never consented to the creation of the image, but they didn't seem to care. She said:

> I'm really not happy. They put me on the cover. They say they did a shoot with me but they didn't. They air-brushed my body and changed my body shape. I didn't give permission for anything. . . . There I am with a shirt that has actually been digitally altered to go to just below my chest, with a stomach that I don't recognize. I don't like being misrepresented to my fans. You work hard to represent a certain thing and have a certain image and somebody can take it all away with the cover of a magazine.[6]

The practice of digital disrobing and alteration is so common that Libertee Muzyka, who previously worked with *Stuff* and *Maxim* magazines said, "I would love to have her abs, and guess what? So would she."[7]

Do you know anyone who believes that she has a perfect body? If you did, you'd probably be nauseated by her narcissism. Really, though: How many girls do you know who even *like* their body? Most girls could name a dozen girls whose bodies they'd love to have, but very few love their own.

Think of the happiest person you know. Does she have the perfect body? Probably not. Her joy has nothing to do with the shape of her body. Now think of the happiest married couple you have ever known. Do they starve themselves? Do they have perfect bodies? I'm willing to bet that they're pretty average-looking people. Look around and you'll see that average-looking girls who possess deep self-respect are more likely to find enduring love than runway models.

We all assume that if we have the ideal figure, we'll earn the ideal love. This pernicious lie drives millions of people into the vicious cycle of self-hatred and self-destructive behavior. One young woman said to us:

> I hate my body. Every time I look in the mirror, all I think about is what I wish I could change about myself. I started eating less in junior high, and there are days where I barely eat anything. I just play with the food on my plate and hope that nobody will notice.

There comes a point where a woman must step back and ask herself: What's the point of all this? Why are we so obsessed with external beauty? Is it simply because we want to be loved by others, or is it something deeper? Could it be, perhaps, that we've fallen for the lie that if we obtain a perfect body then we'll suddenly begin to love ourselves?

This is the core issue. How can a woman develop a healthy self-love? Where does self-worth come from? According to magazines, it's from the amount of approval you receive. The message given to women through the media has been summed up well by psychologist Mary Pipher: "Don't worry about feeling good or being good—worry about looking good."[8] Those who follow this worldly recipe for fulfillment end up, in the words of Pipher, with "hair and smiles in place and a terrible deadness underneath."[9]

How does one avoid this? One female college student offered a practical suggestion:

> Accept that other women will be prettier, smarter, and more popular than you are, and that's fine. It's a big world with lots of opportunities. The goal is not to stand on the top of the pile. The goal is to hold yourself to a personal standard and become someone you would respect if you were someone else.[10]

What this college student discovered was that love wills the good of another—even when that other is you. If you wait until the day your emotions tell you to love yourself, you may be in for a long wait.

Therefore, guard against self-loathing. Because we often have a hard time loving ourselves, we sometimes assume that no man would love us either. Such negative thinking patterns set up a woman for being used, because she'll fall for the first cute guy who expresses an interest in her. In her mind, any physical attention will translate into immediate emotional gratification. It feels like a bodily affirmation of her worth. But when she realizes that he never wanted her in the first place, her self-love will sink lower than before.

Choosing to love yourself can be difficult when you've looked with disdain upon yourself for years. Therefore, if you struggle with an eating disorder or hatred of your body, have the courage to seek help. Talk to a family member, teacher, or counselor. Some girls eternally postpone treatment out of fear that they will be forced to gain weight. Suffering in isolation, they try to convince themselves that they'll be able to pull themselves out of their condition. Yet it lingers for years without lasting improvement. Those who struggle with obesity may also avoid help, sinking into greater despair and contempt for the way the world views them.

When a girl seeks counseling, she'll gain fresh insight. She may discover that she's been trying to make herself desirable to others because she doesn't accept herself. Or perhaps because other parts of her life are out of control, she obsesses about her weight in an effort to feel a sense of control. One girl said, "When I was starving, I couldn't think about . . . the fact that I was young and scared and sexually threatened and angry."[11] Such women reduce all the issues in their life to one: their weight. Through therapy, the deeper issues can be resolved so that the young woman will experience true control over her life.

When a woman develops a critical view of her body, it can become like an abusive relationship. Imagine if a man were to call his girlfriend "fat" and "ugly" every day for several years. The emotional toll of these words would be severe even if she considered herself tough enough to ignore it. It would be like water dripping on a stone. Given enough time, it leaves a deep impression and can pierce through the rock. In the same way, when a woman stands before the mirror and mentally utters insults at herself, she becomes her own abuser. Such wounds require a time of healing and a counselor skilled in peeling away the labels a woman has given herself.

A good counselor will help a woman to see one thing above all: a glimpse of what God sees when He looks upon her. God sees things in the fullness of truth, and declared that the creation of the woman was "very good."[12] The creation of every woman since the first is no less good.

If you wish to see what God sees in you, look for your reflection in His eyes. Gaze into that mirror, for once. Come to Him in prayer and allow Him to gradually reveal your worth to you. Be patient in the healing process. Perhaps you have spent years muttering to yourself, "I hate my nose. My stomach is fat. I wish I were taller. I'm not pretty enough." Wounds take time to heal, especially when you inflict them upon yourself.

If you spend time in the presence of God, you will eventually learn how a father adores his daughter. I (Jason) have a daughter who is only a toddler. As an infant, she didn't have the slimmest figure. Her thighs and forearms had as many rolls as a croissant. And I was entirely in love with her. My only hope is that she will love herself as much as I do. God's hope is no different for you. Once you discover your value in His eyes, you'll learn to resist the urge to beat yourself down.

Instead of looking at yourself and launching mental insults or pointing out a defect in the handiwork of God, try something different. When the urge arises within you to critique yourself, say something different in your mind, such as Psalm 139:14: "I praise you, so wonderfully you made me; wonderful are your works!" Or you could say something in your heart as simple as "God doesn't make junk." What matters is that you begin the process of loving yourself.

You cannot love yourself and hate your body. To hate the body is to hate the person. You don't need to be infatuated with your figure. You just need to declare a ceasefire against yourself. As one woman summed up, "I'm not obsessed with getting skinny. I just want to be healthy." Take on this mentality and you're well on your way.

Cherish Your Body

In his letterman jacket, Matthew approached me following my lecture at his affluent suburban high school. He asked if we could talk in private, so we walked into an empty classroom and turned two desks toward each other. We sat down, and he looked at me with sullen eyes. His jaw began to quiver, but no tears fell as he rolled up his sleeves and asked me, "What does God think about . . . mutilation?" Pointing to scars that littered his forearms, he said, "This one was caused by a lighter. That's a knife. That one's a stapler. That one was a cigar. A pencil. A paper clip . . . "

"Why?" I asked.

Matthew then began to explain how he fell in love with a girl, pressured her to have sex, got her pregnant, talked her into having an abortion, and then cheated on her. He began dating the second girl, and cheated on her as well. Now they both hate him, but he wants to commit to the first one and hates himself for what he did to her. The self-harm is his way to punish himself, because he knows how he's punished her.

Elsewhere, at a campus in East Chicago, Jasmin sat before me in tears, showing me her scars:

> Just last night, I got back from this guy's house where we hooked up again. I was so mad at myself, I cut myself again. I looked down at the palm of my hand, and it was filled with a pool of my own blood. I just sat there and asked myself "Why am I doing this to myself?"

Many cut in order to smother emotional pain. One girl lamented:

> I'm a hypocrite and I know it. I live two different lives. I wear a mask when I'm around people and act like life is wonderful. The me that no one knows struggles with an eating disorder, cuts herself all over her body, and does anything possible to numb the pain of being me.[13]

Others cut in hopes that someone will notice their pain. "[It's] just like bringing the scars to the outside," one girl explained.[14] Sometimes cutting is a form of stress relief or self-punishment. Other times it's used to see signs of life. "My emotional pain is so deep that I feel dead. When I cut myself and see the blood dripping down my arm, at least I know I'm alive."[15]

In all these cases, young people cut because they don't know how to process the suffering in their lives. One girl explained, "I didn't know what to do with all that hurt. It just wouldn't go away. It kept growing and gnawing at my insides."[16] Another young woman told me she needed to go deeper each time she cut in order to get the pain and anger out. Some people may wonder how cutters can endure the pain they inflict upon themselves. But what they fail to realize is that for these young people the external pain pales in comparison to their internal anguish. In a gesture that is rather symbolic of how they handle emotional suffering, many young women habitually pick at their wounds, preventing them from healing.

Most women who self-harm hate their habit but aren't sure how to break free. In order to stop cutting, it's necessary to uncover the reason for the behavior. Because self-injury is often used as a distraction, it never removes the core problem. When the physical pain subsides, the emotional pain returns to fill the void. It's a vicious cycle.

Consider the young woman above who filled her hand with a pool of her own blood after returning home from a meaningless hookup. After injuring herself, was she any closer to the finding the love she was created for? Not in the least. If a woman wants a guy to cherish her and treat her body with honor, she must do the same.

When a woman feels tempted to harm herself in order to numb her pain, what should she do? The first suggestion is for her immediately to have recourse to God in prayer. Just a simple "God give me the grace not to do this" is a good place to start. She could also say a prayer to her guardian angel, who never leaves her side.

Secondly, she needs to resist the urge to turn inward. When a person cuts, it shows that she is pulling away from her friends and family in order to cope with—or escape from—life's problems. If cutting is a problem for you, resist the temptation to isolate yourself. You have a decision before you. What will you choose: solitude or community? If you feel like you have no one to turn to, surely there must be someone. Because the teenage years are often spent in isolation from one's parents, teens often deprive themselves of a network of love that would otherwise help them cope with the pain. Although not all families are intact or supportive, the first safety net in times of trial should be our family or relatives. You could also turn to an adult at church or school in order to find support and strength. If you don't live with your family, become active in your church community to find fellowship.

Perhaps you fear approaching those who could help you the most. You ask yourself, "What will they think of me?" But haven't you spent enough of your life being haunted by that question? When a girl constantly lives under the fear of what others will think, she paralyzes herself.

If you confess your cutting problem, what will they think? If they have any human decency, they'll feel honored that you trust them enough to come to them and they'll admire the fact that you have the courage to overcome your struggles. If you wish to stop harming yourself, you must first accept the love of others. It helps to have someone who loves you when you have trouble loving yourself.

With their help, you can learn how to deal with the stress in a way that will make your life better. Instead of coping with suffering in a destructive way, you can learn how to deal with it in a productive way. That way, when you feel the urge to cut, you can ask yourself, "Why do I feel the need to do this? What's going on in my life that makes me want to act like this? If I cut, will my problems be any better, or will I just be worse off?" With the help of others, address the core issue and set up a strategy to heal it. Instead of causing external wounds, heal the internal ones.

If you cut in order to punish yourself, know this: If you deserve punishment for your behavior, Jesus has already paid the price. As the prophet Isaiah foretold, "But he was wounded for our transgressions, he was bruised for our iniquities; upon him was the chastisement that made us whole, and with his stripes we are healed."[17]

If you are working to overcome the habit of cutting, make sure not to lose sight of the spiritual dimension of the struggle you're facing. In 1 Corinthians 6:19, St. Paul tells us, "Do you not know that your body is a temple of the Holy Spirit within you, which you have from God?" Because your body is a temple, cutting is not merely a psychological problem. It's also a spiritual one, and we would be naïve to dismiss this reality. If the human body is the dwelling place of the Holy Spirit, wouldn't the devil take delight in profaning the temple of God? This is why Scripture explicitly forbids self-harm. For example, Moses commanded the Israelites, "You are children of the LORD, your God. You shall not gash yourselves."[18] Elsewhere, the prophet Jeremiah pleads, "How long will you gash yourselves?"[19] Historically, these passages refer to ritualized forms of self-harm, but modern-day cutting leaves the same scars.

We quote these passages not to condemn depressed women, but to remind them of their value. One girl who contacted us about her struggles with cutting said that she would often find consolation and strength when reflecting on the idea that her body was a temple of the Holy Spirit. The more you can internalize this truth, the more you will begin to cherish the body God has entrusted you with.

Love Your Life

Seventeen percent of young women seriously contemplated suicide in the past year.[20] Two percent attempted to take their lives, and fewer than one out of 25,000 committed suicide.[21] Upon learning this, some people wonder why young people are so obsessed with death. We see the opposite. Why are they so obsessed with life? The fact that so many contemplate suicide while so few take their life tells us that very few people want to die. They're just tired of living.

One reason for the despair is the fact that young women experience a hormonal shift during adolescence that often makes them strangers to themselves. One minute life is beautiful and they bubble over with joy. The next minute the world is conspiring against them and they cry for reasons they don't fully understand. These shifts in emotions are a result of the fact that the main neurotransmitters of the adolescent brain all have a major impact on mood. Especially for a teenage woman, fluctuating levels of estrogen and progesterone exert a powerful influence over these neurotransmitters, creating a perfect emotional storm.[22] It's helpful when a girl can be informed of these facts prior to adolescence so that she doesn't think there's something wrong with her if she finds herself in tears during a television commercial.

As if these physiological factors aren't difficult enough, women's lives are often spiced up with unstable relationships, gossip, strained friendships, family issues, and a host of other problems. It's hardly a smooth ride. A college survey revealed that 47 percent of college female students felt so depressed during the previous year that it was sometimes hard for them to function.[23] When you add sexual activity to the equation, teenage girls become more than three times as likely to be depressed as abstinent teens.[24] One student e-mailed me after a broken sexual relationship to say, "I feel like the gross stuff in the road after the snow is kinda melted and cars have been driving on it for a while."

When you look into the lives of depressed women, you will notice a common theme of a lack of love. They may be surrounded by friends and family, but they feel isolated in the midst of the company. Because they feel starved for authentic intimacy and affection, they may attempt suicide as a desperate plea for attention. They're not declaring that they want to die. They're announcing that they want a reason to live. While they seek consolation in receiving love (as they should), a quicker solution can be found in giving love.

Whenever we are tempted to despair, it is easy to focus on how others have failed to love us. Although part of the blame lies in others—especially for victims of abuse—sometimes part of the blame lies in us, in how we fail to look beyond ourselves. If our life is not lived as a gift for others, where is the meaning in it? Are we living in hopes that others will live for us?

When we step back, we see that God has blessed us with much to be thankful for. We'll also notice that there are countless people whose situations in life are more unfortunate than our own. If we desire to be loved, imagine how much stronger that desire is in others who are less fortunate. These people are not simply to be found in homeless shelters or refugee camps in foreign countries. They're in your family, in your workplace, and in your dorm. They, too, are thirsty for love, and it is within your power to give it to them. When you choose to love, you will find that there is joy in the giving.

For this reason, suicide is ultimately a selfish act because the world needs to be blessed with your life. God has a future for you, even though it can be difficult to believe during times of sorrow and confusion. He did not create you to live a meaningless existence. By the way you live, you can set into motion a chain of hope or a chain of despair. Even if your suffering seems unbearable, know that it will not last. As one high school student eloquently said to us, "Everything will be all right in the end. If it isn't all right, it isn't the end."

If you are struggling with thoughts of depression or suicide, do not keep these thoughts to yourself. Talk to an adult, or call a suicide help hotline such as 1-800-448-3000. Choose to hope, and do not give in to discouragement. Cling to others who stand ready to love you, and trust the word of God, which says, "Study the generations long past and understand; has anyone hoped in the Lord and been disappointed?"[25]

Love Your Fertility

I (Jason) thoroughly enjoy watching television commercials for birth control. Gleeful models prance down a runway or ballerinas dance through the forest to the sound of tranquil music . . . while a voice in the background mumbles minor details about brain hemorrhages, strokes, heart attacks, and nausea. It's too bad they don't have the actresses dramatizing these things in their tutus. Such commercials are about as realistic as the STD medicine commercials in which a woman riding a mountain bike looks ecstatic to be dating a man with herpes. The couple looks so in love that it almost makes you wish that you were infected, too.

The media has done a stellar job presenting birth control as something that's as natural to a woman's body as water, food, and oxygen. It's always celebrated as a liberation from the way your body unfortunately functions. Whenever a new birth control drug or device hits the market, you may have noticed that the advertisers say something to the effect of, "Now, women have a new way to experience greater reproductive freedom, without having to worry about blah, blah, blah." The latest trend is to ingest synthetic hormones in order to get rid of those pesky periods.

But what's so wrong with fertility? Shouldn't a woman take drugs when she's sick, and not when she's healthy? What many women do not realize is that the sale of hormonal birth control is a multibillion-dollar industry. With such money at stake, it's no surprise that the ethics of such a business have been marred with controversy and corruption, showing little regard for women's health. For example, the makers of the birth control shot (Depo-Provera) were fined $2.3 billion by the federal government for illegal drug promotions.

Within the drug industry, companies hire pharmaceutical sales representatives to pitch their products to doctors. Normally, these business meetings take place in the doctors' offices. However, Pfizer reps have been caught wining and dining the doctors. In an effort to butter up the doctors to prescribe drugs such as Depo-Provera, Pfizer sales reps were caught paying for doctors to receive free golf, massages, and resort junkets. Thankfully, the government caught the company in the act (for the fourth time in the past decade), and will now be monitoring their marketing strategies.[26]

Meanwhile, if you were to walk into most gynecologists' offices, you would only see posters of happy models with bright smiles promoting the newest contraceptives. While sitting in my obstetrician's waiting room, I (Crystalina) noticed a large poster informing women about the threat of osteoporosis. Right below the poster was an information rack with an advertisement brochure for Depo-Provera. I find this ironic, considering that the FDA placed a "black box warning" on the shot because it thins a woman's bones and can cause osteoporosis. Near the osteoporosis poster was another, reminding women to get screened for breast cancer. Of course, this was located just a few feet away from the advertisement for the birth control pill, which increases a woman's risk of breast cancer.[27]

By law, the pharmaceutical companies that make birth control must include an information sheet with each drug, outlining the possible hazards. This sheet is usually written in cryptic medical terminology, using microscopic print. Women don't bother to read it because they assume it's up to their doctor to inform them of possible risks. However, most doctors leave it up to the patients to do their own homework and make their own decisions.

One young woman e-mailed Jason after hearing him explain the potential side effects of the birth control pill. She wrote:

> I remember you said you don't want anything in your wife's body that would be bad for her. When you said that, I could see the way your wife was looking at you with such peace, happiness, and love. She knows you have her back, and that's a good feeling. I want that for myself someday.

My hope is that you would have this feeling toward your own body. If you truly love your body, you will live in accordance with the way it has been created. There's no need to ingest, inject, or implant artificial chemicals and devices to render yourself infertile. A woman's body is perfectly made. Her fertility is a wondrous thing, not a disorder that needs to be cured by synthetic sex hormones.

Through pregnancy, a woman's womb becomes a tabernacle for life. Although this may be news for some, women do not become pregnant during intercourse. Fertilization typically occurs hours or even days after the sexual act. As Dr. Alice von Hildebrand points out, "God therefore 'touches' the female body in placing this new soul into the temple of her womb."[28] Imagine if women believed that their fertility was a gift rather than a risk.

Because of the sexual revolution, many women have been taught that they should be free to have sex like a player—with minimal emotional attachment and no risk of pregnancy. This is hardly sexual liberation. Liberation is believing that your body is perfectly made. If you're not ready for a baby, the solution is not to take drugs and have sex. It's to wait for sex until you're ready for motherhood.

Such a proposal might sound simplistic, but consider the wisdom of simplicity. One woman commented:

> I volunteer at a crisis pregnancy center. A sixteen-year-old girl came in for a pregnancy test. As we waited for the results she was visibly trembling and near to tears. When the result was negative, she began to cry and laugh and bounce up and down. I asked her why she was

so happy. She looked at me like I was a total idiot, and in that "Duh, you're so stupid" tone that teenagers do so well, she answered, "I'm way too young to have a baby." I leaned toward her and said, "Then you're also too young to be doing what makes babies." For a long moment she stared at me with her mouth open and not breathing, then in a very small voice she said, "No one ever told me that before."[29]

There's no need for women to live in fear of pregnancy. One single man confessed, "If it's a girl I just met in a bar, I used to wake up in a cold sweat worrying about pregnancy."[30] What's the point of living in such terror of sex? We should be excited to flip over a pregnancy test. Our hearts should be racing with anticipation. We should be thinking, "If we're pregnant, I can't wait to surprise my parents with the news. I'll give them a pair of little blue booties and watch the reaction!" If such a thought is laughable and you're not ready to see the outcome of a positive pregnancy test with joy, then save sex for the day your husband will be by your side to view the results.

Besides, if you're seeking a soulmate, birth control isn't likely to be much help. Not much reflection is needed to notice that many men are likely to postpone marriage if they can enjoy the pleasure of sex without the responsibilities of fatherhood. Imagine how much more serious men—and women—would take the sexual act if making love meant making life! There's a reason why life and love are naturally united within the womb. What God has joined, we ought not separate.

If a woman disregards the way her body is made, nature rebels. A young woman shared with us that she slept with her boyfriend before he headed off to college. She said, "I wish I could go back and think this over. It was almost like I wanted to convince him to marry me but he was not interested." She ended up becoming pregnant, but was told by Planned Parenthood that her pregnancy test was negative. To celebrate the negative results, she and her friends partied with heavy drinking. Her e-mail continued:

About a week later, I woke up in the night with horrible cramps. My roommate's mom was a nurse and helped me go to the Emergency

Room. They said that I had miscarried and admitted me to the hospital for a D and C.

When a woman is sexually active while hoping not to become pregnant, her life is a contradiction. If she sets her will against life, where does this leave her when a pregnancy "accidentally" occurs? Often, the woman is told that she can simply choose to terminate the pregnancy and move on with her life.

Is it so simple? If abortion solves the "problem," why do studies show that women who elect to have abortions are seven times more likely to commit suicide within a year of the abortion as compared to mothers who gave birth?[31] One researcher noticed a significant trend to many of these deaths: A disproportionate amount of them occurred seven to ten months after the abortion. The researcher noted, "This may correspond to a negative anniversary reaction related to the expected due date of the aborted child."[32] Postabortive women are also more likely to require psychiatric hospitalization than the mothers who gave birth to their children.[33]

One woman recalled the day she had planned to have an abortion. She said, "I was summoned to the room where the abortions are performed. I could hear a woman sobbing hysterically in the recovery room. That memory haunts me still."[34] The depths of the other woman's sobs drove this woman from the clinic, and she chose to keep her child. For those who don't make the same decision, the remorse is often not easily forgotten.

The effects of abortion are not merely emotional. One woman e-mailed me to ask I if would share her story with other women. She wrote:

I had three preemies because of the abortion, with our second child being seven-and-a-half weeks early because my cervix was damaged by the abortion. I recently had a total hysterectomy and had all kinds of problems dating back to the abortion and I am in my forties. So abortion is not a simple solution for ridding a "problem." It creates new ones. Pregnancy is not the worst thing that can happen to women. To be frank with you, I had an STD (chlamydia) and an abortion. And looking back, if I had to choose one over the other I would choose the STD. I was able to be medicated to get over the STD but the abortion invisibly shaped my future. It changed the way I parented my future children. It changed the way I felt about my self and my mother and it severed my relationship with my God. How could I ever face God again with what I had done? So I self-medicated and self-destructed.

Among those who promote the "freedom of choice," why are such stories never publicized? Also commonly ignored is the fact that the father of an aborted child will also suffer from the loss. Six years after an abortion, one man said, "Every time I see children of the approximate age of the two lost ones, I cry, no matter where . . . church, the mall, the park, the library. I want to call their names."[35] For everyone's sake, there has to be a better way than abortion to deal with an unexpected pregnancy.

If you have suffered through an abortion, know that God longs to heal you, forgive you, and give you the grace to forgive yourself. Take advantage of the services offered by postabortion healing ministries, such as Project Rachel and Rachel's Vineyard. There you will find compassion and support, not condemnation or shame.

Protect Your Fertility

Erin approached me (Jason) in tears after the speech I gave at her high school. She had lived a wild life the first few years at school and was now paying a heavy price for it. After being infected with a virulent strain of human papillomavirus (HPV), doctors performed four surgeries on her cervix in order to remove the cancerous tissue. Because they had removed so much of her cervix, she now has what doctors call "cervical incompetence." She sobbed, "If I ever become pregnant, I won't be able to carry the pregnancy to full term without having a miscarriage. Now I'll never be able to have kids." After I offered her as much consolation as I could, I gave her a hug and watched her wipe the mascara from her cheeks as she walked toward the hallway, melting back into the crowd of students who knew nothing of her suffering.

Imagine if she could rewind her life to the night she contracted HPV. If she knew then what she knows now, how easily she would have chosen to be abstinent! How liberating the decision would have seemed to her! How inconsequential would a few minutes of pleasure have seemed when compared to the gift of her fertility!

This young woman is only a representative of the millions whose fertility has been damaged because of STDs. You've probably never considered this, but can you imagine how many people do not exist today because an STD destroyed their would-be mother's fertility? While some sexually transmitted infections cause minor irritation and inconvenience, others have the capacity to alter the course of human history. This is no exaggeration. If an STD impairs a woman's fertility, and a single child does not come into being, neither will his children or grandchildren. In time, it creates a ripple that prevents the lives of dozens and even hundreds of other people.

Therefore, when a woman practices the virtue of chastity, she not only safeguards her own body. By protecting the treasure of her womb, her abstinence becomes an expression of maternal love that guards the existence of countless generations. If only the idea of purity were expressed to young girls in such a way, how much easier would it be for them to see the connection between love and chastity!

The world considers such logic silly. "Don't be so uptight. Just use protection." Those who promote the outdated concept of safe sex make two grave mistakes. First, they overestimate the effectiveness of the condom in preventing disease. In one study, scientists followed four hundred college girls for a period of about five years. During that time, 60 percent of the girls contracted HPV. The scientists noted, "Always using male condoms with a new partner was not protective."[36] It's too bad that the scientists didn't inform the women about the limitations of the condom before they volunteered for the research.

Secondly, it's a dangerous exaggeration to call sex "safe" because a piece of latex is involved. Imagine if a young woman approached us in tears after a broken sexual relationship. Let's say she had given away her virginity and felt devastated upon seeing her ex-boyfriend flirting with other girls weeks after telling her that he "never felt this way about a girl before." Now imagine if we consoled her by saying, "Hey, cheer up. You're not pregnant. You didn't get an STD. You're safe!"

Safe? She's destroyed.

Promoting safe sex makes as much sense as telling a child to wear a helmet if he's going to play in traffic. Just as a helmet would only provide partial protection to part of the body, the condom only offers partial protection to the whole woman. In fact, the idea of safe sex is degrading because it reduces a woman to her genitals: As long as they're protected, she's safe. How about keeping the rest of her safe?

Some may object to such an idea, arguing, "C'mon. Nobody is saying the condom protects you from the emotional aspect of sexuality." But the problem is that nobody seems concerned about that. The culture has become so jaded that we spend billions of dollars handing out condoms without teaching people the difference between love and lust.

Despite all the information offered in sex ed, the one thing lacking seems to be awe. The modern concept of sexuality is so deprived of reverence and mystery that it's no surprise that more people seem dissatisfied than ever before. *Cosmopolitan* offers a hundred new lust lessons with every issue, claiming that the sheer memorization of sexual techniques will lead women closer to the satisfaction for which they yearn. Maybe a guy worth marrying isn't really that concerned that you know how to "perform." Personally, we think any guy worthy of you would be romantic enough to throw your *Cosmo* in the trash so that the two of you as husband and wife could teach each other the mystery of human love.

Defend Yourself

Although few people seem to notice, nothing on earth is more assaulted and degraded than the body of the woman. The media focuses upon environmental hazards as the greatest injustice on our planet. While that issue deserves our attention, a more serious war is being waged against women's bodies.

Consider all that afflicts it: anorexia, bulimia, cutting, sexual abuse, STDs, chemical contraception, abortion, degradation through pornography, prostitution and the sex trade, obsessive cosmetic surgery, and so on. Why is it that these things afflict women far more than men? Why are the threats against the woman's body so insidious?

One gentleman in his twenties e-mailed us a letter he wrote for women, praising their goodness and beauty. In it, he offered an insightful explanation of why hell seems so hell-bent on destroying the woman:

> Satan attacks most viciously that which has the greatest ability to lead us to God. I hope you know that he *fears* your beauty. He knows it can lead people to God, who is the fulfillment and source of all beauty. And if you believe that he was once the angel of light surpassing all others in beauty, then you should realize that you are the image to him of everything that he lost. He has taken aim at your beauty and has set his plan to ruin God's plan for it.

The devil knows the untapped potential of every woman to lead souls to God. Because he fears your beauty, he'll seek either to destroy it or to hide it from you. Heaven and hell understand the value of your body and the power of your beauty. Do you?

FIND YOUR BRIDESMAIDS, THEN YOUR GROOM

"Hey Jason!" I looked over my shoulder while working the combination on my high school locker and saw my best friend approaching with a grin on his face. "Guess what I got Rachel to do with me." Nathan would gleefully update me on the progress he made wearing down his girlfriend's morals. I wasn't particularly interested, but he didn't seem to mind. In his spare time, he would visit adult bookstores and often boasted of the fact that his mom paid for him to have a subscription to *Playboy*.

I finished collecting my books out of the locker and we began walking toward our first period class. A few moments later, I heard "Vote for Trevor," and looked up to see another classmate passing out pornography from his locker to anyone willing to vote for him in the upcoming school elections.

Needless to say, I hadn't made the best choice of friends. But I figured: Being a teen is hard enough with the friends I *do* have. The last thing I'd want to do would be to lose them. They may not be perfect, but they're not *that* bad. After all, I can name dozens of guys who are worse than they are: Stalin, Hitler, Pol Pot, Genghis Khan, and so on.

Toward the end of high school I made better friendships, but then headed off to college and needed to start the process again. I wanted friends who brought out the best in me, instead of acquaintances who brought out the worst. Finding such friends is not always an easy task, but it is always worth the effort.

When I (Crystalina) began my conversion as a seventeen-year-old high school student, my friends rejected me the first night I decided not to go clubbing with them. That evening, I wrote in my journal:

> I'm slowly starting to feel like a stranger to my friends. Is all this trouble, tears, and sadness worth it in the long run? Do I really know what I'm doing? I know there is something better than this, and I'm trying to see that. But at times like this, it's hard.

By breaking off those bad attachments, I opened the door to build new friendships. Within a few months, a friend invited me to a retreat, which eventually led to me doing a year of missionary work overseas, volunteering at a school for young girls. I decided to spend this year of service after high school because I knew that I needed a time of serious formation before college. Through this missionary program, I met the friends who would eventually introduce me to Jason. By saying one small "yes" at a time, I created a better environment for myself.

In order to find good friends, it's necessary to turn down the opportunity to hang out with those who will wear down your morals. Don't fear this. Your social life won't end because you respectfully decline the opportunity to attend a certain party. Before my conversion, I assumed that if a woman was pure, it meant that her life would be a bore. But after my conversion, I realized that hookups and hangovers weren't that much fun anyway.

While I was immersed in a lifestyle of booze and boys, it seemed that the more often I hooked up, the higher the amount of drugs or alcohol I ingested. My friends and I escaped into an empty bliss of drugs and drunkenness because we couldn't live with ourselves otherwise. After a while, I lost the desire to fight for anything noble. This spiritual laziness—sloth—has been defined as the sadness arising from the fact that the good is difficult. Instead of improving our lives, we remained submerged in our vices out of mere convenience. But we'd still find ways to congratulate ourselves for not being worse.

At every party, the people who weren't drinking thought they were role models for drinking water instead of beer. The people who were buzzed were busy laughing at the drunkards, while the drunkards thought themselves ethical because they weren't high. The potheads were so giddy and philosophical from the effects of marijuana that they prided themselves for not tripping on acid. Meanwhile, those on acid were too fried to notice the nondrinkers, who thought their sobriety would be an inspiration to all. We were all a bunch of puppets, so consumed with looking at those beneath us that none of us noticed how far we had all fallen. It dawned on me how many people get drunk because they know they wouldn't enjoy the other person's company if they were sober!

Pulling away from such bad company tends to happen naturally when a person makes a real commitment to God. It doesn't mean that you simply turn your back on old friends, but that the things that were once common pastimes (such as drinking) cease to be a mutual interest. You might think, "But I don't want to sit around on Saturday nights or hang out with losers." However, not all people outside your circle of friends are losers. Start looking, and don't be afraid of what you will lose. Hope in what you have to gain.

Iron Sharpens Iron

A teenage guy once told me (Jason) that it was a constant battle for him to maintain his virginity: "Last weekend, my friends got me drunk and tried to get me to sleep with this girl I barely knew." Thankfully, he was beginning to see that he was causing his own problems. With friends like his, who needs enemies?

Those who complain the most about how difficult it is to practice chastity often surround themselves with friends who erode their resolution to lead a pure life. Living a moral life has never been easy. But one of the things that can make the journey smoother is to find decent friends. When you find good ones, you create your own subculture in which it is easier to be good. In order to build solid friendships, enjoy your singleness. One high school girl, who possessed wisdom beyond her years, once said to us, "You don't go through high school looking for a husband. You go through high school looking for your bridesmaids."

The wisdom literature from the Old Testament contains a gold-mine of advice when it comes to friendships:

A faithful friend is a sturdy shelter: he that has found one has found a treasure. There is nothing so precious as a faithful friend, and no scales can measure his excellence.[1]

Though a man might prevail against one who is alone, two will withstand him. A threefold cord is not quickly broken.[2]

Iron sharpens iron, and one man sharpens another.[3]

Where do you find friends who will be a shelter to you, who will give decent advice and sharpen your character instead of dulling it? If your high school offers prayer time in the chapel each morning or during lunchtime, go. Get involved in campus ministry or retreat teams. If you're at a public high school, get involved in a Christian club on campus and a youth group at church. If you're in college, get involved in campus ministry. If you've finished college, volunteer as a leader in a local youth group or find a church with a thriving young adult community. If your church doesn't have one, start it. Instead of complaining that you feel alone in your struggles, go out of your way to find better fellowship. You may be surprised how many people your age are also looking for a better alternative to clubbing every weekend. If you're not the type to start a group, share this book with a friend and make a resolution to hold each other accountable to high standards.

Some hesitate to join religious groups because they've seen too many hypocrites. Indeed, it's scandalous when people professes Christ with their lips on Sunday and deny Him with their behavior the rest of the week. But if you wait until all members of a religion are perfect in order to join their church, you'll never join—because no such church exists. This is why it has been said that the Church is more of a hospital for sinners than it is a museum of saints. We're all in need of redemption, and we're not alone. This is why the Bible commands us: "We should not stay away from our assembly, as is the custom of some, but encourage one another."[4]

Faithful Are the Wounds of a Friend

"Come on, be cool. Everyone's doing it." It sounded like a ridiculous peer-pressure public service announcement for teens, but I (Jason) was listening to these exact words coming out of my best friend's mouth in high school. Some friends and I were pressuring a buddy to take what he thought was an illegal drug. It was actually a Tylenol, but we didn't want to bother him with the facts. We just wanted to see how far he'd go to fit in.

"Do it, man. You'll really like it."

"Are you sure, guys? I don't know."

"C'mon, dude. We all took one. It's amazing."

"All right, then! Gimme it!"

He popped the pill and downed it with a few sips of soda. After a few suspenseful moments, we asked, "Do you feel it yet?" His eyes darted around, "Uh, no. . . . Feel what?" We burst into laughter and told him the truth. He hollered, "You idiots!" and took a few punches at us, but we thought the prank was entirely worthwhile.

Could you ask for worse friends? Probably not.

The book of Proverbs contains a peculiar verse that reads, "Faithful are the wounds of a friend."[5] What this means is that a friend will speak the truth to you, even if it might hurt to hear. The wound is faithful, like one made by a surgeon who needs to make an incision in order to save a patient's life. In the above story, my friends and I did the opposite: We told a lie at the expense of another.

Many "friendships" are based on similarly weak foundations. The people involved might spend massive amounts of time together, but they don't have the best interests of each other in mind. A prime example would be the teenage girls who have said to me, "My girlfriends are encouraging me to lose my virginity before I go off to college. They say I should just get it over with." With the language of "getting it over with," one would think they were talking about getting her wisdom teeth removed. But where will these girlfriends be if she becomes pregnant from the hookup?

No matter who our friends are, our minds will be filled with their ideas. Worldly friends may offer flattering words and superficial joys, but they tend to blur our vision because we compare ourselves to them. If they're getting drunk every weekend, we think we deserve a halo for staying sober. But if our friends are close to God, we feel a desire to improve our faults. Because we become like our friends, we ought to choose them wisely. After all, the ultimate purpose of friendship is for people to perfect each other.

Take a look at your circle of friends and ask yourself if they are true friends. If you haven't made the best choice of companions, you're like millions of other women who find themselves in the same predicament. Go find each other.

How Do I Fix My Friend?

If you have a friend who is making horrible decisions or is in a dead-end relationship, what can you do to rescue her? This is perhaps the most common question we receive from women. Here are ten ways to help her.

1. Don't preach what you don't practice. Take a look at your own life and make sure that you're setting a decent example. Many women are desperate to rescue their friends from terrible relationships without realizing that their own relationships are equally bad. Such women will have a difficult time helping anyone because they're as useful as lifeguards who can't swim.

2. Don't be afraid to be honest with her. Like love, the value of a friendship can be determined by the amount of responsibility people feel for each other. The true friend is willing to speak the truth to you, no matter the cost. Even if it means losing you as a friend, she'll do what's best for you. If you were hurting yourself and were in denial, wouldn't you want a friend who loved you more than you loved yourself? Perhaps you are the only such friend for someone. Do not be afraid to speak the truth. What's a friendship worth if you're afraid to tell someone the truth?

Therefore, charitably explain why you're afraid for her. Explain that you've seen her change because of her relationship, and that she deserves to be in a relationship where she feels peace and joy, not fear and sadness. If you don't know what to say to her, suggest she watch some of the videos at chastity.com or have her read "The Top Ten Guys to Avoid" section in Chapter 1. Better yet, give her the whole book.

3. Don't get dragged into her lifestyle.   There's no problem with helping people who need help. But if you find yourself getting pulled down as a result, take a step back. One young woman told us that in an effort to her help her friend stay safe at parties, she would often accompany her. She confessed, "I would tag along, swearing not to drink, but that ended quickly and one turned into two, and then a few more." She became drunk, lost consciousness, and was sexually assaulted. Protect yourself from such heartache, and don't lose yourself in the quest to seek and save another.

4. Don't blame yourself if she rejects your advice and isolates herself from you.   Sometimes girls are so insecure that they are willing to toss a friendship under the bus for the sake of having a boy by their side. Even if she abandons you now, in the end you will have won her trust. Proverbs 28:23 says that the person who rebukes another will get more thanks in the end than the one who flatters.

5. Pray for her.   Each time your mind is tempted to worry about her, take that as a reminder from God to pray for her. Your anxiety does nothing for her, but your prayers have an infinite value.

6. Get others to pray for her.   Ask the holiest people you know to pray for her. The book of James says that the fervent prayer of a righteous person "has great power in its effects."[6] If you do anything on this list, this one is the most important. After all, you are not only trying to persuade your friend with clever arguments. There's a spiritual power you're coming up against that needs to be confronted with grace and prayer. Whether you realize it or not, a battle is taking place for your friend's soul, and you would be wise not to ignore some of your greatest allies.

7. *Fast for her.* Some may wonder what good it would do a friend if you fasted for her, but Jesus clearly stated in the Gospels that some spiritual battles can only be won by prayer *and* fasting.[7] This should be done in moderation, according to your state in life. For example, a teenage friend of ours was so excited about the idea of fasting that he decided to give up meat and vegetables for forty days. He ended up becoming so malnourished that he passed out and fell off the bleachers during a high school football game. This would be a good example of what not to do. Instead, try giving up soda for a week, or skipping seconds at a meal. If you're able, talk to a spiritual director (and physician, if necessary) and do what the early Christians did: fast on bread and water for a day. Fasting is a sacrifice that when offered to God in love has tremendous efficacy for helping souls.

8. *Deepen your friendship with her.* An anti-drug commercial recommends to parents: "If you talk to your kids about everything, you'll be able to talk to them about anything." The same goes with you and your friend. Take a deeper interest in her whole life, not only her dysfunctional relationship. Talk about her work, her school, her shoes, and her interests. Not every conversation needs to be about her deadbeat boyfriend. This way, you earn the right to be heard. She probably won't feel as defensive when you bring up her dating life since she knows you truly care about her.

9. *Get help.* If she's in an abusive relationship or is doing something that could potentially cause serious harm to her, don't hesitate to tell her family. This is not easy, but you would certainly regret your silence if something worse happened to her. Such situations are difficult because she might alienate herself from you and her family. Abusive boyfriends often go to great lengths to separate a woman

from those who love her. Therefore, do everything in your power to stay united with her.

10. *Don't give up on her.*   When we try these things and nothing seems to happen, we wonder what we're doing wrong or what we're forgetting to do. Remember that God is answering all your prayers and giving her the graces of conversion. But God has also given her the gift of a free will. When she turns her heart to God, all these graces will be waiting for her. See the mercy and patience of God as an example. Keep up the prayers and love and do not let go of hope. She needs to know she can always come back.

Convincing a friend to leave a bad relationship is usually a frustrating endeavor. You may hear things like, "He's not that bad. I can change him. He really does love me." Such phrases are hard to hear, because you know how bad he is—and you know she's the only one being changed by the relationship. Often a woman will refuse the advice of her friends and family. She may need to hit rock bottom before she wakes up. But when she does awaken, make sure you're there to offer her support, helping her to love herself again.

MEET THE PARENTS

When a boyfriend meets your family for the first time, does your dad bring a firearm to greet your potential suitor? If so, make sure to give your dad a big hug the next time you see him.

Why is he so uptight and protective? As they say, the opposite of love is not hate, but indifference. In other words, the opposite of love is: "I don't care who you're going out with, what you'll be doing, or when you're coming home." Your dad is probably more like this:

> Who are you going out with? What are his license plate and social security numbers so I can do a background check? Is he an Eagle Scout? Where does he think he's taking you? Do you mind if I plant this microchip in your purse so that I can monitor your location on my GPS?

The reason why parents are protective is because people protect what is priceless. You might say, "I'm a big girl, and I can make my own decisions now." But the bigger the girl you are, the more you'll care about your parents' opinion of another man. Even if you've graduated from college and are living as a single professional, have the humility and wisdom to run potential guys by your parents.

We know of a father who has five daughters and no sons. Whenever one of his daughters brings a date over to the house, he sits the young man down in private and asks him, "What's your ultimate dream car?" The young man pauses and then gasps, "Ooh, I'd want a Hummer." The dad replies:

"Okay. Now let's say you were given the truck as a gift and you waxed it up, polished the rims, and started cruising around the neighborhood. You pull up to a mall and you park away from the other cars to keep it from getting a ding. As you get out, you see me approaching. Even though we've never met before, I ask you, 'That's a nice truck. If you're going to be in the mall for a few hours, do you mind if I drive it around?' Would you give me the keys?"

Understandably, the young man replies, "No. I don't even know who you are!"

The dad insists, "But what if I showed you my driving record. I've never even had a parking ticket!"

Unfazed, the boy shakes his head, "Nope."

"Okay," the dad answers, "but now I'd like you to explain to me why I should entrust you with my daughter tonight—who means infinitely more to me—when you won't even let me borrow your imaginary truck." And he makes the boy answer him.

Although the daughter probably threw a fit over this interrogation process, you can be sure that the young man did not soon forget it. The dad wasn't telling the guy that he was forbidden to love the daughter, but that he would be devastated if the young man failed to love her as she deserved.

Don't Hide

While speaking at a high school that had eighty-seven pregnant girls on campus, I (Jason) encountered a teenager who was seven months pregnant. For the last several months, she managed to hide her belly under loose clothing and sweatshirts. Her parents didn't know about it until a few days before, when she broke the news to them. But this was only half the story. What her parent's didn't know was that her boyfriend lives in her closet. Yup. He has been living in her closet for nearly a year! She brings him food from the fridge and he hops out the window when he wants to hang out with friends. Since he's a high school dropout, he doesn't have much to do during the day. He roams around the house and plays video games while her parents are at work. Needless to say, she wasn't quite sure how to tell her parents about this minor detail of her relationship.

This bizarre situation highlights some of the problems with sneaking around. If a girl hides a relationship and hopes it will last, how will she reveal the deception? Eventually it will become impossible to conceal. When the truth is revealed and the parents discover how long they've been deceived, they will resent her boyfriend all the more. If he's hoping to have them as his in-laws one day, this is not going to score him any points. But he's not thinking about them or about the future. He's thinking about himself and what he wants today. But if a guy really loves a girl, would he do something with her that would hurt her parents? If he loved her, he would understand that it is an act of honor to a woman to love and honor her family.

Obviously, not all guys or girls think this way. More often than not, they wonder, "Why can't this relationship just be about us?" However, any relationship divorced from the influence and direction of the family is unhealthy. For example, I met a devoutly religious mom whose nineteen-year-old son was cohabiting with his girlfriend. Her eyes welled up with tears as she explained to me how the relationship unfolded, despite the way she had raised him. Her son didn't live in an isolated universe apart from his family, as much as he probably wished that was the case. His mom's heart was broken, but he didn't seem to care. It was all about him and the girlfriend. In his mind, his mom was just being emotional and had no right to impose her ideas on the way he wanted to live.

While such a son might not be interested in what the Bible has to say on parent-child relationships, Scripture says:

> With all your heart honor your father, and do not forget the birth pangs of your mother. Remember that through your parents you were born; and what can you give back to them that equals their gift to you?[1]

The Bible does not tell us merely to obey our parents, but to honor them and bring them joy. God's word doesn't simply prohibit disobedience. It invites us to love. Even though adult children do not have to obey their parents, they still are commanded to honor them.

When a girl's feelings for a guy run deeper than her respect for her parents, she'll ignore their wishes and pursue the relationship. She'll think, "My parents are so ridiculous and controlling. They don't trust me, and they hardly know my boyfriend. He's really a good guy. I'll be moving out soon anyway, so who cares if they don't like him?"

What's a woman to do, then, if her parents don't like the guy she loves? When I (Crystalina) was dating the wrong guys in high school, I did everything in my power to hide the truth from my mom. I would think, "How do I get her to change her mind about him?" If this is your dilemma, realize that if you really want to change your parents' opinion of a guy, then you have to do the one thing you dislike the most. Obey them. The more you defy or deceive your parents, the more resentment will exist between you and them. How is your boyfriend supposed to win their respect while openly going against their will? Besides, the more you resist your parents, the more opposition you will meet. They'll see your stubbornness as a further indication of immature rebellion.

Quit trying to convince them how great he is. If he is a gentleman of character, purity, faithfulness, and honesty, then these qualities will become obvious. Instead of playing tug-of-war with your folks, try to see why they don't like him. Maybe you know exactly why they disapprove of him, but you don't see it as a problem. Or perhaps you think he'll change, and you're hoping to improve him.

When you're in a relationship, it's easy to see only the positives, while those on the outside see things from a different perspective. One teenager e-mailed us to say:

> My parents weren't being stupid by being protective; they were show-ing the kind of love I should be looking for in my future spouse. I just didn't see it at the time. After realizing these things, I began to see this boy in a whole new light, and he didn't look as good as he did months ago, or even days ago.

The more you accept your parents' authority within the home, the more likely they are to think you will be trustworthy when you're away from them. You may think, "I am trustworthy. I'm not going to run out and get drunk and pregnant. They're just overprotective."

But your maturity level is only half of the equation. The other half is the maturity (and testosterone) level of guys.

Some teens have given up the hope of winning their parents' trust. The main reason for their despair is because they're discouraged by the effort that a trustworthy life would require of them. As an act of rebellion, some girls deliberately make stupid choices in an attempt to get back at their parents for any number of reasons. This may bring sorrow to the parents, but the girl is the one who ends up with the greatest suffering.

Many young women ask us, "Why won't my parents trust me?" We typically respond, "Well, if they knew everything you did when they aren't around, would they trust you more?" The answer is always "no." There's only one way to win a person's trust and that is to become trustworthy.

Admittedly, sometimes parents will forbid their daughter from seeing a wholesome guy. This can be especially difficult to accept, because it's harder to understand. Early in the twentieth century, a man by the name of Pier Giorgio Frassati lived in Turin, Italy. He was a stunningly handsome tournament skier and mountain climber known for his laughter and charity. As a young man, he fell in love with a girl named Laura Hidalgo, but his mother did not approve of her. Why? The girl was from a lower social class.

Obviously Pier Giorgio had every reason to protest this superficial reason to deny a relationship. But he didn't. He accepted his mother's wishes in order to honor her. In a private letter to a friend, he wrote of his reaction while reading an Italian love story, *Ho Amato Cosi* (*I Loved That Way*). Pier Giorgio said of the author:

> He describes in the first part his love for an Andalusian woman and believe me I am moved because it seems like my own love story. I too loved that way, only that in the novel it is the woman who makes the sacrifice whereas in my case I will be sacrificed. But if that is how God wants it, His holy will be done.[2]

Six months later, Pier Giorgio contracted polio from the poor he ministered to and died at the age of twenty-four. Some may look at this and think he missed out on love. But God had known all along that Pier Giorgio would not remain on earth for much longer.

Had he married Laura, he would have left a widow and perhaps an orphaned child behind. Instead, he maintained a friendship with her, and the providence of God worked even through the biased wishes of his mother. Through his experience, Pier Giorgio discovered that "one of the most beautiful affections is that of friendship."[3]

"Help! My Parents Won't Let Me Date."

Some teenage girls feel that their parents stifle their chances of finding love. They might say, "How am I supposed to learn how to relate to guys if they won't even let me date?" Don't be afraid. Men are not complex beings, but we are very different than women.

For starters, girls often judge the quality of their relationships by the quality and quantity of time they spend communicating with one another. That's why they're perpetually on the phone exchanging thoughts and feelings. Men don't. In college, I (Jason) remember a group of female friends who went on an all-girls retreat for the weekend. When they returned I asked one of them how the weekend went.

"Oh, it was wonderful!"

"Really? What did you guys do?"

"We just talked."

"Huh? You guys were there for forty-eight hours."

"Oh, I know. It was *so* much fun!"

To me, the idea of spending two days in a cabin talking to people seems tortuous. When I went on an all-guys retreat a few weeks later, we spent as much time outside of the cabin as possible. The only time we spent indoors was devoted to eating, sleeping, or playing practical jokes on each other (i.e., throwing pancake batter over the shower curtain when a friend was inside). For men, this is bonding.

Women may struggle to understand this. When I returned from an afternoon of golf with a friend, Crystalina asked, "Did you guys have some good talks?" I tilted my head, squinted, and tried to remember if we had a single meaningful conversation during the five hours of golf. "No," I replied. She said, "Then what did you guys talk about?" "I don't know. Just stuff." She asked, "Are you guys getting along okay?" All I could remember is that we drove the golf cart down a steep embankment through the sprinklers and spun a few doughnuts in the mud.

The point of all this is to help you understand that men bond through activities more than through communication. When you begin dating a guy, make time to share in the activities that he loves. Hopefully, he'll understand your desire for communication as well, and will gradually learn to speak in complete sentences.

Be patient with our inability to express our feelings. We're not like you. In fact, *USA Today* reported that a study of more than one thousand women revealed that one in four women admit to crying after getting a haircut.[4] Men aren't like this. We only cry over serious, life-altering tragedies, such as when our team loses the World Series or NBA Finals. Despite our differences, don't worry that you won't be able to relate to us if your parents have quarantined you during your teen years.

You don't need to date in order to learn how to love. In fact, I think the women least prepared for lasting love are those who have had the greatest number of relationships. They're expected to break up with every man in their life except for one—and that one's supposed to last until death do they part? While there's nothing wrong with being in different relationships prior to marriage, people tend to overestimate the value of passing relationships in preparing you for lasting ones. If you really want to learn how to love, try loving your family members. If you can love them, you'll be able to love anyone on the planet!

It has often been said that the family is the "school of love." But if your upbringing was anything like mine (Crystalina), then you know this doesn't mean that our families will always set the best example of love. Because of such things as abuse, neglect, alcoholism, infidelity, and divorce, many of us witness the opposite of love. Many women raised in broken homes have no desire to get married. Who can blame them, after all they have seen? If this is the case with you, do everything in your power to find good examples of married love. How refreshing it is to meet married couples who love each other with tender faithfulness and respectful reverence!

Many girls feel lonely and assume it is because they don't have a boyfriend. In reality, the real cause is that they probably lack a sense of being connected to others who do love them. Therefore, if there are family wounds that have never been healed, don't be passive. Begin by forgiving in your heart those who have hurt you. But don't stop there. Go to the family members whom you have hurt, and seek their forgiveness. But don't just say "I'm sorry." Ask for forgiveness. Use the word.

If your family situation is the opposite of everything you would ever hope for in your future marriage, do not be afraid that you are doomed to repeat the same problems. Use your hurt as motivation to build something better for your future. When it comes to your future spouse and family, you have the freedom—and the great responsibility—to choose a worthy spouse and future father.

If you want to build a family of your own eventually, you cannot run from the issues in your family today. You may not be able to resolve every problem, but there's a lot you can do. Don't be discouraged by what's beyond your control. Do the little things and let God take care of the rest.

God Honors Those Who Honor Him

In *Boy Meets Girl*,[5] Joshua Harris writes about a couple, Rich and Christy, who were high school seniors deeply in love. Instead of merely sending text messages and e-mails back and forth, they handwrote their love letters. Unlike so many relationships marred by drama and regret, their love was wholesome and innocent. However, when Christy's father realized how attached the two were becoming, he decided to intervene. While driving alone in the car with Rich, the father asked, "So what's this I hear about you and Christy?" He went on to inform Rich that he would prefer they not date. He wasn't boorish about his wishes, but spoke with kindness about the risks of getting too emotionally involved when marriage is still many years away.

Initially, Rich saw the wisdom behind his words and agreed that he and Christy would just be friends. Such a resolution was easier said than done. It wasn't long before they began seeing each other behind her parents' backs. The secret relationship continued for a few months, but neither of them was at peace. Rich told Christy, "We have to tell your parents. We can't go on like this." But before they had the chance, Christy's father overheard her telling a friend about the relationship.

Rich was heartbroken and ashamed that he had deceived her parents and lost their trust. A few days later, he met with them and promised that he would never do it again. But he knew that their feelings were too strong to merely be "just friends." They had to make a clean break. As a sign of his commitment to step back, he asked Christy to return to him all the love letters he had written her.

That night, Rich returned to her house at 3:00 A.M. with a shovel. Quietly, he dug a hole in her front lawn and buried in it a box filled with all the love letters they had exchanged—over one hundred pages. He closed the lid, took one last look at the box, patted down the dirt, and looked up at her quiet house. Speaking in his heart to God, he said, "If you want to dig this up some day, I know you can. But if not, this is where it will stay." He knew that the only reason God would separate him from Christy permanently would be that God had better plans in mind for the both of them. This was hard to imagine, but he trusted that God would know what was best. He knew that if it was God's will for them to be together, honoring her parents could never stop that.

A month later, Rich and Christy headed off for separate colleges without saying goodbye. Almost two years later, the two still had not seen each other or even talked over the phone. Then, unexpectedly, Christy's father called him and asked if they could meet at his office. When Rich arrived, the father expressed gratitude for his integrity and character. By letting go of Christy, Rich proved that he valued a father's love for his daughter even above his own desires and hopes. Before their conversation ended, Christy's father told Rich that he thought the couple was in a better place to begin a relationship.

The two began their friendship anew and eventually began courting. A few months before college graduation, Rich celebrated Christmas morning with Christy's family in Virginia. That morning, he handed her a small box that contained a tag from a nursery for a red maple tree. She wasn't expecting a tree for Christmas, and did her best to act impressed. The family knew of his plans and could hardly contain their excitement. Her father said, "Why don't you go plant it in the front yard?" Rich grabbed Christy's arm and they walked outside to where the tree and a shovel were waiting.

Rich stood over the place where he had previously hidden the box of letters and began to dig while Christy stood by, breathing in the crisp winter air. His heart must have raced as his shovel finally reached the box. He couldn't wait for her to see one more letter that he had added to the box when he buried it four years earlier. This love letter said everything about his love for her. It was a marriage proposal. As she read the words, he dropped to one knee and presented her with an engagement ring. Needless to say, she said "Yes."

Let there be no doubt that God honors those who honor Him, and that He always gives His best to those who leave the choice with Him.

Don't Play House

Once upon a time, there was a young couple we'll call Lauren and Rob. They met as sophomores in college, and began hanging out on a regular basis. Eventually, they spent less and less time with other friends, and began talking and texting incessantly. Their friendship soon became physical, and since they were basically acting like a boyfriend and girlfriend, they decided after a long talk that they might as well make it official. Lauren felt a sense of relief that they now had a title because she was beginning to feel uneasy about how close they were becoming without officially dating.

After a year of dating, Rob felt that they were ready to "take their relationship to the next level." While sitting on a couch after a late-night movie, he brought up the physical aspect of their relationship. "We've already gone pretty far. Going all the way isn't much further." She hesitated to concede his point, but couldn't argue with his logic because they had basically done everything other than sex. They had already talked about being together forever, and she had a hard time imagining her life with anyone else.

Before long, they were sleeping together. A few semesters passed at college, and although they had a few rough spots and brief breakups, they stuck together. During his senior year, Rob rented a house and Lauren began spending much of her time studying, cooking, or hanging out at his place. Before she knew it, they were practically roommates. They agreed that it was pointless for her to rent an apartment while spending most of her time under his roof. Because she spent the night at his place so often, her toiletries were sitting on his sink and her clothes were hanging in the closet. It seemed as if the only thing that was missing was her furniture. Gradually, as more of her possessions and clothing moved in, she did too. Just as they slid into dating and slid into sex, they slid into cohabitation.

She had always hoped for an exciting courtship, an unforgettably romantic marriage proposal, and a new life in marriage, but as time dragged on she began nagging him about a wedding date. Eventually, he figured, "We've already lived together for a while. We might as well just get married." They did, and lived somewhat happily ever after. The end.

Odds are, this is one of the less enchanting love stories you've read in a while. One reason why this tale is so drab is because lacks any sense of mystery or anticipation. No one is being wooed or pursued. The couple almost appears to be floating down a river without any sense of direction. Every stage in their relationship was remarkably the same as the stage that preceded it: Their dating life wasn't much different than the time they spent being friends with benefits. Their sexual intimacy wasn't much more intimate than what they had already done together. Their time of cohabitation was hardly distinguishable from their frequent sleepovers, and their marriage felt identical to their time of cohabitation.

They became husband and wife, but felt like they had already been married for years. As newlyweds, they reached a goal desired by so many young couples, yet the journey had seemed so uneventful. The moral of the story is that if you want a romantic and enchanting love story filled with anticipation and hope, don't shack up.

What to Do before "I Do"

Surely, you've seen cars on the road with "Just Married!" written on the back window in shaving cream or shoe polish. Empty soda cans drag in tow behind the car, and the couple inside is bubbling with joy. But have you ever seen a cohabiting couple so enthused about their relationship status that they did the same thing, writing "Just Cohabited!" on the back of their car? Neither have we. The excitement isn't there because every ounce of anticipation has been spent.

I (Crystalina) know of a woman who took this exact approach to finding love. She and her boyfriend shared physical intimacy before dating, sex before marriage, and cohabitation before the wedding date. But their story didn't end happily ever after. When she became pregnant after seven years of living with her boyfriend, he announced that he wasn't ready for that level of commitment and broke up with her. He's now dating someone else, and she's a single mom. She isn't alone. In fact, the majority of cohabiting moms never marry the father of their children.[1]

It doesn't take a guy three years of shacking up to know if he wants to marry you. If anything, cohabiting will delay a man's decision! According to a survey of unmarried men, the most common reason they were delaying marriage was the availability of sex without commitment.[2]

The second reason men delayed marriage was that they could "enjoy the benefits of having a wife by cohabiting rather than marrying." According to the researchers,

> They can avoid the time-consuming effort of searching for a sex partner when they have one living at home. . . . They don't want to 'settle' for second best in their choice of a marriage partner, though they don't have the same standards for a choice of a live-in girlfriend. Indeed, in some cases, they see her as a second best partner while they continue to look for a soul mate.[3]

Therefore, by practicing chastity and refusing to shack up, a female removes the top two reasons why a man would delay marriage.

The third reason was that they wanted to avoid divorce and its financial risks. If this is the case with your man, perhaps the best way to get him over his fear of divorce is to offer him the opportunity to lose you now instead of later. Another reason the men offered was that they were waiting for the perfect soulmate and she hadn't yet appeared. I'd say that such guys should just propose to their mirrors and live happily ever after.

There's a reason why God explained that a man should first leave his father and mother, cleave to his wife, and only then become one flesh with her.[4] When we take these steps out of order, chaos often ensues. All too often, a couple becomes one flesh, and then hopes for marriage. However, it rarely works out in their favor: Fewer than half of cohabiting couples end up getting married.[5] Of those that do go on to marry, the majority will be divorced within fifteen years.[6] In fact, out of every ten cohabiting couples, only about three will develop marriages that will last more than a decade. A majority of young adults think that cohabitation is a good way to avoid an eventual divorce, despite the fact that marriages preceded by cohabitation are far more likely to fail.[7]

Nonetheless, cohabitation precedes most marriages today. In fact, in a survey of single men aged twenty to twenty-nine, 44 percent of them said they would only marry a woman if she agreed to live together first.[8] In today's culture, cohabitation has become so commonplace that some question the common sense of those who jump into marriage without first testing their compatibility. In the words of one bachelor, "It should be a law, you should move in together and have a one year trial period."[9]

As the logic goes, "Who would buy a car without first test-driving it?" The obvious problem with such a question is that a person is not a something that you can return to the used-car lot if you aren't satisfied with its performance. A spouse is not something you trade in after ten years, when newer models appear on the market. Furthermore, while compatibility makes marriages more enjoyable, the survival of a marriage depends more upon the couple's ability to work through their incompatibilities.

One single man explained that he assumed cohabitation would predict greater stability in marriage because, "If you are truly compatible, then you don't have to change."[10] Such a comment reveals an immature view of human love. One of the purposes of marriages is sanctification. Through marriage, one's faults rise to the surface like oil in water so that the couple can correct them, thus growing in love and holiness. Such a purification of one's love might be a painful process, but it will forge a marriage that can last for ages. If a man is unwilling to change and be refined by the fire of authentic love, how will he last through good times and bad, sickness and health?

Underneath the irreverent question of "test driving" is an understandable fear. Many young couples today have witnessed the separation of their own parents and have no desire to relive that experience in their own relationships. Many are hesitant about the seriousness of a marriage commitment, and this is partly a good thing. Marriage is not something to be taken lightly.

But the question is this: Does cohabitation assist a couple in making a wise marriage decision or hinder their ability to do so? Those who live together prior to marriage typically don't foresee how much more difficult they are making their own lives if their relationship doesn't work out. Just imagine how much harder it would be to break up with your boyfriend if half of his apartment was filled with your furniture and you needed a moving company to leave him! Consider how much harder it would be to break up if you had nowhere else to go. You don't want to find a new roommate or move back in with your parents, and you don't want the hassle of moving all your stuff again.

Cohabiting couples who have rocky relationships often stay together because they already feel emotionally, financially, and physically married. If such relationships do end, the separation can be just as painful as a broken marriage. Because cohabitation isn't exactly a fruitful season of marital discernment and preparation, it has earned the less-than-noble nickname, "shacking up."

Living with a boyfriend often creates tension within families because parents usually aren't excited about the arrangement. Most mothers and fathers would prefer that their daughter find a man who finishes college, finds a stable profession, asks their permission to wed her, sweeps her off her feet with his wedding proposal, and then brings her into his home once she has become his bride. That's the kind of son-in-law they hope for, and I would imagine that you would prefer the same thing. This isn't an outdated social expectation. It's the honorable thing to do, and you deserve a guy who wouldn't think of doing it any other way.

Therefore, prepare for your marriage with a noble and holy courtship. If a man is not your husband, don't gradually dole out to him the intimacies that belong to your future spouse. If he *is* that man, then he can prove it by waiting with you for the sacrament to which God has called you. In the meantime, don't pretend to be his wife when you're not. Don't play house.

If you're already living with a guy, move out. Even if you're living with a male roommate whom you're not dating, find another place to live. Don't offer as an excuse that you can't find a female roommate. There are more than three billion other females on the planet. Surely you can find one to split the rent with you. Don't complain that moving out would be too complicated. It's not. Just do the same thing you did to move in, but do it backwards.

Don't Rush the Ring

Virtually every young girl dreams of her wedding day. She envisions the dress, the flowers, the church, and the groom-to-be. To look forward to marriage is a good thing, and you should never let anyone tell you otherwise. However, this God-given desire can sometimes drive young women to accept marriage proposals too soon. I (Jason) once met a fifteen-year-old girl who was on her third engagement. Thank goodness none of the relationships worked out, or someone with a driver's license would have had to drive her to pick up her marriage license! I also remember meeting a young man who wanted to propose to his girlfriend, but he needed to save up enough money for a ring. But if he can't afford a ring, how's he supposed to afford a wife?

Such examples are obviously a bit extreme, but many young couples begin talking about their dreams of marriage and family life when they've only known each other for a few months or years. All the starry-eyed daydreaming about the new home and white picket fence causes them to overlook the fact that they can't even afford a white picket fence, let alone a house. Seriously: One hundred feet of nice vinyl fencing costs about $2000! Such young couples may think:

We might not have a lot of money, but we can either be poor alone, or poor together. We've never felt this way about anyone ever before, and we know we want to be together forever. So what's the point of putting off marriage?

Some couples have enough wisdom to admit that they're not ready for the responsibilities of married life, so they enter into an eternal engagement. The boyfriend gives her a promise ring, and they consider themselves engaged despite the fact that they have no wedding date. This is not an engagement. A real engagement is when the boyfriend asks the parents' permission, pays for the ring, and then the couple sends out invitations, registers for wedding gifts, and sets a wedding date within a year.

When these things are not happening, it only means one thing: the "engaged" couple are dreaming about the permanence of marriage and using a ring to make themselves feel romantic and hopeful. What they need to realize is that engagements are for people who are ready to get married, not for people who can't wait to get married.

When a couple does not understand this distinction, they tend to see courtship as an annoying burden that stands between them and the intimacy they long for in marriage. All serious couples anticipate marriage, but their courtship should not be rushed because of this. If they hope to have a solid marriage, the best thing they can do is to take advantage of these years, using them to build an even more solid friendship.

If a couple rushes toward marriage, it may be a sign that the relationship lacks stability, and may be based on infatuation. In her book *But I Love Him*, Dr. Jill Murray offers a list of warning signs that a relationship is clouded by infatuation. Some of these include:

- Physical and sexual attraction is central.
- They are characterized by urgency, intensity, sexual desire, and anxiety.
- They are driven by the excitement of being involved with a person whose character is not fully known.
- They involve nagging doubts and unanswered questions; the partner remains unexamined so as not to spoil the dream.

- They are consuming, often exhausting.
- They entail discomfort with individual differences.[11]

If you ever find yourself in a relationship in which these signs are present, don't rush into a deeper level of commitment. Also, don't accept a wedding proposal, hoping to resolve serious relationship issues before the wedding date. Deal with them now, instead of hoping that the glitter of a diamond and the romantic thoughts of marriage will make your problems disappear.

Too Young for Marriage?

In biblical times, young women would marry in their early teens, soon after becoming able to bear children. Nowadays the median age at which a woman first marries is twenty-five, which is the oldest age in American history.[12] In many societies around the globe, boys become men as teens. They get their jobs, learn to take care of themselves, and prepare to carry the responsibilities of a family. In America, we've got twenty-eight-year-old men who live in their moms' basements and play video games until one in the morning. As a result, the goals of a mature life, including marriage, tend to get pushed back.

This can be a challenge for couples because our bodies desire marital intimacy about a decade before we're ready for the responsibilities that follow. However, the delay can also be a good thing because it allows many women to pursue their college dreams and career goals. It's also beneficial because the place in the brain where reasoning and judgment take place is not fully developed until a person reaches his or her early twenties.[13] When a woman waits until she's twenty-four or twenty-five to get married, she's neurologically able to make a more informed decision because her brain is more capable of making wise choices. If she marries as a teenager, she's more likely to regret the decision and later wonder, "What was I thinking?"

This brain research isn't just a matter of speculation. Look at divorce rates according to the age of the bride: If a woman is married before her eighteenth birthday, she has a 48 percent chance of being divorced within ten years of her wedding. If she waits until she is twenty to twenty-four years old, it drops to 29 percent, and if she waits to marry until she is twenty-five or older, her odds of divorce in the first ten years of marriage drop to 24 percent.[14]

Young marriages are not necessarily doomed. Many people today have grandparents who married young and enjoyed lasting marriages. However, they matured at a younger age and lived at a time when divorce was less prevalent. Regardless of what happened two generations ago, today's woman would be wise to avoid rushing down the aisle. If she marries too young, she often gets a bit "itchy" after a few years. She looks around at women her age, and begins to think:

> I never got the degree I dreamed about. I never traveled to Europe with my friends. I never even dated around much. My whole life has been about him. We spent so much time dreaming about ourselves that I forgot about myself in the process.

The lack of fulfilled hopes and goals may cause her to resent her husband and children. What she realizes too late is that her marriage would have been more stable and secure if she had fulfilled these wishes prior to becoming a wife and mother.

It's easy to find marriages that are troubled because the decision was rushed. But it's hard to find ones that were weakened because the couple didn't marry soon enough. Therefore, know that if it is God's will for you to be with a particular man, taking more preparation time for marriage will only strengthen the union.

15

Break Up, Even if He Smells Good

All along, I (Crystalina) knew something wasn't right. When I would call Nick's phone, he wouldn't pick up. When I found hair ties and makeup in his car, he would tell me that they were mine, or say that his friend and his girlfriend had borrowed his car and left them there. I wanted so badly to believe him because for the past two years I had given him everything I had.

My relationship with God was dead, but I still muttered an occasional prayer that He would show me the truth. Then out of nowhere, while hanging out at my cousin's house, her phone rang.

"Hey, this is Liz. Is your cousin Crystalina still dating that guy Nick?"

"Yeah, why?"

"Uh, then why is he on a date with another girl at the movie theater near school?"

My cousin hung up and was scared to speak. I knew something was wrong, and demanded, "Who was that? What'd they say?" She relayed the message, and a few moments later she was clinging to the handles in my Jeep as I squealed out of her driveway toward the movie theater.

Upon arriving at the lobby of the theater, I found Nick with his buddies . . . and his date. His friend was the first to notice me storming into the building like a one-woman S.W.A.T. team, and stared at me with bulging eyes. Trembling and screaming at Nick, I poured out my rage and created quite the scene.

That night at my cousin's house, I bawled uncontrollably. I couldn't imagine my life without him, because I had made him my life. For two years, I chose to be blind, so as to spare myself from this inevitable pain. Yet even after witnessing all of this, I went back to him in a vain effort to prove to myself that he wanted me more than her. But in the end, no effort on my part could create a love that never existed.

Whether or not a breakup involves infidelity, most of us know the pain of giving away our heart and receiving it back in pieces. You get so close to a guy, sharing laughter and memories. Slowly, you share yourself, and the two of you become part of each other's life. Somewhere along the way, something changes. Something that was so wholesome and good begins slipping away, evolving into something different. At times, it happens at a rapid pace and everything changes overnight. But usually the change happens gradually, until what you once had with him becomes unrecognizable. There are small bits and pieces of what once was, but the picture has changed. The question is: Did the relationship change, or are you finally seeing it for what it is?

At the beginning of a relationship, there's so much fog and smoke; the newness is intoxicating. A false utopia surrounds you both. It's safe—or at least you think so. As time goes on, you go deeper. Slowly, what's fake is gone and you begin to see what lies beneath the surface. Certain things are revealed, and you begin to see them in the light. You know, I know, and everyone knows deep down that it's not okay. Something's not right, but you want to hope. You ignore. You focus on the good and stay at the surface, because the deeper you go, the darker and more sobering the reality becomes.

Once the façade is lifted, the pain sets in. The beautiful image that you once had is gone. You wonder: Was it ever true? Was it ever real? Or did I fall in love with the surface, while deep down knowing the truth all along? Afterward, you wonder: Can I really trust in people, even if they are family, friends, and loved ones? Do I give away my heart? Trusting in someone can be an unpredictable thing that can make or break a person and destroy the spirit.

We all know the truth. We can run and hide. We can live our

lives ignoring it. But it always calls us back to what is real. Do we really want to know the truth? Can we even handle the truth about the man we loved, trusted, and let in? We bonded with the person that we hoped he was. We gave our hearts to the man we dreamed he could become. But that hope is not the reality of who is before us.

The truth is always in front of us; we just have to stop trying to look at it with human eyes and ask God to show us the truth through His eyes. When we allow Him to do this, not only will He reveal the truth to us, He'll give us the grace to face it with courage and hope.

Facing Your Fears

Sometimes a woman can't wait to dump a guy. But more often than not, it's something she dreads. She feels torn and afraid. Many see this anxiety as a sign that they should stay put. Because a breakup would be difficult, they put their life on hold. To overcome these difficulties, a woman must overcome any number of the following fears.

1. "I'll never find someone like him again."   This emotion is most common in young girls, who also say, "I've never felt this close to anyone before. I'll never love anyone like I loved him." Because they are new to the experience of falling in love, the novelty of the relationship leads them to believe that such intimacy could never be surpassed. In reality, her emotion says nothing about the future. All it means is that she's never been so attached in the past.

If you can relate to this, understand that breaking up will not be a total loss. You don't need to toss aside all the good times and forget the positive qualities that he may possess. Instead, appreciate the good memories of him and expect your future boyfriends to possess similar qualities. Meanwhile, evaluate the bad aspects of the relationship and remind yourself that you won't settle for those in the future. When you acknowledge the things you've learned through this relationship, the breakup becomes somewhat easier to accept.

2. *"I'm afraid of being alone."*   Woven deeply into the fear of breaking up is the assumption that no one else would want us. The fear of loneliness was something I felt while trying to leave a relationship back in high school. I felt like I couldn't. I was scared to death that if I left him, I'd miss out on love. I couldn't see that I was already missing out on love by staying with someone who valued pleasure more than he valued me.

3. *"I'm afraid of hurting him."*   While this motive is compassionate, it usually harms the guy more in the end. Why? If a relationship is wrong for you, then the longer you remain in it, the harder the breakup will be for him. Let's face it: There's no way to break up with a guy that will leave him feeling warm and fuzzy. It's going to hurt. But it often has to be done. Trust me that he'll eventually get over it. When you do break things off, don't drag on a semi-relationship. Doing so only makes things more difficult.

4. *"I'm afraid I never should have dated him."*   A final fear that grips women is that of admitting the truth. A common example of this is the girl who loses her virginity in the relationship. She may cling to the guy for years, regardless of how bad the situation becomes.

She can't bear idea of the relationship failing. But if the relationship is not of God, then it failed when it began. The only thing that's happened since then is that she has distracted herself from the truth. To move on, such a woman must admit that she made a mistake that won't happen again in the future. She needs to accept the loss and trust that God would never ask her to let go of something unless He wanted to give her something infinitely better, namely Himself.

If you feel unable to make the break and are confused about what to do, begin by doing what you know is right. If you've physically gone too far in the past, be pure. If there's been deception in the relationship, be honest. If you do this, your decisions will become clearer as you persevere in doing what's right.

If you're in the wrong relationship and are afraid to call it quits, remember: "Courage is not the absence of fear, but rather the judgment that something else is more important than one's fear."[1] In your case, that something else happens to be the future that God has waiting for you. Be not afraid. Your life is too short to spend it with a guy who was never meant for you.

How to Let Go of a Guy

In order to catch monkeys in Africa, certain tribes of hunters hollow out a large hardened gourd, and insert tinfoil through a small hole. When the monkey sees the shimmering foil, it reaches inside. When he clenches his fist around the foil, his hand becomes too large to pull out of the hole. Because the vegetable is so heavy, the monkey will be unable to walk. The frustrated primate will pull and pull until he starves to death, or until the hunters capture him. If he would only let go, he would be free. But the monkey craves the worthless piece of tinfoil so much that it costs him his life.

The same is true with the woman who clings to a bad relationship. Because she's so consumed with grasping what she thinks is good, she loses the opportunity to pursue what is great. But until her hands are empty, God cannot fill them.

How does a girl let go?

First, listen to your gut. Many young women learn volumes by watching the disastrous relationships of their parents. One teenage girl e-mailed me (Jason), sharing her sorrow over the end of her parents' twenty-year marriage:

> I never realized how one situation, and a word as simple as "yes," could have so many terrible effects on a person. My mom's mistake of saying yes to my dad, marrying my dad, truly has had traumatic effects on her. Now I see the reason why all of this happened. Even when she knew something was wrong, when she got that feeling every woman has in her heart when she is being controlled and used, she continued to say yes. To think that one word could've stopped my mom's life from virtually falling apart is mind blowing. It's never too early to start thinking about your future, and your family's future. My mom is a prime example of what can happen if you say yes to the wrong person, and continue to say yes after you *know* you need to say no.

232 How to Find Your *Soulmate* Without Losing Your Soul

If your boyfriend has qualities that you know would damage a marriage, step back. Imagine ten years from now, being married and having two young children. But instead of having a peaceful marriage, your relationship is no different than it is today. If the thought of raising kids in such an unhealthy environment makes you cringe, then it's time to end this relationship. Take to heart the wisdom of one teenage girl who said, "I can't always cater to what I want because I have to remember what I deserve."

The second step in letting go of a guy is to find a breakup buddy. When you know you need to end a relationship, few things are better than a solid friend or family member by your side. When you're alone, it's easy to second-guess yourself. Even after the breakup, you may wonder why you left and be tempted to fall back. Therefore, when you feel weak and you want to call him in the middle of the night or reply to a text message, call or text your breakup buddy instead. You might also need a shoulder to cry on. You'll also feel less guilty for downing a gallon of ice cream when someone else's spoon is in the carton.

Finally, break the news. You can do this any number of ways. Chat with your breakup buddy, and come up with some bullet points that you want to express to the guy. If things get argumentative, you'll know what to say because you've prepared your words. And be honest. Don't give bogus reasons for the breakup. Don't tell him that you just need a break when what you really need is a breakup. As much as you can, give him the news with class and dignity.

As to where you break up, pick a location that is neither at your place nor his. It's best to pick a spot where you feel safe and you can easily leave if things get heated. If you don't want to talk with him face to face, you can always write him a letter to explain your reasons. Or, if you're dating "Mr. I-Don't-Have-Enough-Social-Skills-to-Meet-Girls-without-the-Internet," you can always notify him by e-mail that you've updated your Facebook status to single.

Stick with Your Decision

Think of all the relationships you've seen in your life. Who holds the record for having broken up the most times? It becomes so confusing that I've seen couples break up with each other when they weren't even dating! Instead of taking the break to grow in independence and maturity, they waste months or years of their lives going nowhere. Therefore, if you find yourself breaking up with your ex-boyfriend, it's time to make a commitment . . . to saying no.

The initial weeks and months of a breakup are the most challenging because you're tempted to fall back into the consolations of the relationship. We all know that absence makes the heart grow fonder. Even if you're the one who ends the relationship, you may still miss the person. Because a reunion might be only a phone call away, you might think, "Well, I know the relationship wasn't perfect, but having someone is better than having no one. We did have some good times, and he looks so miserable without me." Resist the temptation to go back unless years have passed and the guy has resolved all his unhealthy qualities.

If you can't get your mind off the guy, do not take this as a sign that you're supposed to be with him. It's just a sign of how emotionally attached you became to him. It's an indication of the past, not a guide to the future. No matter what happens, don't let him make you feel as if you're failing to love him by leaving the relationship. Sometimes the most loving thing you can do for a guy is to break up with him.

If he does not respect you saying no to this relationship, then it is yet another sign that he does not love you. If you know it's time to end things, do it quickly. Don't flounder around. You've doubted yourself long enough. Besides, how many girls do you know who regret breaking off a relationship? Now, how many do you know who regret waiting too long to break one off?

If he refuses to accept the breakup and continues to call, text, or stalk you, tell him clearly to stop doing this. Just because he misses you does not mean he is mature and godly enough to love you properly. Let him know that you will not be returning his messages or answering the phone. Eventually, he'll get the hint. If he shows up at your house, follows you around, and makes you feel unsafe, you may want to obtain a restraining order. If you're still living at home with your parents, tell them what is going on. If you've moved out, tell a roommate, neighbor, family member, or friend who can come over if necessary.

What are you to do in the meantime? Stay busy. Don't sit around and give yourself a chance to mope. Do things that you've wanted to do for a long time. After all, when was the last time you did something just for you? It's time for you to enjoy the single life without the drama of an unstable relationship. If your relationship was bad, then it probably dictated to you what kind of day you would have. If things were good with him, I imagine your days were great. When things turned sour, you were probably miserable. Now it's time to regain custody of your heart. No guy should be allowed to dictate to you what kind of day you're going to have. As one teen girl said to us, "The only guy worth your tears is the one who would never make you cry."

As you pull away, draw closer to those who love you and will support you (God, family, and friends), not just your breakup buddy. Enjoy the peace of their love and friendship. Times may come when you wonder if you did the right thing by breaking off the relationship. But if you're close to those who love you, they'll help you to get through those times.

Sometimes breakups are easy. One girl shared with us, "I had absolutely no idea how good it would feel to let him go." Other times, it's not so simple. Don't be surprised if it takes a while to get over him. It may feel like an eternity before you can go a day without thinking about him. How do you cope with this? Each time you think about him and are tempted to feel sad, say a quick prayer for two intentions: For him, and that God's will be done in your life and his.

After a painful and drawn-out breakup, one college girl e-mailed us the prayer she offered for her ex before she would go to bed each night:

> God, please just help James to know your will for him in all aspects of his life. Increase his self-control, and please help him to understand my morals, not just agree to live by them. Help him to want to live

according to my morals out of love for you. And even if we aren't meant to be, please lead him to the right girl.

What a remarkably mature and beautiful prayer! One can be sure that she didn't arrive at this level of spirituality overnight. She certainly spent her share of time wrestling with God over her broken heart. But the trials made her stronger.

By praying for your ex, you are loving him. You may want to love him in a more tangible way (or you may want to slash the tires of his car), but by giving him the grace of your prayers, you are again doing what is best for him. By doing this, you'll begin to pull yourself out of the anxiety regarding the future and regret about the past. Depending upon how attached you were to him, this is going to take some time. If you can accept that from the start, you'll be more patient with yourself.

At some point in life you need to decide who will make the decisions: Will it be you or your emotions? When the emotions reign, your life becomes full of drama because your decisions are based on impulse instead of wisdom. When you know what needs to be done, sometimes your emotions kick and scream. The person without wisdom will always see this as a sign that they made the wrong decision and will cave in to appease their feelings. Have courage, because the further you pull away, the more you will discover yourself again! As the saying goes, "He is no fool who gives what he cannot keep to gain that which he cannot lose."[2]

Moving On

When it comes to breaking up, there's no easy way to do it. It's usually messy and painful. If he initiates the breakup and you wish to stay friends, then you experience the anguish of hoping for more while watching his life go on without you. If you make a clean break, then it's difficult in a different way. Letting go is not easy, but sometimes you just have to move forward and let your heart catch up when it's ready.

Especially if you've been sexually intimate, the breakup will be painful. Such couples have been as physically close as a bride and groom are on their wedding night. Therefore, don't expect an easy transition. But don't let this keep you from doing what needs to be done.

If you're in an unhealthy relationship, do nothing else physical with him. No kissing. No holding hands. No nothing. This man is not your future husband, and your affections do not belong to him. Any more affection you show him is simply leading him on.

If he's the one who is breaking up with you, then don't blame or torture yourself over what you should have done differently. If you've clearly done something wrong, such as cheating on him, then losing him will be a painful lesson on the importance of fidelity in future relationships. But if his reasons for leaving you are less clear, try—although this may seem impossible—not to analyze the relationship to death. Sometimes God's greatest blessings are when He takes something away that we desperately want. At the time it feels like an amputation, but everything happens for a reason. As painful as this experience may be, it is better that it happens before marriage as opposed to after.

Sometimes we think we know our future and everything seems clear. The next moment our lives can be turned upside-down. At times like this our faith becomes most real. God alone knows your future, and He knows well the plans He has in mind for you—and they are full of hope (Jer. 29:11-14). This is an actual promise of God. No matter how dark things may seem right now, it's not going to be this way forever.

If your relationship was an unhealthy one, eventually you will look back and say to yourself, "What was I thinking, being so distraught about it not working out?" Once you meet a man who truly cherishes you and shares your values, you'll realize that the end of this relationship was the best thing that could have happened to you. May the end of it be the beginning of the fulfillment of God's will in your life.

16

FORGIVE YOURSELF

When Megan was fourteen years old, her parents took her to the mall to buy a purity ring. The idea—and the jewelry—were not imposed upon her. In fact, she loved the thought of waiting for marriage and giving the gift of her virginity to her husband on their wedding night.

However, as the years passed, her resolve grew weaker and her romantic notions faded. As a junior in high school, she realized that nearly all her friends had already become sexually active. She met a senior named Josh through a mutual friend, and they seemed to hit it off immediately. Because so many of her friends were constantly in relationships, she often felt like she had been missing out. She'd sit at the lunch table and listen to all the drama and gossip, feeling she had little to offer.

Her relationship with Josh grew physical before it had even matured into a relationship, but Megan didn't seem to mind. As any girl does, she questioned her attractiveness at times. But when she and Josh were close, all these questions seemed to melt away. She went to church and considered herself more conservative than the rest of her friends. Unlike some of them, she would never think about having a one-night stand or hookup. She knew that she and Josh cared about each other. As time passed, the two became more physically intimate. Then one night, it happened. It wasn't planned, but "one thing led to another."

Upon losing her virginity, she realized that it wasn't the romantic and blissful experience she had anticipated. Josh's immaturity only deepened this realization. She recalls:

> I bought the ring and in my heart I knew that it was something that should be important. After the first time, we were laying there, and he looked at my ring and said, "Wow. I guess I just crushed that idea." And he laughed. I was so hurt when he said that because I realized that he was right. He had crushed my gift. Something I should have had complete control over was crushed just for the feeling of being loved. I thought that there was no hope and I kept going on with this lie that we loved each other and that was all that mattered. I referred to the ring as my ticket out of the house. I figured if my parents thought I was being good I could get away with it. But I can't get away from myself or the horrible feelings that went along with it. I cry way too much for a girl that has a great life.

When the relationship ended and Josh left for college, Megan was unsure what to do with herself. She had formed an idyllic notion of a white wedding and romantic honeymoon where she would give her purity ring to her groom as a pledge of her undivided love. Now, she was watching the boy to whom she had given her virginity walk out of her life. He had slept with others before, and would probably continue the pattern in college. She wondered, "Was I just a number to him? I can't believe I did that. I know they say that everyone has second chances, but I really don't think I deserve a second chance."

For months, she was more upset with herself than she was with Josh. She knew he didn't force her to do anything. He always made sure to say that they would go at her pace. Yet here she was, less than a year after having met him, wondering how everything happened so quickly. The relationship took off like a rocket, and came down like one. Now she was left alone, sifting through the wreckage.

Healing the Past

What is a woman to do with regret? How does she cope with disappointment when she begins to blame—or even despise—herself for the mistakes that have been made? It's insufficient to tell her,

"Everyone messes up. Do be so hard on yourself. Dust yourself off, and try to be better in the future." In the case of Megan, she wasn't simply upset about the past. Perhaps she was more devastated about what it meant for her future. She had never wanted to be with more than one guy. She never wanted to tell her future husband that she didn't wait for him.

Perhaps the first step such a woman should take is to bring all her suffering to the only one who can quiet her worries and answer her questions—God. Referring to the unconditional love of Christ, Mother Teresa once wrote:

> He loves you always, even when you don't feel worthy. When not accepted by others, even by yourself sometimes, He is the one who always accepts you. . . . Only believe—you are precious to Him. Bring all you are suffering to His feet—only open your heart to be loved by Him as you are. He will do the rest.[1]

When you don't accept yourself, it helps to know that someone still accepts you. Yet how often do we feel as if God is the one who is *most* disappointed in us? Theologians tell us that God's greatest attribute is His mercy. But do we believe this? If you struggle with accepting the fact that God loves you in the midst of your imperfections, consider the love I (Jason) have for my daughter. It has been said that for parents, having a child is like having your heart walking around outside your body. How true! As I write this, my daughter is sound asleep in her crib. However, it hasn't been such a peaceful week. In the past seven days, she has awakened Crystalina and I numerous times, tossed her dinner, spilled her juice, soiled her diapers, drooled on me, pulled my hair, wiped her nose on my face, and playfully smacked me repeatedly—while smiling.

Yet tomorrow morning at 5:45, she's going to crawl into our bed with her nappy, tangled hair, wrap her arms around my head, and wake me with a hug, and everything will have been forgotten. Her love melts me. Don't be fooled into thinking that God is any less ravished by your love. As the Song of Songs reads, in prose that reflects the love of God for us, "You have ravished my heart."[2] I once read a quote about fathers that said we have, "Wills of iron, nerves of steel, and hearts of pudding." God's heart is conquered infinitely more easily than that of humans. There is nothing you can do to make Him love you more, and there is nothing you can do to make Him love you any less.

When you accept the love of God, you increase your own capacity to love others. In the Gospel of Luke, the story is told of a repentant prostitute who fell at the feet of Christ and bathed His feet with her tears. When a Pharisee witnessed the act, he thought that Jesus should have known better than to have such a woman touch Him. Jesus not only defended her, but added:

> "Do you see this woman? I entered your house, you gave me no water for my feet, but she has wet my feet with her tears and wiped them with her hair. You gave me no kiss, but from the time I came in she has not ceased to kiss my feet. You did not anoint my head with oil, but she has anointed my feet with ointment. Therefore I tell you, her sins, which are many, are forgiven, for she loved much; but he who is forgiven little, loves little." And he said to her, "Your sins are forgiven."[3]

Although you may have read this passage before, have you considered how the prostitute felt about herself after this personal encounter with the living God? Do you think she walked away from this experience thinking, "I'm so dumb for having been a prostitute. Who would love me now?" Because she allowed herself to be loved by Love, her past without God seemed insignificant when compared to the future that He opened up before her. Imagine her going to bed that night, lying awake and reliving in her mind the moment He looked into her eyes with pure compassion and respect. Perhaps no other man had looked at her in such a way. She knew that her life was not over because of her mistakes. Rather, because of God's mercy, it had just begun.

In the Gospels, this is not an isolated event. It's a pattern. While giving a retreat to college women, Karol Wojtyla recalled the encounter Christ had with the Samaritan woman. You may recall the event from the Gospel of John, when Jesus meets a woman who had had five husbands and was living with yet another man. Wojtyla remarked:

> There must have been something in this conversation which did not humiliate or mortify her, crushing her, but relieved her. . . . In every

Gospel episode involving meetings with women, they find their independence at Christ's side. . . . There are no slaves at Christ's side. The
public sinner becomes a promised bride, a sister.[4]

When a woman discovers her identity in God, she is prepared
to face the future—as well as the past. Without this, she may fall
into the habit of defining herself by her failures. In the words of
one woman who e-mailed us, "How do you change when you can't
change the moment that made you who you are?" Her wounds were
so deep that they had become her identity. In such cases, a woman
must reject the temptation to label herself. Instead of identifying with
her guilt, she must act upon it.

Modern culture often tells us that guilt is unhealthy, especially as it
pertains to sexual matters. Some have even said that the real problem
with sin is the people who say it exists. The idea goes something like
this: The real cause of women's guilt and shame is the sexist idea that
they should be pure. If we liberate females from the unrealistic and
burdensome ideals of chastity, nobody will feel remorse and regret.

This would be like saying the problem with breast cancer is mam-
mograms: If we could rid ourselves of the people who promote breast
cancer screening, women would be liberated from the anxiety and
fear caused by cancer. Obviously, anyone who loves women would
consider such advice ludicrous.

Guilt is not harmful. What's unhealthy is shamelessness. Guilt is a
gift from God. It's an alarm clock that awakens us when we're not
living as we ought. The dissatisfaction and emptiness that follows
every sin is a call from God to return to Him, who alone can satisfy
our deepest desires. If you feel ashamed, thank God your conscience
is alive, and come to Him to be cleaned. If you feel sorrow because
of your past, allow yourself to weep if you feel the need. There's a
period of mourning that a woman goes through when she recognizes
a great loss. It's a necessary part of the healing process. As painful
as this may be, the tears are healing.

The Bible says that when the Holy Spirit convicts us of our sins,
He is also the comforter. The devil is the accuser, while the Holy
Spirit is the advocate. The term "advocate" comes from the Latin
advocatus, which was often used in a legal context to refer to some-

one called to your side to defend you in court. Even when you're the one accusing yourself, God stands by your side.

There is nothing you could have done that cannot be forgiven. The reason we delve into this is because it becomes easier to forgive yourself when you know that God is willing to forgive you.

Choosing to Receive Forgiveness

Love is not something you simply choose to give. It is also something you must choose to receive. In the case of God's love, He does not give what we do not wish to receive. He will not force Himself upon us. Like a true lover, He extends a proposal that the beloved is free to accept or reject. Should you wish to receive the proposal of His mercy, what should you do?

You do not need to wait another moment to return to God. Even as you read these words, you can turn your heart toward Him again. As Psalm 51 reads, "A broken contrite heart you will not spurn." Do not think that the number and gravity of your sins is the measure of your distance from God. Rather, your union with Him is determined by one thing: the desire you have to return to Him. A lukewarm soul that attends church every weekend does not possess as much intimacy with God as the prostitute in the Gospels who bathed Christ's feet in her tears.

You may think, "I feel bad about what I did, but I don't feel *that* bad." When we look to the example of the repentant prostitute, we might feel discouraged because we lack her zeal and supernatural love. Don't worry. If you lack a contrite heart, just give God what you do have. If you feel you have nothing, give *that* to Him! If you don't possess a heroic love for God, you can at least desire it. In His eyes, the desire to love Him *is* to love Him.

No Regrets?

We once received an e-mail that began, "Is it wrong to not regret losing my virginity? I really do love the guy." However, by the end

of the letter a different tone was evident. The girl concluded her
e-mail by writing, "Sometimes I find myself crying at night trying
to figure out how I could have done such a stupid thing. After almost a year I have come to the point where I feel as though I can't
forgive myself." If this is not regret, it's hard to imagine what is.
Another girl e-mailed us and said, "As I look back on this now I
do not regret it. However, I do wish it hadn't been done."

When a woman gives away too much but claims to feel no remorse, she usually falls into one of three categories:

Some cling to their relationship out of fear that if it ends they
will have to face enormous regret. To avoid this, they prolong the
inevitable separation. In such cases, the absence of regret is a sign of
the presence of denial.

Other times, women find it difficult to bond because they have
lived through so many broken sexual relationships. Because they feel
emotionally detached, they see no reason to regret what they've already done many times before.

Finally, other couples find themselves in sexual relationships where
no such abuse or manipulation is present. Compared to the superficial
flings they witness among their peers, they appreciate the fact that
their consensual union is meaningful to them. Because their closeness
is more tangible than the idea of disobeying a commandment, the
idea of "being sorry for your sins" seems vague. But the fact that a
woman feels no regret today is no guarantee that she will not feel
it in the future. More often than not, the regrets surface after the
relationship ends.

What women in all three cases should realize is that repentance is
not always about feelings. Even when you know an action is wrong,
this does not mean that you will feel guilt. We should be sorry for
our sins, but God does not limit the grace of forgiveness to those
who truly perceive the weight of their offense. If you lack feelings
of regret for what you did, don't let this keep you from seeking
God's forgiveness. Some might think that such an apology would be
insincere. It is not. If you apologize without feeling sorry, it means
that your request for forgiveness is rooted in the knowledge of your
offense. If you know that you hurt someone you love, then it is

an act of love to mend that wound, regardless of how guilty you feel.

When a person approaches God with a spirit of humility, she begins to see what had previously been hidden. While in a darkened room, the air appears clear. When rays of light penetrate the darkness, the smallest specks of dust appear. In much the same way, the blemishes of sin are difficult to detect when we hide from the light, but become apparent when we invite God to open our eyes.

Although it may be hard to admit, perhaps it is time to seek forgiveness from others as well as from God. If you have sacrificed friendships for the sake of passing relationships, seek forgiveness from your friends. If you have deceived your family and lost their trust, have the humility to apologize. Even if you have hurt ex-boyfriends or a current one, perhaps you will find healing in seeking their forgiveness. Every situation is unique, and perhaps others owe *you* a number of apologies. Instead of focusing on those wounds, look at how you might take an active role in your own healing process.

Forgiving Yourself

For some women, it's easy to ask God for forgiveness. The real challenge is granting the same forgiveness to themselves. Forgiving yourself is not a one-time act. It's a process of learning to accept yourself and your past. In the words of one woman:

> I'm trying to learn that I am lovable, and that I am not used, or damaged. But it is hard to see yourself through the eyes of another, because in my own eyes, I don't think I'm worth anyone's time. It is something that I am striving to overcome, because as soon as I can learn to love myself, then and only then will I be ready to love another. I know I am worth more than my body, I am worth more than my mind, I am worth someone's everything. I am worth love.

When a woman makes a regrettable sexual decision, she may think, "Once it's gone it's gone. What good guy would want me now?" She then falls more easily into the same mistakes with men in the future. To prevent this, look back at how you fell, and what led up to that.

What could you have done differently? Had your prayer life dropped off or altogether disappeared? Were you with a guy who didn't have the same standards as you do? Were you hiding things from family or friends who love you? The purpose of examining the past is not to relive it, but to learn from it in order to become stronger in the future.

The best way to heal the past is to purify the future. This may seem like a daunting task, as if you are standing at the base of a towering mountain. But with one "yes" at a time, the mountain will begin to shrink. With each step upward, the summit becomes closer. Do not worry about what lies ahead. Instead, focus only on today. When you're ascending out of a bad lifestyle, the first steps of the journey are often the most difficult. Fresh memories may entice you with temptations, previous relationships may linger, and the undying cycle of gossip and rumors may cause you to question whether such a change is possible.

However, the battle will not always be this fierce. It may seem like you're moving from one slavery to another, but reflect on when the Israelites were led by Moses away from the slavery of Egypt. At first, Moses was their best friend. When things became rough, they whined and groaned about how their previous life of slavery was better than being lost in a desert. They wondered, "Is there a promised land, or is this all there is?" In the same way, when God draws us into the desert of purification, we must have faith that this is not the end. He did not "bring us out here to die," as the Israelites feared.

Painful memories can only be healed when they are used as motivation to build a better future. After making enormous mistakes, a woman may wonder, "How can I start over?" But how can she not? It is never too late to turn around, because every morning, God's mercy is new.[5]

17

CHOOSE TO HEAL

When she was nine years old, Sarah was kidnapped by a stranger and driven hundreds of miles away from her family. As her parents frantically organized search teams and prayer vigils, she suffered abuse from a man she had never seen before. Days later he began thinking of ways to dispose of her. Driving past an empty construction site, he pulled his car into a dirt road and up to a latrine. Taking one last look to make sure nobody was watching, he pulled his victim from the vehicle, and threw her into the sewage. As she stood half submerged in the human waste, she shivered and listened to the gravel crunching under his tires as his car sped away.

There she remained overnight, too afraid to climb out or even call for help. When morning came, a worker at the construction site discovered her and called the fire department. When the truck arrived, a fireman was lowered into the pit to retrieve her. When she saw him descending toward her, she began throwing waste at him and crying out, "Get away! Just leave me here!" She had been so traumatized that she no longer knew who to trust, and wanted to remain in the latrine. The man had to forcibly grab her in order to bring her to safety and eventually home to her family.

We have lost count of how many heartrending stories of sexual abuse we have heard. Most are not this gruesome, but the victims share enough in common. They feel tortured by questions as they try to make sense of what happened. They think:

It's probably my fault that this happened. If only I didn't put myself in that situation. What do I do now? I don't want to tell anyone. What will they think of me? Will they believe me? Will they blame me? Can I ever trust a guy again? Will I ever be able to move past this? The thoughts keep haunting me. Maybe I should just keep this a secret and deal with it on my own.

When a girl has suffered any form of sexual abuse, what can she do to heal? Here are five ways she can begin the process.

Don't blame yourself

"I was so stupid to get in that truck with him. I knew he was drunk and all my friends said he was bad news. It just seemed like it would be fun and exciting." A young high school girl wiped the tears from her cheeks as she recounted to me (Jason) how a friend of her older brother invited her on a drive during a party. As soon as she hopped in the car, he locked the doors, sped off to an isolated area, and took advantage of her. Afterward, he drove her back into town and told her to get out of the truck, about a mile from home. Clutching her torn clothes to her body in an effort to keep warm, she sobbed un-controllably as she walked home under the streetlights. She didn't want to face her parents, so she curled up under a blanket and spent the night on the porch. When morning came, she sped upstairs and stood in the shower for an eternity. When she came downstairs she told her parents that she spent the night at a friend's.

For weeks, she battered herself with reminders. "I could have avoided everything if I just skipped the party or just hung out with guys my own age. This is my fault. If I tell anyone, they'll just say I deserved it for putting myself in that situation." Hypothetical scenarios of how she could have prevented the abuse haunted her, causing her to forget that every rape is the fault of the rapist. Even if she did put herself in a dangerous situation, she never gave him the right to violate her. Every woman should be safe in the presence of a man, no matter the circumstance. Sadly, every woman knows that this is not always the case.

Through counseling, she was able to come to grips with the fact that while she cannot change the past, she can avoid bad situations in the future. She can gain wisdom from the suffering. At least some good could arise from the pain of her experience. However, nothing good would come if she continued to blame herself.

Don't hide

Could you imagine getting into a massive car accident on the freeway, sustaining a few broken ribs and a concussion, and telling the paramedics:

> Don't worry about me. I'm fine. The hospital doesn't need to know, and they would just blame me for driving too fast. Besides, I can't stand needles and they're just going to prick me with an IV and injections of pain medicine. I can heal on my own.

Would you survive? Perhaps. But you would heal more quickly if you showed your wounds to the physician. The same could be said of the girl who has suffered the trauma of sexual abuse yet plans to heal alone in silence. The hospital exists for a reason, and so do family, friends, and counselors.

From a scientific perspective, it's interesting to note what happens in the mind of young women who suffer abuse. Researchers from the University of Texas Southwestern Medical School discovered that traumatic intimidation through abuse and violence leads to high levels of stress that trigger excessive levels of brain-derived neurotrophic factor (BDNF) to be released in the brain. When this happens, certain genes in the brain are turned on, causing the victim of abuse to experience social withdrawal, depression, fearfulness, an increased tendency toward addictive behaviors, and a decreased ability to enjoy intimacy in the future.[1]

If you have been sexually abused and are experiencing these consequences, you are normal. But take a step in faith and find an adult in whom you can confide. It can be a family member, relative, teacher, counselor, youth minister, pastor, or anyone who is trustworthy and loving. If you can't think of whom to tell, pray to God that He will show you the right person.

Ideally, you want to be able to tell your parents. Just think: If the same trauma happened to your daughter one day, what would you want her to do? You probably want to tell them, but you're afraid. Perhaps you're afraid that they might look at you differently or get upset with you. Your worries are understandable. But do not allow your fears to become an obstacle to your healing. If you have hidden your wound and the memories are not going away, it just means you should try a new way to heal.

If you're an adult victim of sexual abuse, then regardless of when the abuse happened in your life, don't deprive yourself of the healing you deserve. Ignoring memories of abuse won't make them disappear or aid the healing process. It only holds you back from being who you were before the tragedy. When physical wounds are neglected, they often lead to infection and unnecessary pain. The same is true of wounds of the heart.

To open up to someone about sexual abuse is not easy. Recounting the events will likely bring tears and a host of emotions. Such a process can be intimidating, and you may be tempted to think, "Why do I need to dig up those old wounds? It hurts just to think about what happened, and I've been through enough hurt. I just need to be strong and move on." However, refusing to mourn is not a strength. It is a weakness. It requires tremendous courage to weep and allow yourself to be consoled by another. Who knows, you may discover other women who have survived the same experiences and are willing to offer compassionate suggestions based upon how they found healing. You're not alone: More than thirty percent of women have been coerced into some form of sexual activity against their will.[2]

Some women have grown so accustomed to hiding the hurt that they don't know how to express sorrow about it. They may go so far as to minimize the abuse, maintaining a stoic attitude: "It's all in the past. I'm fine. It wasn't a big deal." If you have been abused, then what happened to you matters. Grieving over it allows you to admit this. Part of the healing process is allowing these feelings to come to the surface and allowing someone else to validate your pain and empathize with you. You may think, "Well, what's that going to do? What's happened has happened. Nobody can change it." While it's true that no one can change the past, the memories can be healed and your heart can be renewed. Sometimes it takes a leap of faith to believe that healing is possible.

Another difficulty in disclosing sexual abuse is that it requires risk: Will they believe you? Will the police get involved? Do not allow these fears to stop you. It is true: Sometimes a girl will confide in someone who does not believe her. This may happen when a girl tells her mother that a family member or relative abused her. As if the abuse wasn't hurtful enough, sometimes the mother might defend the abuser. She may say things such as, "You're just making that up to get attention or because you don't like him." She probably believes the daughter but is afraid to deal with reality. Every mom has maternal instincts to protect and nurture her children. This is why it is so tragic when mothers stand by the men who harm their children.

What is the girl to do in this case? She should not give up, but should go to another adult who won't be biased about the situation, such as a counselor. She should also remember Psalm 27, which reads, "Even if my father and mother forsake me, the Lord will take me in."[3]

When it comes to getting the police involved in a sexual abuse case, many victims are understandably terrified that their situation will become public knowledge or dragged into lengthy court battles. However, when you speak with a trusted adult, you can discuss how you want to proceed. In making that decision, recognize that most sexual offenders are prowling around today because no one brings them to justice. If every one of their victims pressed charges against them, the rates of sexual abuse would plummet. Sexual abuse would not disappear, but countless future victims would be spared the pain you have experienced. Most abusers don't hurt only one victim. If someone has abused you, you were probably not their first victim, nor are you likely to be the last. For this reason, we encourage you to be brave and bring them to justice.

Don't bury your wounds

Haley sat on the bleachers of her high school gym, quietly telling me how she slept with countless men after having been raped. In the middle of our conversation, she asked if I would come with her to see her self-portrait hanging in the school's art exhibit. Together we walked through the hallways as she shared her story with me. We arrived at the classroom and she pointed out her charcoal drawing. "Here it is."

The image on black canvas was of a girl with angel wings that rose gracefully above her. She sat in darkness, with her head bowed down in despair. Her forehead rested upon her folded arms, which rested upon her knees. Streaks of black water that resembled tears poured down the canvas in the background. After our conversation, she e-mailed me a copy of the portrait, and I still have it framed and sitting on a bookshelf in my office, as a reminder to pray for her.

But aside from prayer, how does one convince such a girl that she deserves to be treated like a princess? Every voice in her head would protest against such an absurd idea. How do you tell her that she no longer needs to run from her past? If you attempt to talk a woman out of a destructive lifestyle, she may dismiss all consolations, thinking, "This is just the way it has to be."

A woman's heart is inseparable from her womb. When she bears life through pregnancy, she forms an indescribable bond with her child. Through the gift of sexuality, a wife becomes one flesh with her husband. The womb is meant for life and for love. Her body is a sacred place, because it is within the woman that the marriage is consummated and human life is created. Because of its sacred purpose, it demands tremendous reverence.

However, when a woman's sexuality is desecrated, the wound is especially deep. This explains the profound brokenness expressed by one young woman who e-mailed me to say, "I was raped last year, and since then I have wasted my body because I have felt worthless."

When a woman suffers sexual abuse, her abuser sends her a vivid message that she does not deserve to be loved, cherished, or protected. If she does not seek help in dealing with the abuse, she may begin to integrate this message into her soul. Her life will soon begin to reflect the belief that she does not expect to be loved. She may begin to give away her body to men who are as lustful as the man who abused her. But this time, she consents and even initiates such encounters. One wound is buried under another. She thinks she has discovered a way to prevent being hurt by guys. Her body may be available to them, but her heart is locked up and she gives it to no one. She won't let anyone hurt her—because she's too busy hurting herself.

The victim asks herself in silence, "Who would want me now?" What she does not realize is that the kind of guy she really wants —a respectful and loving gentleman—would not love her any less because of the abuse she has suffered. If anything, he would want to love her more, to make up for what she has suffered. I cannot even conceive of a man so heartless that he would think, "You were abused when you were younger? I don't want to be with you." Do not think that you are worthless or worth less because of the past. No matter what has happened, you still have yourself to give.

After a woman has suffered sexual abuse, it's best for her to take a time of healing for herself before she enters a new relationship. If she doesn't take the time to be made whole, she might begin using relationships to soothe her pain. In a sense, she's attempting to fill a container that's been broken. As a result, she'll wonder why she feels so empty after trying so hard to be filled.

Learn to trust again

It is not uncommon for a young woman who has been abused to feel that she'll never be able to trust guys again. She may wonder, "Am I ever going to be able to have a normal relationship with a guy? I'm terrified of being alone with a man. Is intimacy going to be possible for me?" Following the abuse, some girls cease to be interested in men altogether, guarding their hearts against any relationships. These reflexes are understandable reactions to shelter one's heart from further pain.

If a woman does not gradually learn how to trust again, her ability to give and receive love will atrophy. In the words of C. S. Lewis:

To love at all is to be vulnerable. Love anything, and your heart will certainly be wrung and possibly be broken. If you want to make sure of keeping it intact, you must give your heart to no one, not even to an animal. Wrap it carefully round with hobbies and little luxuries; avoid all entanglements; lock it up safe in the casket or coffin of your selfishness. But in that casket—safe, dark, motionless, airless—it will change. It will not be broken; it will become unbreakable, impenetrable, irredeemable. . . . The only place outside Heaven where you can be perfectly safe from all the dangers and perturbations of love is Hell.[4]

The person who guards herself because of sexual abuse is not doing so out of selfishness, but the end result is the same. She closes herself off from what can ultimately heal her—love. A woman wisely remarked:

The worst harm you do yourself is if you cease to love, because you might be hurt or you have been hurt. You shrivel up like an old prune. Don't do that. Be willing to be hurt. The pain of trying to keep yourself from being vulnerable is much greater than the pain of loving and losing. Remember that.[5]

By this, she does not mean that a woman should be careless with her heart. She means that we cannot live without love, and love requires a certain level of receptivity and openness. Certainly, a woman will feel distrustful toward men after suffering abuse. She rightfully guards her heart. But by trusting her intuition and slowly developing simple friendships with decent men, she can learn to trust again. From the start, it is wise for her to communicate to any potential pursuers that she is deliberately taking a time of singleness in her life. Being in good friendships and eventually holy relationships will help her to see that she can feel safe again, although the process takes time. There is no wound so deep that it cannot be made whole through God's grace.

Find healing through mercy

In order for the healing process to be complete, a victim of abuse must choose in her heart to forgive her abuser. Such an act of mercy might seem impossible to you, considering the pain that you have endured because of him (or her). However, when you refuse to for-give, you only harm yourself by holding on to bitterness. Love alone is victorious over evil.

You have assuredly heard the saying "forgive and forget," but we say forget that. Your job is to forgive. The whole idea of forgetting an injury makes it sound like if you really forgive someone then you'll suddenly have amnesia. In other words, if you still remember the hurt that a person caused you, that must mean that you haven't completely forgiven that person. Nothing could be further from the truth. Forgiveness does not mean forgetfulness. It just means that you no longer hold it against the other person. You do not wish them harm. This is why Scripture often refers to unforgiveness by using the metaphor of debt. Forgiveness is when you write off the amount others owe you.

When one person refuses to forgive another, the person who caused the wound often doesn't seem to care; however, the unforgiving heart grows hardened over time. Holding on to the sins of another is like clinging to a burning ember. Let it go, because it will only wound you more, as long as you refuse to surrender it.

Once you have forgiven the other, take one last step: Replace ha-tred with charity by praying for whoever has hurt you. Desire his conversion instead of his condemnation. God will ensure that justice will come to him. You don't have to worry about that. One day, he will see the evil he has inflicted upon himself, and that alone will be pain enough. At that moment he will realize that he cannot escape what he has brought upon himself. Your task, in the meantime, is to pray that his heart will change and be healed.

If the memories of the past continue to haunt you, bring them to God during your prayer times. Talk to Him, heart to heart, about it. If God can heal the blind and raise the dead, He can heal your memories as well. It may not happen overnight, but trust in His promise: "Behold, I make all things new."[6]

RISE ABOVE THE GOSSIP

It all started at about 9:00 at night in my (Jason's) dorm, with my college roommate Jason playfully thumping our friend Raphael on the head with a broken TV antenna. Raphael was immersed in his studies, and chose to ignore the irritating assault. Jason persisted with a few more taps. The stoic silence of his unwilling playmate only fueled Jason's desire to continue, hoping for a reaction. Eventually Raphael snapped, "Cut it out!" Jason was feeling rather frisky, and so he tapped away a few more times, pretending Raphael's skull was a snare drum. That did the trick.

Raphael arose with such wrath that his chair slid forcefully behind him and into the wall with a crash that echoed down the dorm's hallway. He shoved his torturer and a fight ensued. Jason rushed Raphael, without remembering his opponent's expertise in martial arts. The commotion caused a few students to peek out of their rooms, just in time to see Jason fly backwards across the hallway and into his own room, without ever touching the floor in between. Raphael later explained that he learned that particular kick to the torso from a Bruce Lee movie. Upon realizing that he was outmatched, from across the hall Jason began hurling a few choice words, a few objects out of his refrigerator (including a jar of mayonnaise), and the broken television antenna. By midnight of the same evening, the two were laughing it up over a meal of pepperoni calzones.

This is one of the benefits of being male. Fights typically last a few minutes and lifelong friendships sometimes form as a result of them. Have you ever noticed how a pair of boxers will stare each other down and spew hatred at one another prior to their fight, yet hug and kiss each other afterward?

Female fights typically work in the opposite order: Hugs and kisses come first, but when a fight breaks out, it is followed by months or years of stare-downs and hatred-spewing. The emotional and verbal fracas can last for decades. I recall speaking at a pair of high schools where the all-boys school enjoyed massive financial support from its alumna, while the all-girls school struggled to make ends meet. An administrator said that when the telemarketers call their former female students, they hear complaints like, "No, I don't want to make a donation to the school." She then mumbles something about the trauma that was inflicted upon her twenty years ago when her sophomore English teacher made a joke about her hair.

The nature of the female fight is something that transcends species. In his research on chimpanzees and Rhesus monkeys, one Dutch primatologist noticed that male apes are quick to reconcile after a fight.[1] After getting involved in a violent skirmish, the two can often be found embracing and grooming one another. The females, on the other hand, tend to simmer for years after crossing one another. Once they fight, the friendship is history. The researcher described them as "vindictive and irreconcilable." They might shove and slap one another, and refuse to come to an ex-friend's aid. Their animosity toward one another can be sparked by things such as a rivalry over a particular relationship (sound familiar?), or if a single treat is tossed into the habitat and only one female comes out the winner. Thank goodness they don't know how to use Facebook, or who knows what they'd do to each other!

While this may seem amusing, the wounds inflicted by gossip and verbal abuse are hardly a laughing matter. Newspaper headlines frequently report about teenage girls who commit suicide because of gossip or online bullying. Incriminating photos are plastered on the Internet for all to see, with corresponding stories, damaging labels, and lies. Ex-boyfriends retaliate with ruthless rumors, and parents are at a loss for ways to console their thirteen-year-old daughter after her reputation has been shredded by a clique of backbiting "friends." Few young women escape the gauntlet of the teenage years unscathed. Unfortunately, the problem of gossip often continues into college and beyond, with rumors floating even around the workplace.

What is a woman to do?

Don't Gossip

Everyone complains about the widespread evil of gossip, yet how many people confess it? Before we can fix the fault in another, we must realize our own guilt. Who hasn't said something about another person that you would not say to his or her face? When it comes to gossip, we've all been the victim and the victimizer. Why do we do it? The root of gossip is the presence of pride and the lack of charity. Its fruit is bitterness, pain, and division. Its antidote is love and humility, coupled with forgiveness.

You may have noticed that humble people have no need to gossip. They're aware of their own mistakes in life. Instead of relishing the downfall of another, they seek to build up others. This partly explains why gossipers are often miserable people. Joy only comes from loving, and one of the greatest acts of love you can do on a daily basis is to keep your mouth shut when you are tempted to say what should be kept secret. One spiritual writer explained: "The really spiritual man is known by the kindness of his speech, and still more by the kindness of his silence."[2]

When we gossip, it is as if we ascend to the top of a skyscraper and open a feather pillow, waving it in the wind until the contents are emptied. Even if you wanted to gather the feathers together, it would be impossible. No one knows where they have gone. The same goes with the dispersion of rumors. Once we unzip our mouths, the damage is irreversible.

But it is not enough to avoid spreading gossip. We must avoid listening to it as well, by having custody of our ears, guarding ourselves against insatiable curiosity. Cut conversations short when you hear another person cut down. Defend those who are not present to defend themselves. Furthermore, choose your friends wisely. Those who gossip to you will gossip about you.

How should you deal with the problem of gossip? Meditate upon the following verses from Scripture:

> He who repeats an evil report has no sense. Never repeat gossip, and you will not be reviled. Tell nothing to friend or foe . . . Let anything you hear die within you; be assured it will not make you burst. When a fool hears something, he is in labor, like a woman giving birth to a child. Like an arrow lodged in a man's thigh is gossip in the breast of a fool. Admonish your friend—he may not have done it; and if he did, that he may not do it again. Admonish your neighbor—he may not have said it; and if he did, that he may not say it again. Admonish your friend—often it may be slander; every story you must not believe. Then, too, a man can slip and not mean it; who has not sinned with his tongue?[3]

> I tell you, on the day of judgment people will render an account for every careless word they speak. By your words you will be acquitted, and by your words you will be condemned.[4]

Down through the ages, Christian writers have praised the wisdom of keeping our mouths shut:

> Silent lips are pure gold and bear witness to holiness within.[5]

> Silence is the cross on which we must crucify our ego.[6]

> Preserve silence like a key of gold that locks up the great treasure of the other virtues that God has given us.[7]

Don't Empower Them

For as long as you live, you'll have to deal with gossip in one way or another. No matter how perfect you are, it will happen. Even Jesus endured frequent calumniation and slander. He didn't do anything wrong, but others were jealous of his status. Similarly, in the world of female bullying, many girls will tear down another not because she did something wrong, but because she didn't! If she has something they want (such as a boyfriend, popularity, or beauty), envy will trigger their malice.

If you pour out your tears and energy trying to correct every lie and explain every rumor, you'll wear yourself out. There's a better way to combat it. Ask yourself, "Does this person deserve to have control over my day?" Do not give him or her power over you. Although you may be hurt by what was said, you can still choose to retain your peace. This is easier said than done, but it begins by an act of your will. You may even need to say to yourself:

> I'm not giving that person control over my day. If she (or he) wants to spread her rumors, she'll end up with the worse reputation for being immature, mean, and untrustworthy. I'm not going to stoop to her level by gossiping back, nor will I allow her to define the way I look at myself.

This last part is key: Do not allow gossip to shape the way you view yourself. So many young women have said to us in private conversations, "I figured if everyone thought I was a slut, I might as well act like one." This is giving others control over you. It is pure submission. Don't allow yourself to be defined by those who do not love you. Your identity is a daughter of God. That's who you are, regardless of your past. When you know who you are, you'll have a shield to protect you from the hail of gossip.

The people who weigh you down with their hurtful words will not be in your life forever. If you are in high school, realize that I (Crystalina) graduated from a school of over three thousand students, and am in touch with none of them. Jason graduated with a class of one thousand, and he's still in touch with two. Sometimes it's hard to see beyond the four walls of your school or workplace, but don't let the rumors defeat you. Your life is bigger than your reputation.

Finally, remember that anyone who says damaging things about you—whether they be true of false—is hiding her own pain. Therefore, pity the person who gossips about you. Instead of letting the rumors rob you of your peace, pray for whoever is spreading them. You've got to be pretty sad to ruin other people's lives in order to think yours will improve. As strange as it sounds, gossipers deserve your prayers. If only we all prayed for others as quickly as we judge them.

Be Classy, Not Catty

Imagine if God allowed you to pour burning coals onto the head of whoever gossiped about you. If that sounds like an enticing offer, here's how you can do it without having to go apologize afterward. St. Paul explains:

> Bless those who persecute you; bless and do not curse them. . . . Repay no one evil for evil, but take thought for what is noble in the sight of all. If possible, so far as it depends upon you, live peaceably with all. Beloved, never avenge yourselves, but leave it to the wrath of God; for it is written, "Vengeance is mine, I will repay, says the Lord." No, "if your enemy is hungry, feed him; if he is thirsty, give him drink; for by so doing you will heap burning coals upon his head." Do not be overcome by evil, but overcome evil with good.[8]

When you have an enemy and the battle is a war of words, don't attempt to overcome her with clever arguments or vicious words. The Bible tells us, "Do not argue with a chatterer, nor heap wood on his fire."[9] Instead, practice the virtues that are the opposite of her vices. Instead of entering into the wrath of another, be the classy one. After all, there is no comeback to charity.

Perhaps the greatest act of love that you can do for the one who hurts you is to forgive him or her. The person may never ask for forgiveness—or even think that he or she did anything wrong. But this is not something you can change. Although it is especially difficult to forgive another person while you still suffer, do not delay. Christ forgave those who crucified Him—while He was still hanging upon the cross. Even His closest friends betrayed and abandoned Him. Similarly, the wounds of gossip are often caused by those closest to us, because they typically know our deepest secrets.

Follow the example of Christ: Do not simply leave the judgment to God, but call down His mercy for those who have wounded you. Such love is heroic, but it is also healing. It raises you above the petty gossip and you gain merit in heaven for the way you have chosen to respond to suffering. Besides, upon what grounds can we ask God for forgiveness if we will not forgive others for the harm they have caused us?

The Best Revenge Is a Good Life

If your acts of charity and prayers do nothing to calm the storm of gossip, do not give in to discouragement. Disprove the gossip with the witness of your life. You can't instantly change the way people view you. To lose your good reputation, perhaps you made some bad decisions, or maybe just one. Or perhaps you did nothing! Either way, make wise decisions to earn a good reputation. As we all know, it takes longer to get a good reputation than a bad one. Be patient.

If you've made some mistakes, feel free to admit them to yourself: "Okay, dumb move. Now I know better, and it's not going to happen again." Or, in the words of one woman who e-mailed us, "I have a lot of regrets right now, but at least I'm not making any more for later."

In time, your example of purity will speak louder than someone's mouth, no matter how gapingly large it might seem. Don't be afraid that your identity will be tarnished forever. You haven't lost your chance to find your soulmate. If a guy really loves you, then he'll be able to see beyond rumors about your past—true or not—to see who you are today.

19

Enjoy the Season of Singleness

With a sack lunch in his hand and a science book tucked under his arm, a seventh-grade boy approached me (Jason) after I spoke at his middle school. In a cracking voice that signaled the dawn of puberty, he inquired, "I started dating this one girl when we were in third grade, and we were pretty serious for three years. I broke up with her last year, and now I'm wondering if I should ask out this other girl." After I gave him what advice I could, I pondered what a "pretty serious" relationship meant for a pair of eight-year-olds.

There's no denying it: From our youngest years, we've all felt at some point that everyone in the world has a date . . . except *you*. Girls suffer the most from this modern phenomenon because guys are the ones who traditionally make the first move. If no guy is sending text messages to a girl's phone, she'll assume that she's not only incomplete, but defective. After all, if she doesn't have a boyfriend, there must be a reason, right?

There's no use comforting her. In her mind, she's alone, she's unlikable, and nobody pursues her because she's unlovable: she'll probably grow old alone and live in an apartment with twelve cats.

What's worse for any woman than feeling unwanted and unnoticed? To remedy the situation, she may take matters into her own hands, changing the way she behaves in an effort to gain the attention of men. She may lower her standards and hook up with guys, assuming that they "just have needs." But by doing so she knows she's giving up—and giving in. By throwing herself at a guy, she's announcing to him that she doubts he would otherwise pursue her. She'll tell herself that she's experimenting and having fun, but she's losing herself in the process.

In today's culture, does a single woman have any other option? Indeed she does. Instead of measuring her worth by the number of men who are interested in her, she can embrace her "season of singleness," developing the virtue of patience and a sense of purpose. Her patience shows that she won't give in to a shallow relationship in order to pacify her desire for the real thing. And her purpose announces to a man that she's not waiting for him to come along before she begins to live her life.

Patience

It was about ten o'clock on a Saturday night when my high school friends and I got home from the batting cages. As we walked through the kitchen to load up on free food, we all gave my mom a polite hello as she ended a conversation on the phone. "Who you talkin' to?" I asked. "Oh, it was Andrea's mom. Andrea is really upset and crying." With the sympathetic tenderness of a sixteen-year-old guy, I inquired, "What's her problem?" My mom replied, "Nobody asked her to the dance tonight." Our response? "Oh, there was a dance?"

With that, we all shrugged our shoulders and went into the back yard to play basketball. Meanwhile, some cute girl on the other side of town was having enormous self-esteem problems when in reality she had nothing to worry about. She was cute. But we were clueless.

Don't beat yourself up if you don't have a boyfriend. Regardless of your age, realize that some guys don't have the guts to ask anyone out and are too immature to love a woman properly. Meanwhile, some men are shallow and won't bother to pursue a woman who has standards because she won't let herself be used. As a result, many women have complained to us that there seems to be only two kinds of single men in existence: wimps and jerks. Neither is desirable for obvious reasons.

Because the pickings seem slim, many women find themselves alone and frustrated. The high school girls feel left out when all their girlfriends seem to have someone taking them out on Friday night. The college girls who secretly hope for something more meaningful than a pointless hookup sit alone in their dorms having another date with their textbooks. The single adults return from work to find a big, depressing "0" on the answering machine.

What are they to do? The high school girl should understand that regardless of her perception of other people's dating lives, the vast majority of teenage girls are not in committed dating relationships. As for the college girl, she should remind herself that she's more likely to find love by becoming an intelligent woman than by making dumb mistakes at a party. What about the flustered professional who comes home to that answering machine solemnly reminding her "You have no new messages"? She would do well to pick up the phone, call a friend, and do something to better her life.

When your fellow classmates, friends, and co-workers are jumping headlong into intense relationships, you may get the feeling that you're moving too slowly. The reality is that they're probably going too quickly. They often break up again and again, as they learn the habit of failed relationships. From the outside looking in, it appears that all is well with everyone but you. You see couples in love, holding hands, and gazing into each others eyes . . . and you envy that. But in the long run, people who engage in repetitious romances are likely to envy you because you have not given away as much as they have. Some of them have never been engaged but feel like they've already lived through several broken marriages.

You may think, "I don't even want some intense physical relationship, but just someone who will call out of the blue to talk or hang out, someone who actually cares how I'm doing." If that's how you feel, know that there are millions of people feeling the same way you are. While that may not make life any easier, it will at least let you know that something is not desperately wrong with you. You're not a freak of nature because you're single.

For most women, the idea of singleness is frightening. Although you might long for marriage and loathe being single, keep in mind the wisdom of one marriage counselor, who said, "It is better to be single and wish you were married than to be married and wish you were single."[1]

While singleness may have always struck you as a curse, we invite you to see it as a choice. In fact, we recommend that you deliberately not date for a while. You may think, "Um, thanks for the suggestion, but I've been single long enough." However, there are benefits to choosing the lifestyle as opposed to resigning yourself to it. Because you've taken the dating pressure off yourself, you can focus on relating to guys as friends. This will serve as a better foundation for love, when the time comes. You're also likely to meet more members of the opposite sex because all your time isn't absorbed with one. Finally, you'll have more time to enjoy your girlfriends and the experience of being single.

Take some time for yourself in order to put life in perspective. Doing so will not harm your chances of finding love. It will help them. After all, independent women are the most alluring to men. When a woman looks like she's waiting to be asked out, it makes you wonder why she hasn't been. On the other hand, if she's happy with her independence, she doesn't appear to be as accessible. She's a challenge. It's as if she's saying, "I don't need you to complete me, but you're free to try." She seems content with herself. Such a positive demeanor naturally draws others in. But this happiness must be an authentic joy. It cannot be a happy mask worn to become more likeable.

Everyone wants love, and we usually spend an enormous amount of energy and anxiety trying to make it happen. Because of this, the idea of finding your soulmate by deliberately not dating might sound counterproductive. But one reason we suggest this is because it's what Crystalina and I were doing when we met each other.

Each of us had dated around for years, looking for "the one." But we didn't find each other until we took a break from it all and focused our attention on God alone. In our own ways, we asked, "God, what do you want in my life?" Once we did this, it was surprising how His will unfolded in our lives.

Focus on what God wants of you today and let Him worry about tomorrow. Sure, that's easier said than done, but the Lord gives us a time of singleness to serve Him, and many of us either fill it with passing relationships or spend it miserable because a future relationship hasn't unfolded according to our plans. When we busy ourselves with the things of God, we learn to look beyond ourselves to serve those whose needs are far greater than ours.

Let's say you give this a try. A few months pass by and not much happens. What are you supposed to do? Be patient. Let's say you try patience and nothing happens. Then what? Patience. What better practice could there be for marriage than patience, patience, and patience? However, all the waiting can sometimes make a girl ask, "Lord, if you're all-powerful, then how come I'm not getting what I want?"

I (Crystalina) would argue that the most difficult virtue for a woman to practice when it comes to relationships is patience. Purity, honesty, compassion, humility, and all the other ingredients of love are easier for us to develop. They might come naturally for some. However, when it comes to patience, this is usually not the case. The reason for this may be our fear that we may miss out on love if we don't grab onto whatever comes along. It is this impatience that often lies at the root of so many poor decisions we make —especially sexual ones.

I've lost count of how many times we've heard girls say, "I can't stand being alone." But the surest way for a woman to end up alone is by allowing the fear of loneliness to dominate her decisions. Because this phobia is so common, it's essential that we conquer it— or at least not allow ourselves to be conquered by it.

Purpose

At the age of seventeen, Ashley left her family and ran off to Las Vegas to marry her twenty-four-year-old boyfriend. She stood before me (Jason) in an empty hallway of her high school, sobbing as she rolled up her sleeve to show me a bruise on her arm in the shape of her husband's hand. Earlier that week, the two of them had gotten into an argument because he blamed her for the miscarriage of their twins she had recently suffered. Before meeting him she had contracted an incurable sexually transmitted disease that impaired her ability to carry a baby to full term. He knew she caught the STD because she was raped, but blamed her anyway.

As I looked into her eyes, swollen with tears, I asked only one thing: "Ashley, what is your dream in life?" Her eyes brightened as she explained that she always wanted to pursue a career in theater and dancing in New York. She told me, "I even got a letter of acceptance from NYU!"

"What's keeping you from going?" I asked.

Her expression dropped. "Nick won't let me leave Texas."

"Look, Ashley," I said to her, "you're not in a real marriage. Leave this guy, move back in with your parents, get your feet on the ground, finish high school, and then get on the next plane to New York City." I kept in touch with her for a while to make sure she left the abusive situation. A few years after our exchange, I received an unexpected e-mail from a university student in New York who was majoring in dance. She said, "Whenever I have my first performance on Broadway, I want to send you tickets to the show."

You'll notice that what saved her from throwing her life away was the fact that she dreamed of something bigger and better for herself. When a girl lacks dreams and an identity, she makes boys her dream and seeks to find her identity in them. If her primary concern is to be accepted and wanted by a man, her long-term goals tend to fade into the background and may disappear altogether.

If a girl finds a guy before she finds her purpose in life, she's more likely to invest everything in him, as opposed to investing in herself. As the relationship progresses, she may begin to feel a sense of discontent because she never took the time in life to pursue her own interests apart from him. For these reasons, a girl must take the time to discover her purpose in life if she wishes to give and receive true love. In fact, a woman is not ready for a boyfriend until she can live happily without one.

The idea of being happily single may seem paradoxical to women who look to the affirmation of men for their sense of self-worth.

Many singles will struggle with the concept because of the ache they feel for a relationship. But before a woman fills this void with a man, she must ask herself, "If God put me on earth for a reason, what is it? What am I doing to make the world a better place? Am I pursuing my passions in life or just living a soap opera?" When she seeks the answers to these questions, she'll find herself in the process.

Are You Single . . . or Singular?

While flipping through a magazine, I noticed the familiar face of one of my classmates from college. "What's she up to?" I thought to myself. The article explained that while Shannon was in college, she read a book that described the suffering of a Chinese mother as she lived under the government's one-child policy. She began praying for the country, but never imagined how God would use her to answer her own prayers.

A year and a half after finishing college, Shannon was praying one morning and asked God, "How can I get into an orphanage in China?" Ten minutes later, her phone rang. It was a friend offering her an invitation to volunteer at an orphanage . . . in China. She packed her bags and before long she was flying overseas without even knowing the language.

One day an unnamed famished baby with a cleft palate was dropped off at the orphanage. Shannon had picked up enough Chinese to understand when the staff told her not to become too attached to the child because he would soon die. She begged to differ and later said, "I was convinced God sent him to us not to die, but to live."[2] She named him Max and began using a dropper to give him his milk, because his facial deformity prevented him from being able to drink from a bottle. In order to ensure that he ate, Shannon slept with him and nurtured him back to health.

A few years later, Shannon began working for another orphanage that cared for babies who were abandoned because of their disabilities. Since the government only allows parents to have one child, couples sometimes reject the unhealthy ones. Because of the extreme poverty in some areas, some mothers abandon their children in hopes that someone will care for them. For these reasons, Shannon's orphanage often had more children than they could handle. Some of the babies were so ill that they would only live a matter of weeks or months. For this reason, some workers questioned whether the orphanage should accept the infirm. Instead, they suggested that the orphanage should be reserved for those who were likely to survive.

Because Shannon couldn't bear the thought of these children dying without love and affection, she opened her own home to dying orphans. Shannon's new orphanage, Loving Heart Home, now accommodates eleven babies, and she is preparing to expand and double the capacity. With a team of fifteen Chinese women, she cares for the infants until they recover or return to God. In her spare time, Shannon raises money to pay for the children to have life-saving surgeries.

Some people may read her story and can only imagine how difficult it would be to become a mother to a dozen dying children. Although the work is sometimes overwhelming, Shannon said that her goal is to fill the short lives of the babies with love and happiness. One of her staff members, when asked why she worked there, said, "If I were dying, I would want someone to be with me, to love me, to care for me. These children deserve no less."[3]

Now, rewind the story and change some details. Imagine Shannon ten years ago. But instead of kneeling for her morning prayers, seeking to know how she could serve God, she was doing something else. Imagine her loafing on a couch with a gossip magazine on her lap, sipping a latte and complaining on her cell phone to a friend that all guys are total jerks and that she's upset she doesn't have one to call her own. While she's yapping away, she notices a call on the other line. "Hold on," she interrupts. "I got another call." She clicks over, and it's a friend inviting her to China. I can hear her now:

"Uh, thanks, but I'm kinda busy. Good luck, though."

Click.

"Hey, that was a church friend. She wanted me to go to China with her. Whatever! So anyway, did you hear that Daniel told Brianna that Kayla said Zach didn't want to see Alyssa anymore?"

You have been created to live for something greater than yourself, and it is only through the complete giving of yourself that you will find yourself. The Creator of the universe has created you for a specific purpose. Do you believe this? One man discovered, "The place that God calls us is that place where the world's deep hunger and our deep desire meet."[4] Or in the words of a young woman:

> I realized how perfectly each person's vocation matches his or her personhood. I finally understood that discernment did not mean figuring out some cosmic plan; it meant figuring out the glory for which God had specifically created me.[5]

God has given you qualities that He has given to no other. As a woman, you have been blessed with certain gifts that only a woman can offer. Your job to is to discover those and place them at His disposal.

Therefore, during your single years take the time to focus on your purpose while growing in patience. As you do so, be prepared for sacrifice. In order to attain these qualities, every girl will pay a price. Because of her dreams in life, she'll need to place her goals above guys for a while. Because of her desire to grow in patience, her standards will be tested during times of loneliness. Instead of being swayed back and forth between the fear of loneliness and feelings of impatient expectation, she will become balanced and hopeful. Dawn Eden, author of *The Thrill of the Chaste*, remarked:

> A woman with the courage to step out into the unknown, risking temporary loneliness for a shot at lasting joy, is more than a "single." She's *singular*. Instead of defining herself by what she lacks—a relationship with a man—she defines herself by what she has: a relationship with God.[6]

The season of singleness is not about being passive and waiting around for the next guy to call. It doesn't require total isolation, but rather a healthy detachment from all the unnecessary drama. It's a time for enjoying life and prioritizing it. If the idea intimidates you, take to heart the consoling words of one man, who said, "Be courageous, fear nothing, and you will not be disappointed."[7]

20

BELIEVE AGAIN

Imagine God sitting alone at a table in an elegant restaurant. Across from Him is an empty seat, reserved for you. As time draws on, He wonders why you haven't responded to the invitation. He takes a peek outside the door of the restaurant and hears a noise coming from the back parking lot. Recognizing the familiar sound of your voice, He follows the sound until it leads Him . . . to a dumpster.

Behind the rusted metal wall, He can hear you talking to yourself: "Ooh. Pizza crust. Sweet! There's some chocolate left on the inside of that candy wrapper!"

Despite the location, He's glad to have found you, and He calls you by name. You cautiously poke your head above the dumpster, and God looks at you with love, and a little sad smile. He's sad that you're in the dumpster, but He's smiling because you don't realize there's an entire banana peel in your hair. Hiding within the security of the massive container, you're hesitant to hear what He has to say. But you're curious.

"I have a feast waiting for you inside. There's Australian lobster tail, white wine, crème brûlèe . . . There's even a little card at your place with your name on it. But your seat was empty. So I came looking for you. Would you come inside with me?"

You're silent. But your mind is whirring with doubts. You squint your eyes at Him and reply, "I can't see any lobster. I don't even smell the food. How do I know you're not just going to pull me out of here so that you can starve me to death?"

Before giving Him a chance to reply, you drop back into the dumpster and stare at the familiar rusted walls. Perhaps you've been in the dumpster so long that you hardly notice the stench. You reason to yourself, "It's not that bad in here. At least when I'm in the dumpster, I know what to expect. I'm on my own, and I can do it myself. I don't need anyone's help." But as hard as you try to convince yourself otherwise, you know you're still hungry. You wonder, "Maybe He's telling the truth. Maybe there *is* something better."

But as soon as you begin to hope, a voice inside shuts you down, "No. Even if He is telling the truth, I don't belong in that restaurant. Look at me. Everyone will stare. Everyone will cringe at the smell of me. They'll all know where I've been. I can't fool them. I should just stay here."

Sitting on a mound of leftovers, you listen for the footsteps of God walking away, but He isn't moving. He's waiting. Minutes pass by, and you hear nothing. Your breathing slows down, and then you hear Him again.

"Trust me and take my hand. I know you can't see what I want to give you. The only way I can give you what will satisfy you is if you trust in me completely. I love you as you are . . . but, sweetheart, I can't roll your dumpster into the restaurant. If you want to come with me, you need to let go. I won't force you to do anything. I can only ask you to trust."

Notice, God does not shame you. He doesn't say, "Look at yourself. You should know better!" He does not motivate you with fear: "If you stay there, you're just going to end up getting burned at the city dump!" Instead, He loves you. He knows that if you encounter His love, your life will never be the same. He can only wait and hope that you'll remember the promise made thousands of years earlier through His servant David in Psalm 84, "Better is one day in your house, than thousands elsewhere."

Take His hand and do not be afraid to hope. Your future depends upon it.

Accepting the Invitation

Do you believe that God has an invitation waiting for you? If not, why? Perhaps the suffering you have experienced in life has caused you to doubt God's existence. You may have thought, "If God is so good and loving, why have so many bad things happened to me? If He is so powerful, why didn't He stop those things from taking place?"

Unexplained suffering has led many people to dismiss the idea of a personal, loving God. Others assume that God no longer loves them because of the things they've done in the past. In both cases, many sum up their thoughts of God by saying, "I'm not really into the God thing."

Perhaps the analogy is simplistic, but for a person to claim that she is not into the "God thing" could be compared to the acorn that claims it's not really into the "soil thing." In other words, "I'm not that interested in where I came from or where I am going. I'm not interested in the only thing that can give complete meaning to my life or fulfill my very existence." If we have been made by God and for God, then our lives will not make sense apart from Him. If we lose sight of our origin, we'll miss our destiny. We're made for more than this world can offer.

Imagine shopping in an unfamiliar mall and walking up to the directory. When you look at the map, it doesn't say where you are, or show the names of any stores. Your shopping experience would be frustrating as you wandered aimlessly through the mall. Or maybe this would be heaven for you, I don't know. The point is this: We don't have to wander through life wondering if it has any meaning. God has a specific plan for why He created you. Your existence is not an accident, and your future is in good hands—if you're willing to trust Him with it.

Trust is the key that opens the door to God's plan for your life. If you are afraid of the plans He has in mind for you, look at the origin of these fears. At what point in your life did God lose your trust? Upon reflecting about this, some might be able to identify a tragedy that caused them to lose faith in Him. Many people have difficulty believing in the idea of a loving God because they've witnessed a profound lack of love from the people who were supposed to reflect His love to them. All too often, a father or other male is the root cause of such hurt.

It is often said that a person's relationship with God begins where their relationship with their dad ends. This is not always the case, but if you have a father who is abusive, absent, or impossible to please, it's easy to impose these qualities onto your idea of God. If you feel as if your earthly father is always disappointed in you or is emotionally unavailable, it becomes difficult to envision a God who loves you unconditionally and is closer to you than your own breath. Some may ask, "How am I supposed to trust a God who I don't see when I can't even trust the people I do see? If God is love, and I don't believe in love any more, how am I supposed to believe in God?"

Your feelings about God are not the measure of His nearness to you. His love does not need to be earned. It is a gift. Try to wrap your mind around this: Not only does God love you, He likes you.

"I Know, I Know. God Loves Me. But I Want a Guy to Love Me."

The Hebrew word for soulmate is *b'shert*. A Jewish woman once explained to me that she understood the word to mean that one's soulmate is only visible to the person who is living in the will of God. You could live next door to him your whole life and never know it, unless you were living as God was calling you to live.

How do you conform your life to His will? In the Gospel of Matthew, our Lord says, "But seek first his kingdom and his righteousness, and all these things shall be yours as well."[1] However human the temptation may be, we can't say, "Okay, God. If I need to put you first in my life in order to get what I want, then I hereby declare you first. Now can I have what I want?" It doesn't work like that.

Spiritual maturity emerges only through patient suffering. Seasons of waiting, wondering, and hoping may need to pass by as you cling to Him in faith, allowing Him to shape your hopes and even your very desires.

If you are frustrated with God because you haven't found your soulmate, perhaps there's a reason why the time hasn't come. Sometimes we make a god out of human love, and the idol needs to be broken. Human love is a beautiful thing to desire and to find. The dream of love does not need to be abandoned. But when it becomes the center of our longings, the cause of our joy or despair, and the ruler of our hearts, it needs to be handed over to God, who alone can fulfill our deepest desires.

Because the human heart is made for love, we seek it tirelessly. But perhaps we would encounter it more quickly if we let *it* find *us*. What we mean is this: You will become more attractive to the person God has in mind for you when you become the woman that God is calling you to be.

Therefore, keep your eyes on heaven rather than earth. Odds are, we're more likely to miss "the one" if we're constantly trying to find him. We're paying more attention to what we want than to what God wants. Trust us: You won't miss "the one" if you keep your eyes on Christ. He won't let it happen. But if your focus is not on God, then you're guaranteed to waste a lot of time with guys who aren't meant for you. When we don't trust God, we often take matters into our own hands. It's then that we become our own worst enemies. When we begin to view God as an obstacle to our deepest longings, we can be sure that we're a long way from finding them.

Perhaps you have assumed that God would lead you away from guys, just as guys typically lead you away from God. It isn't supposed to be this way. God shouldn't be viewed as a third wheel or an obtrusive guest in a relationship. He is the source of love. To the degree that a woman loves God, she is capable of loving a man. And to the degree that she loves a guy, she will lead him closer to heaven. When couples discover that God alone can perfect their human love, they'll find themselves closer to each other than ever before.

Walking with God Means Walking in His Ways

Have you ever had a girlfriend who was in a terrible relationship? Despite the fact that you and all of your friends begged her to open her eyes and get out, she stayed put. She'd even get upset at you for pointing out the obvious problems, or accuse you of jealousy. You didn't want her to break up because you were jealous or because you wanted her to obey a list of your rules. You just wanted what was best for her. You probably watched her make numerous poor choices, while wringing your hands in frustration, wishing she would trust you.

In the same way, God does not get angry at us because we aren't following His rules. He wants to see us happy and He knows what will ultimately bring us joy or despair. There's a tendency in all of us to believe: "God is out to get me. He's holding out on me. He's stingy." But as we look within our own hearts and begin to spend more time in prayer, we discover that we are the ones who are being stingy with Him. If only we would give everything to God, we would realize how generous He has been trying to be toward us all along. Because of our stubbornness, we often cling to what we don't really want because we doubt that anything better exists.

Such a distrustful disposition must be surrendered. Instead of seeing obedience as something that requires our submission and God's domination, we need to see that our obedience to God is an expression of loving trust and abandonment. Divine laws are created by love and should be obeyed in love.

A life of happiness is not based upon "Thou shalt nots." Jesus Christ did not die on a cross in order to give us more rules to follow. He died in order to save us and to obtain for us the graces necessary to love as we were created to love. Instead of thinking of God as a law-giver who sits aloof upon a throne waiting to judge you, let go of these ideas for a moment. Indeed, God has given us laws. He will be our judge. But in the end we will be judged by a God who is love, on our willingness to reflect His love.

God's idea of spirituality is not something that takes up an hour of our lives on Sunday. He longs for a relationship with each of us that will permeate and transform the way we approach every aspect of life. This includes our work, our studies, and especially our relationships. Because of this, the life of a Christian woman ought to be an expression of her love for God. The same goes with how she uses her body. In a sense, purity is like trusting God with your body. It shows that you will wait patiently for the time God has appointed for you to receive a spouse from Him. In the meantime, you will not run ahead and grasp at the pleasures of marriage.

Purity is not about following a litany of laws. It's about encountering God and wanting to give everything to Him because you realize He has given Himself fully to you. It's not so much about making ourselves perfect for Him. If anything, it's about allowing Him to love us when we're most imperfect.

You may wonder, "But what if I do this spiritual stuff, and I try to get all holy. What's the point if there are no good men out there? What if I stay strong and pure, but he never comes?" We would ask you: What if he waits, and you never show up? What if you lower your standards to find him, and the good one passes you by? You'll always wonder what could have been. Instead of worrying about all these scenarios, here's a better idea: Take care of God's business and let Him take care of yours.

The Thirst for Eternal Love

After a hookup, a college student in Maryland complained to us of an inescapable feeling of dissatisfaction and discouragement. She pondered in her e-mail, "Do good guys actually exist?" In order to cope with the disappointment, she typically found solace in chocolate, shopping, and a girls' night out. Since the stores were mostly closed and she had run out of chocolate, a friend in the dorm suggested they go out for a Saturday night on the town. The two drove down to Annapolis in hopes of meeting some Navy boys.

When they arrived at the bustling seaside town, they decided to begin the night with a quick visit to a nearby church. The two ducked into an adoration chapel located beneath a church a few blocks away from the main strip of bars and restaurants. She explained:

> As I knelt down in the silence, I couldn't help but notice a young couple praying together. The man was kneeling down and praying with his eyes closed. The woman was pregnant. I watched them for a few moments, and suddenly I knew that I wanted that type of relationship. I prayed, "God, please at least show me that there are 'normal' religious guys out there. . . . Lead me to someone that always brings me closer to you. . . . And until you bring us together, Lord, please guide both of us to you."

Not long after this prayer, she met a young man who finally appreciated her values. In the past, she had often been put down because of her morals. But he "unknowingly made every embarrassing experience and every lonely moment of my high school years well worth the struggle." Decent guys do exist. Trust in God, and hold out for them.

Find Yourself in Him

To find love, begin by finding yourself. People often fear that if they draw near to God, He'll wipe out their personality. The opposite is true. Many women have said, in the midst of their sin and despair, "This isn't me. I don't even know who I am anymore." Indeed, the further you get from God, the more you drift from your true identity.

God does not wish to take away your identity. He hopes to fulfill it. If you have not been yourself lately, He'll give you back to yourself. As you grow in your relationship with Him, you'll learn that holiness is not a rare gift given to pious elderly women. It's not about conforming to a mold. It is every person's calling and represents the full flowering—the full bloom of one's personality. The person far from God is like a seed that did not settle in the soil, but rolled off onto a rocky path. The saintly individuals of the world are the seeds who blossomed into roses. Yet each flower—each person—possesses her own unique radiance and reaches her full potential only when rooted firmly in Him. In the words of one man, "The more a woman is holy, the more she becomes a woman."[2]

You will have trouble believing this if you associate holiness with being an uptight prude. But if holiness is the fulfillment of your God-given identity, then only by His grace will you become who you were created to be. Your gifts, talents, and other qualities do not need to be suppressed in order to follow Him. In fact, He may desire to use those gifts for a greater purpose than you ever imagined!

Choosing to live a godly life is something you should do for your sake and for the sake of the world. A great deal rests upon whether or not you say yes to God—not just once, but daily. In her book *The Privilege of Being a Woman*, Dr. Alice von Hildebrand reminds women:

> As long as women are faithful to their "religious" calling the world is safe. But the threat menacing us today is precisely the metaphysical revolt of feminists who have totally lost sight of their vocation because they have become blind to the supernatural.[3]

When women lose sight of their call to holiness, the entire world misses out. If you're going to help save the world (you mistakenly think we're exaggerating), begin by taking the time to make an inventory of your spiritual life. Ask yourself:

- Am I interested in pleasing God, or am I trying to please myself while hopefully not offending Him?
- Am I more concerned with being accepted by men or being accepted by God?
- Whose heart am I trying to win?
- Am I waiting for God, or is God waiting for me?

Also, look at your daily habits, and compare the amount of time and energy you spend on your physical appearance compared to the amount of effort you spend on beautifying your soul. There's no problem with looking gorgeous. Just make sure your soul matches the rest of you.

Perhaps it's time to give your spiritual life a makeover. If you used to have a devotional life of prayer, get back in the habit. If you've never been particularly religious, don't be afraid to deepen your interior life. God isn't hard to find. You're probably the one who has been playing hard to get!

Spiritual Makeover

If the thought of spirituality intimidates you, realize who is pursuing who. God longs for your love. Let Him pursue you. He thirsts for you. At times, when we try to grow closer to God, we feel overwhelmed because we think that our spiritual progress depends entirely upon the quality of our own efforts. At such times, it's refreshing to remember that God is the one who is in pursuit of us.

No one comes to God holy. We all come as beggars. While in college, I (Jason) recall one of my professors explaining our relationship to God the Father in this way: Imagine a little girl who wanted to buy her dad a birthday present. She came to him, and said, "Daddy, I want to buy you a present, but I don't know what you want." Pleased by her thoughtfulness, he said, "I'd love a new tie, sweetheart." She looked at him, and added, "But I can't drive to the store. Will you take me?" They hop in the car and drive to the store together. Upon arriving, she asks him to pick the one he wants, because she wants him to get his favorite. After browsing for a while together, he finds the right one. As they walk toward the cash register, she squeezes his hand, looks up to him with her irresistible brown eyes, and reminds him, "Daddy, I don't have any money. Can you buy it?" The dad gladly pays for his own present, and the two of them leave the store.

On the morning of his birthday, she watches eagerly as he opens the messy wrapping paper on her gift. Upon seeing the gift, his eyes become moist with emotion as he pulls his daughter close and kisses the top of her head, thanking her for thinking of him. This is the heart of God the Heavenly Father. He's not hard to please. Because you're His daughter, He loves you more than even the most tender earthly father ever could. You don't need to come to Him with a halo. Come as you are, because you are the gift He desires. If you've been away from God, haven't you made Him wait long enough?

In order to do give Him the freedom to work in your life, make room for silence. Our lives are filled with so much noise and busyness that we rarely take time to pray. Even though our minds are full of life's questions, how often do we sit still long enough to hear God give us the answers? His voice will not be an audible one. However, when you begin to tune out the constant distractions and quiet your soul, you'll notice that His promptings become clearer in your heart. Don't be afraid to listen to them.

The real reason why people don't stop to listen to God is not because they don't think He'll speak to them. They're afraid He will. They're afraid of what He has to say, and so they surround themselves with more noise, companions, and possessions. Or they get involved in good things like volunteer work in an effort to divert their attention from the one thing God is asking of them. As one young woman said to me, "Praying kind of scares me. I figure that if I pray I will either get an answer that I am not prepared for or an answer that I cannot deal with."

Don't be intimidated by prayer. If you don't pray much, begin talking to Jesus more, reading Scripture, and going to church on Sunday. Go on a retreat if you're able. When you pray, specifically use the name of Jesus, not merely "God" or "Lord." Using His name slows us down and reminds us that we're not rambling to ourselves about our problems. We're talking to a Person. Speak from your heart to His, and He will teach you how to pray. Spend some time with Him in the morning, on the drive to work, and at night before bed. Consistency in simple prayers is more important than praying much irregularly.

We can't expect to grow spiritually if we think that prayer times will just happen. Therefore, set a regular prayer time and stick to it. St. Paul said that we ought to pray constantly.[4] In order to do that, we need to begin somewhere. One spiritual director advised college students, "Pray fifteen minutes every day. Lengthen it if you can, shorten it if you must, but never omit it."[5] Yet another master of the spiritual life recommended:

> Never forget that it is at the beginning of each day that God has the necessary grace for the day ready for us. He knows exactly what opportunities we shall have to sin . . . and will give us everything we

need if we ask Him then. That is why the Devil does all he can to prevent us from saying our Morning Prayers or to make us say them badly.[6]

In your prayer time, don't seek out spiritual feelings or emotional experiences. Seek God. Feelings aren't bad, but they should not be pursued as an end in themselves or else the soul will be restless when they are taken away. When we get too attached to spiritual consolations, we'll make the mistake of thinking that our closeness to God is measured by the intensity of our religious experiences. It is not. In fact, it has been said that real prayer begins when you pray when you don't want to.

You can pray at any time. You can do it right now, as you read! All it takes is that you open your heart to Him. This very moment, if Jesus could speak directly to your weary heart, He might say something like this:

Listen to my words slowly so that they penetrate your heart. Do not lose hope in me. Trust in me alone, and do not despair. My love will never fail you. I know how you desire perfect love. Know that this desire—and its fulfillment—come only from me. Give me your heart completely every day. Make me the object of your hope. If you lack peace, it reveals that you do not trust fully. To the extent to which you know my love, you will trust me. The peace you desire can only be found in my will for you. If you feel pain, anxiety, or worry, immediately give me your heart. Give me those people, those plans, and those concerns that weigh upon you. Give me the past, present, and future. I will cleanse your heart so that you may live with the grace to do my holy and perfect will with a spirit of rejoicing. You have seen your weakness. Come to me without hesitation during your time of need, and I will fill you with my divine strength and love. Fear not. Be patient and know that the troubled waters of your soul will become calm again. Do not be gloomy. Rejoice in your suffering. If only you could see how close our hearts are becoming! If only you knew the joy I have waiting for you. I will not show you that right now. I wish to see your faith. I give you the grace. Accept it, and glorify my Father.

21

TESTIFY

While I (Crystalina) was visiting Jason for the first time in San Diego, we drove to his church to spend some time in the chapel. As we walked from the car to the door of the church, he nonchalantly asked, "Hey, I've got a chastity talk to give at a high school tomorrow. Do you wanna get on stage with me and do your talk?"

Although we had met at a chastity conference a year earlier, he didn't know I didn't have "a talk." Hardly anyone even knew my past—including him! We weren't even dating yet, but it was obvious we had strong feelings for each other. And now he was asking me to get on stage and give my testimony before an entire high school, when he didn't even know what he was about to hear?

I was mortified. I stuttered, "Um, well, if I do the talk, what do you think I should say?" As we approached the door of the chapel, he replied, "I don't know. Why don't you ask Jesus? He'll tell you." With that, we walked into the chapel . . . and into the rest of our lives together.

While in prayer, I poured out my fears to God:

What will Jason think of me if I tell him the truth? He's been saving his virginity for marriage, and I'm sure he assumes that I have too. What will his parents think when they find out? Who am I to give a chastity talk? Who would want to listen to me? What do I have to offer? I don't have a theology degree. I'll just make a fool of Jason and myself! God, how did I get myself into this? How did you get me into this?

After leaving the chapel, Jason and I began the drive back toward his apartment for dinner. Sitting quietly in the passenger seat, I spoke shyly. "Jason, I need to tell you something. . . . You know how I strongly believe in chastity and saving yourself for marriage? Well, I didn't always believe this." With that, I began telling him of my past. Without question, it was the most difficult conversation of my life. There was no easy way to tell him, because it's not exactly the thing you want to bring up when you're falling in love!

In high school, I wanted to impress the boys. I knew exactly what to say and do to win their attention. But the time for wearing masks and playing games was over. I had finally met a man whose opinion of me truly mattered. I didn't want to disappoint him, but I knew I couldn't hide forever. Either he would love me for who I had become, or he would lose interest in me because of how I used to be. I had no choice but to surrender and hope.

I don't think he knew how to react, because I had become such a different person. The only Crystalina he knew was wearing modest skirts, doing missionary work, and reading chastity books. As I told him of my past, I could tell that his heart was heavy. I wanted to comfort him, but before I knew it, he was drying my tears. He was comforting me, and reminding me that I was a new creation.

The next morning, Jason handed me the microphone in front of six hundred wide-eyed teenagers. Just as I had done for him, I poured my heart out to the students, telling them how I had gradually lost myself and then was found by Christ in the midst of my darkest hour.

After the assembly, students poured onto the stage toward me. Many were in tears, hugging and thanking me for being so honest. It was overwhelming because I had no idea how they would receive me. Jason and I drove away from the assembly and he remarked, "I think we'd make a pretty good team."

After I returned home, I began to process what had just happened. As the students poured out their gratitude toward me, it struck me how so many girls are waiting for female leaders. Their hearts are so good, and they're ready to follow. It's almost as if they're waiting for someone they trust to give them permission to rise up. The question

Jason and I have for you is: Are you willing to lead them by the witness of your own life?

Wendy Shalit sounded a worthy challenge to all women when she wrote:

> Consider how girls today need to be thin, available, and always sexy. At the same time they are supposed to have no hopes, no messy feelings, no vulnerability. They must be aggressive, yet somehow inviting. It's complicated, and to rebel against the new bad-girl script takes enormous confidence. But . . . it can be done.[1]

Not only can it be done, it must be done. However, the change must begin within our own hearts. When a British newspaper invited numerous eminent authors to write essays on the theme "What's wrong with the world?" the famous English writer G. K. Chesterton submitted a one sentence essay that read, "Dear Sirs, I am."

It's easy to talk about solving the problems of the world. What requires effort is looking objectively at our own shortcomings. Before we can save the rest of the world, we need to first save ourselves. Sometimes we get so involved in sensuality that it saps the life out of us, and we do nothing noble or great to build up the world. We become so stuck on the emotional comfort of a relationship or the pursuit of pleasure that we become too busy to think about anyone other than ourselves. The world needs your radiance. Now more than ever, a brave generation of women must forge a dynasty, and reinvent a new generation of uncompromising pure womanhood.

Every day, the world mocks the Christian view of relationships, marriage, and sexuality, implying that we think the act of sex is inherently dirty, bad, and deadly. In reality, we're the ones who think it's beautiful, good, and life-giving. In fact, we have no problem with people who glorify sex. The problem is when the world fails to see its glory, forgetting that it ought to be the most beautiful expression of love between a husband and wife. Because sex ought to be so glorious, it's worth waiting for.

This lifestyle is possible for everyone, but many act as if it's out of their reach because they don't want to let go of their current ways. We whimper, "I don't know what to do." But sometimes when we say we're confused, what it really means is that we know exactly what we need to do—but we don't want to do it.

The world cannot afford your fear any longer. In the Old Testament, God raised up a simple Jewish woman named Esther to become the Queen of Persia. Through her courage and faith, she was able to prevent the massacre of a great number of innocent people. Before she stepped out in faith to save their lives, someone encouraged her by saying, "And who knows whether you have not come to the kingdom for such a time as this?"[2]

So have you. God has not only called you into existence, but has chosen for you to live during this moment in history . . . because you are needed for such a time as this in His kingdom. Therefore, no matter how pure or impure your past may be, never underestimate the power of your testimony. If you are united to the will of God, your potential is limitless.

Perhaps more than ever, our world is in need of women who can restore an authentic feminism. Early feminists sought to promote equal rights for women. They spread the word that women are capable and competent—able to take care of themselves without needing men to rescue them from poverty and ignorance.

While it's noble to empower women, some within the feminist movement have made women feel less than womanly if they're hoping for a man. Marriage is sometimes viewed as a hindrance to a woman's full potential. An authentic feminism recognizes that marriage is a healthy dream and a noble aspiration. If a woman dreams of being a single professional, God bless her. If she dreams of being married at home with eight kids, God bless her. True feminine liberation is giving her the freedom to choose for herself without looking down upon her goals. Besides, if she's seeking a soulmate, perhaps the two of them would be able to do more for humanity than either of them could have accomplished alone.

Finding your soulmate without losing your soul is not an easy journey. But even in the midst of your times of loneliness, remember that you are never alone. While journaling during a difficult time in life, I wrote these words that I felt God was speaking to my heart, encouraging me. I share them with you because I know I'm not alone in what I have felt during times of darkness, and you need to remember that you're not alone, either:

Why do you always seek man's approval? You're always wondering: "Do I look pretty enough? Do I sound smart enough?" With a shadow of insecurity hovering above you, you're always trying to keep others interested. Meanwhile, you give yourself away while ignoring your gut. Don't be controlled by the amount of attention and approval you receive, and stop being ashamed of yourself. Your worth can't come from who you're with, what you wear, or what others think of you.

Are you scared to admit your own self-worth? Do you keep your true beauty, gifts, and talents so locked away and hidden from the world that you can't truly see how amazing you are? Are you afraid of shining so brightly that the light will scare others away? Do not shy from who you are because you fear abandonment or the negative opinions of others. You take scraps from the world but I have given you everything you need, deep within you. Everyone's light is different and some brighter than others. But do not be scared of your own light, for it was put in you so that others who are blinded by their own darkness could see your light.

Why are you scared and sad? Why do you belittle yourself and dim your own light? Your light was made to shine—that is its purpose. Your self-worth is within you and has been given to you for a purpose. Your beauty—God's beauty—was given for a great reason as well. The darkness has tried to extinguish this beauty within, but it cannot. It will not be put out.

At times, you allow your insecurities to overpower you, and your thoughts run wild. But with Jesus' love you can control any vice, wickedness, or evil weapon that comes against you. It's time to rise up, unafraid of who you are. Embrace it. Do not lower yourself or hide, because the power of my love and grace will always be there to catch you and show you the way. I will catch you, but will you let me?

Deep down you know who you are and what you are supposed to do. Stop lowering yourself to the world and start rising to heaven. Even though it might seem so far away, it truly is all around you. Heaven is watching, praying, and cheering you on. You have a whole army of angels and saints wanting you to succeed in your battle. But the biggest battle of all will be with yourself. Know who you are and what you are not. You are a beloved daughter of Jesus, He who is God.

NOTES

Introduction

[1] Ian Kerner, *Be Honest — You're Not That Into Him Either* (New York: Regan Books, 2005), xxi.

[2] Ibid., 12.

Chapter 1

[1] Lisa Rubisch, as quoted in Kerner, *Be Honest*, 156, 157.

[2] David Walsh, *Why Do They Act That Way?* (New York: Free Press, 2005), 62.

[3] Teri Figueroa, "Girl's Soccer Coach to Face Trial for Molest," *North County Times*, June 28, 2005.

[4] Edward Marriott, "Men and Porn," *The Guardian*, Nov. 8, 2003.

[5] Douglas T. Kenrick et al., "Influence of Popular Erotica on Judgments of Strangers and Mates," *Journal of Experimental Social Psychology* 25, no. 2 (March 1989): 159–67.

[6] St. Robert Bellarmine, letter to his niece, 1614, as quoted in Rosemary Guiley, *The Quotable Saint* (New York: Visionary Living, Inc., 2002), 166.

[7] William Tooke and Lori Camire, "Patterns of Deception in Intersexual and Intrasexual Mating Strategies," *Ethology and Sociobiology* 12, no. 5 (September 1991): 345–64.

[8] David Blankenhorn, *Fatherless America: Confronting Our Most Urgent Social Problem* (New York: HarperCollins, 1995), 45, 46.

[9] Wendy Shalit, *A Return to Modesty: Discovering the Lost Virtue* (New York: Touchstone, 1999), 7.

[10] Judith S. Musick, *Young, Poor, and Pregnant* (Yale University, 1993), 60.

[11] Benoit Denizet-Lewis, "Friends, Friends with Benefits and the Benefits of the Local Mall," *New York Times*, May 30, 2004.

[12] Suzanne Ryan et al., "The First Time: Characteristics of Teens' First Sexual Relationships," *Research Brief* (Washington, D.C.: Child Trends, August 2003), 2.

[13] National Center on Addiction and Substance Abuse, "National Survey of American Attitudes on Substance Abuse IX: Teen Dating Practices and Sexual Activity," Columbia University, August 2004, 6.

[14] http://en.wikipedia.org/Statutory_Rape.

[15] Louann Brizendine, *The Female Brain* (New York: Morgan Road Books, 2006), 44.

[16] St. Clement of Alexandria, *The Teacher*, as quoted in Guiley, *The Quotable Saint*, 163.

[17] Gen. 3:12 (New American Bible).

[18] Barbara Dafoe Whitehead and David Popenoe, "Why Men Won't Commit: Exploring Young Men's Attitudes About Sex, Dating and Marriage," National Marriage Project, 2002.

[19] Ibid.

[20] Søren Kierkegaard, *Either–Or* (Princeton, N.J.: Princeton University Press, 1946), ii, 2.

[21] Fulton J. Sheen, *Life Is Worth Living* (San Francisco: Ignatius Press, 1999), 61.

Chapter 2

[1] Brizendine, *The Female Brain*, 70.

[2] Joshua Harris, *Boy Meets Girl* (Sisters, Oregon: Multnomah Publishers, Inc., 2000), 51 (emphasis in original).

Chapter 3

[1] Heather Gallagher and Peter Vlahutin, *A Case for Chastity: The Way to Real Love and True Freedom for Catholic Teens* (Liguori, Mo.: Liguori, 2003), 7.

[2] Quoted in Donald DeMarco, "Paul VI versus Playboy," *National Catholic Register*, July 20–26, 2008.

[3] Janie M. Fredell, "Abstinence: The New Pink?" *Harvard Crimson* (March 14, 2007).

[4] Shalit, *A Return to Modesty*, 212 (emphasis in original).

[5] Gen. 4:1.

[6] Hephzibah Anderson, "My Year without Sex! Hephzibah Anderson Took a Dramatic—and Liberating—Decision. So Did It Help Her to Find Real Love?" Mail Online, June 26, 2009.

[7] Warren Throckmorton, "Depression: A New Sexually Transmitted Disease," *Washington Times*, December 8, 2005; Hallfors, Waller et al., "Which Comes First in Adolescence–Sex and Drugs or Depression?" *American Journal of Preventive Medicine*, 29: 3 (October 2005): 163–170; cf. Robert Rec-

tor, "Facts About Abstinence Education," Heritage Foundation, Web Memo 461.

[8] Wendy Shalit, *Girls Gone Mild* (New York: Random House, 2007), xxi.

[9] Dietrich von Hildebrand, *Purity: The Mystery of Christian Sexuality* (Steubenville, Ohio: Franciscan University Press, 1989), 47, 51.

[10] Ibid., 48.

[11] Dawn Eden, *The Thrill of the Chaste* (Nashville, Tenn.: Thomas Nelson, 2006), 124.

[12] Robert Rector, "Out-of-Wedlock Childbearing and Paternal Absence: Trends and Social Effects," Heritage Foundation, July 7, 1999.

[13] Luke 15:7.

[14] Song of Sol. 2:15.

Chapter 4

[1] Tom Stoppard, as quoted at http://www.brainyquote.com/quotes/authors/t/tom_stoppard.html

Chapter 5

[1] 1 Cor. 13:6 (NAB).

[2] Alice von Hildebrand, *The Privilege of Being a Woman* (Ann Arbor, Mich.: Sapientia Press, 2005), 40.

[3] Ibid., 92.

[4] Bartels and Zeki, "The Neural Correlates of Maternal and Romantic Love," *NeuroImage* 21 (2004): 1155–66.

[5] Karol Wojtyla, *Love and Responsibility* (San Francisco: Ignatius Press, 1993), 128.

[6] Ibid., 120.

[7] 1 Cor. 6:9–10, 18 (NAB).

[8] 1 Thess. 4:3–5, 7–8 (NAB).

[9] St. John Chrysostom, *Hom. in Eph.* 20, 8: PG 62,146–47, as quoted in *Catechism of the Catholic Church*, 2365.

Chapter 6

[1] St. John Climacus, *The Ladder of Divine Ascent*, as quoted in Guiley, *The Quotable Saint*, 125.

[2] Eden, *The Thrill of the Chaste*, 9.

[3] John and Stasi Eldredge, *Captivating: Discovering the Secret of a Woman's Soul* (Nashville, Tenn.: Thomas Nelson, 2005), 214.

[4] Anderson, "My Year without Sex!"

[5] Bill Cosby, as quoted by brainyquote.com.

[6] Lakita Garth, as quoted in Shalit, *Girls Gone Mild*, 63.

[7] 2 Cor. 12:9.

[8] 1 Cor. 10:13.

[9] Camille De Blasi, *Modestly Yours* (Snohomish, Wash.: Healing the Culture, 2002), 15–16.

[10] Fredell, "Abstinence: The New Pink?"

[11] Attributed to St. Ignatius Loyola; see Joseph de Guibert, S.J., *The Jesuits: Their Spiritual Doctrine and Practice* (Chicago: Loyola University Press, 1964), 148, n. 55.

[12] James 1:2–4 (NAB).

[13] Gal. 6:9 (NAB).

Chapter 7

[1] Donna Freitas, *Sex and the Soul* (New York: Oxford University Press, 2008), xvii.

[2] Thomas Lackona, "The Emotional Dangers of Premature Sexual Involvement," *The Neglected Heart* (January 30, 2007), 3.

[3] Laura Sessions Step, *Unhooked* (New York: Riverhead Books, 2007), 21–22.

[4] Freitas, *Sex and the Soul*, xiv.

[5] Laura Schlessinger, *Stupid Things Parents Do to Mess Up Their Kids* (New York: HarperCollins, 2000), 167.

[6] Eden, *The Thrill of the Chaste*, 195.

[7] Denizet-Lewis, "Friends, Friends with Benefits and the Benefits of the Local Mall."

[8] Laura Sessions Step, *Unhooked*, 43.

[9] Denizet-Lewis, "Friends, Friends with Benefits and the Benefits of the Local Mall."

[10] John and Stasi Eldredge, *Captivating*, 52, 56.

[11] Josh McDowell, *Why True Love Waits* (Carol Stream, Ill.: Tyndale House Publishers, 2000), 165.

[12] Freitas, *Sex and the Soul*, 154.

[13] Ibid., 131 (emphasis in original).

[14] Ibid., 155.

[15] Denizet-Lewis, "Friends, Friends with Benefits and the Benefits of the Local Mall."

[16] Eden, *The Thrill of the Chaste*, 84.

[17] Joe S. McIlhaney Jr. and Freda McKissic Bush, *Hooked* (Chicago: Northfield Publishing, 2008), 32.

[18] Ibid., 37.

[19] Ibid., 45, 62.

[20] Laurie Turnow, "Ten Reasons I Want ... to Have Sex with my Boyfriend" (Snowflake, Ariz.: Heritage House '76, Inc., 2007).

[21] Louann Brizendine, *The Female Brain* (New York: Morgan Road Books, 2006), 77.

[22] David Larson, as quoted in William Mattox, Jr., "The Hottest Valentines: The Startling Secret of What Makes You a High-Voltage Lover," *Washington Post*, February 13, 1994.

[23] Willy Pedersen and Morten Blekesaune, "Sexual Satisfaction in Young Adulthood: Cohabitation, Committed Dating or Unattached Life?" *Acta Sociologica* 46, no. 3 (September 2003): 179–93.

[24] Christopher West, *The Love That Satisfies: Reflections on Eros and Agape* (West Chester, Pa.: Ascension Press, 2007), 32.

[25] Christopher West, *Heaven's Song: Sexual Love as It Was Meant to Be* (West Chester, Pa.: Ascension Press, 2007, 2008), 129.

[26] Lena Chen, as quoted in Randall Patterson, "Students of Virginity," *New York Times*, March 30, 2008.

[27] Von Hildebrand, *The Privilege of Being a Woman*, 95.

[28] Eden, *The Thrill of the Chaste*, 83.

[29] *Midrash Rabbah* on Genesis 22:6, in *The Soncino Midrash Rabbah* (New York: Judaica Press, 1983).

[30] Raïssa Maritain, as quoted in James V. Schall, S.J., "The Prince of This World," The Catholic Thing, March 8, 2010.

[31] Harris, *Boy Meets Girl*, 154.

[32] Sarah Hinlicky, "Subversive Virginity," *First Things* (October 1998), 15.

[33] West, *The Love That Satisfies*, 79.

[34] Arleen Spenceley, "Why I Will Be a Virgin until I'm Married," *St. Petersburg Times*, September 27, 2009.

[35] Jeffrey Satinover, M.D., *Feathers of the Skylark* (Westport, Conn., Hamewith Books, 1996), 80–81.

[36] 1 Cor. 6:20.

Chapter 8

[1] Denizet-Lewis, "Friends, Friends with Benefits and the Benefits of the Local Mall."

[2] Ibid.

[3] Eden, *The Thrill of the Chaste*, 77.

[4] Anonymous, M.D., *Unprotected* (New York, Sentinel: 2006), 2.

[5] Denizet-Lewis, "Friends, Friends with Benefits and the Benefits of the Local Mall."

[6] M. S. Carmichael et al., "Plasma Oxytocin Increases in the Human Sexual Response," *Journal of Clinical Endocrinology and Metabolism* 64, no. 1 (January 1987): 27–31; M. R. Murphy et al., "Changes in Oxytocin and Vasopressin Secretion during Sexual Activity in Men," *Journal of Clinical Endocrinology and Metabolism* 65, no. 4 (October 1987): 738–41.

[7] Michael Kosfeld et al., "Oxytocin Increases Trust in Humans," *Nature* 435 (June 2, 2005): 673–76; M. Heinrichs et al., "Selective Amnesic Effects of Oxytocin on Human Memory," *Physiology and Behavior* 83, no. 1 (October 30, 2004): 31–38; J. A. Bartz et al., "The Neuroscience of Affiliation: Forging Links between Basic and Clinical Research on Neuropeptides and Social Behavior," *Hormones and Behavior* 50, no. 4 (November 2006): 518–28; B. Ditzen et al., "Effects of Social Support and Oxytocin on Psychological and Physiological Stress Responses during Marital Conflict," *Frontiers in Neuroendocrinology* 27:1 (May 2006): 134; Theresa L. Crenshaw, M.D., *The Alchemy of Love and Lust* (New York: Pocket Books, 1996).

[8] A. Bartels and S. Zeki, "The Neural Correlates of Maternal and Romantic Love," *NeuroImage* 21 (2004): 1155–66.

[9] Brizendine, *The Female Brain*, 68.

[10] Ron Louis and David Copeland, *How to Succeed with Women* (New Jersey: Reward Books, 1998), 206.

[11] Ibid.

[12] *Seventeen* (July 2005), 84.

[13] Jonathan Small, "Ask Him Anything," *Cosmopolitan,* December 2005, 48.

[14] Freitas, *Sex and the Soul*, xvii.

Chapter 9

[1] Christopher West, *Theology of the Body for Beginners* (West Chester, Pa.: Ascension Press, 2004), 110.

Chapter 10

[1] Paula Rinehart, "Losing Our Promiscuity," *Christianity Today*, July 10, 2000, 39.

[2] Jeremy Laurance, "University of the bleedin' obvious," *The Indepenent*, (February 17, 2009); Christine Dell'Amore, "Bikinis Make Men See Women as Objects, Scans Confirm," National Geographic News (February 16, 2009).

[3] History.com, "This Day in History: Bikini Introduced," available at http://history.com/this-day-in-history.do?action= VideoArticle&id=6949.

[4] Shalit, *A Return to Modesty*, 102.

[5] St. Bede the Venerable, as quoted in *Magnificat*, March 2010, 332.

[6] St. Thomas Aquinas, *Summa Theologiae*, ed. Thomas Gilby. Volume 43, Question 144, Article 4.

[7] http://www.lovematters.com/kimalexis.htm.

[8] Shalit, *A Return to Modesty*, 175.

[9] Anderson, "My Year without Sex!"

[10] Shalit, *A Return to Modesty*, 191.

[11] Gal. 5:22–23.

[12] Eden, *The Thrill of the Chaste*, 150.

[13] WorldNetDaily.com, "The Kids Are All Right: Girl Pleads to Retailer for Modest Clothing," May 22, 2004.

[14] Nick Perry, "More Modest Clothing, Please, Girl Asks Nordstrom," *Seattle Times* (May 21, 2004).

[15] Kevin McCullough, "Abercrombie & Fitch to Your Kids: Group Sex Now!" WorldNetDaily.com (November 14, 2003).

[16] Woman and Girls Foundation, "The Girlcott Story," available at http://www.wgfpa.org/girl2girlgrants/section_girlsOurVoices/ girlcott.htm.

[17] Scott Simonson, "Local teens score one for modesty," *Arizona Daily Star* (Sept. 18, 2004).

Chapter 11

[1] Teresa Tomeo, *Noise* (West Chester, Pa.: Ascension Press, 2007), 59.

[2] HealthyPlace.com Staff Writer, "How Many Children Have Eating Disorders?" (Jan. 8, 2009), available at http://www.healthyplace.com/eating-disorders/main/how-many-children-have-eating-disorders/menu-id-58/page-2/.

[3] Leanne Potts, "Carnie Needs To Shed Self-Esteem Bid," ABQJournal.com. Feb. 9, 2003.

[4] Mark Memmott, "Is It Real? Or Is It Martha?" *USA Today*, March 1, 2005; "Oprah! The Richest Woman on TV?" *TV Guide*, August 26, 1989.

[5] CBC Street Cents, "Behind the Hype: Celebrity Image," available at http://www.cbc.ca/streetcents/guide/2005/04/s03_01.html.

[6] "Nelly Stays True to Herself," Chris Santos, SOTR. Jan. 8, 2002.

[7] CBC Street Cents, "Behind the Hype."

[8] Mary Pipher, *Reviving Ophelia* (New York: Riverhead Books, 1994), 40.

[9] Ibid., 44.

[10] Sarah Pevey, as quoted in Shalit, *Girls Gone Mild*, 136.

[11] Caroline Knapp, as quoted in Shalit, *A Return to Modesty*, 59–60.

[12] Gen. 1:31.

[13] Susie Shellenberger and Kathy Gowler, *What Your Daughter Isn't Telling You* (Minneapolis, Minn.: Bethany House, 2007), 106.

[14] Shalit, *Girls Gone Mild*, 270.

[15] Shellenberger and Gowler, *What Your Daughter Isn't Telling You*, 109.

[16] Ibid., 174.

[17] Isa. 53:5.

[18] Deut. 14:1 (NAB).

[19] Jer. 47:5.

[20] Centers for Disease Control, "Youth Risk Behavior Surveillance—United States, 2009," *MMWR*, 59: SS-5 (June 4, 2010): 9.

[21] Ibid.; Centers for Disease Control, "Suicide Trends Among Youths and Young Adults Aged 10–24 Years—United States, 1990–2004," *MMWR* 56:35 (September 7, 2007): 905–908.

[22] David Walsh, *Why Do They Act That Way?* (New York: Free Press, 2005), 63–64.

[23] The American College Health Association, National College Health Assessment, Spring 2006.

[24] Robert Rector et al., "Sexually Active Teenagers Are More Likely to Be Depressed and to Attempt Suicide," The Heritage Foundation, June 3, 2003; Martha W. Waller et al., "Gender Differences in Associations between Depressive Symptoms and Patterns of Substance Use and Risky Sexual Behavior among a Nationally Representative Sample of U.S. Adolescents," *Archives of Women's Mental Health* 9, no. 3 (May 2006): 139–50.

[25] Sir. 2:10 (NAB).

[26] Suzanne Hoholik, "Pfizer Must Pay $2.3 Billion: Upper Arlington Man Helped Blow Whistle on Drugmaker's Marketing," *Columbus Dispatch*, September 3, 2009.

[27] World Health Organization, "IARC Monographs Programme Finds Combined Estrogen-Progestogen Contraceptives and Menopausal Therapy Are Carcinogenic to Humans," news release, July 29, 2005; *Physicians' Desk Reference*, (Montvale, N.J.: Thomson, 2006); Collaborative Group on Hormonal Factors in Breast Cancer, "Breast Cancer and Hormonal Contraceptives: Collaborative Reanalysis of Individual Data on 53 297 Women with Breast Cancer and 100 239 Women without Breast Cancer from 54 Epidemiological Studies," *Lancet* 347, no. 9017 (June 22, 1996):1713–27; Chris Kahlenborn et al., "Oral Contraceptive Use as a Risk Factor for Premenopausal Breast Cancer: A Meta-Analysis," *Mayo Clinic Proceedings* 81 (October 2006): 1290–1302.

[28] Von Hildebrand, *The Privilege of Being a Woman*, 63.

[29] fructusventris.stblogs.org.

[30] Whitehead and Popenoe, "Why Men Won't Commit."

[31] Mika Gissler et al., "Suicides after Pregnancy in Finland: 1987–94: Register Linkage Study," *British Medical Journal* 313 (1996): 1431–34; cf. B. Garfinkle et al., "Stress, Depression and Suicide: A Study of Adolescents in Minnesota" (Minneapolis: University of Minnesota Extension Service, 1986), quoted in David C. Reardon, "The Abortion/Suicide Connection," *The Post-Abortion Review* 1, no. 2 (Summer 1993).

[32] David C. Reardon, "Abortion Is Four Times Deadlier Than Childbirth," *The Post-Abortion Review* 8, no. 2 (April–June 2000).

[33] David Reardon et al., "Psychiatric Admissions of Low-Income Women Following Abortion and Childbirth," *Canadian Medical Association Journal* 168 (2003): 1253–56.

[34] Angela Woodhull, "Testimonies True to Life," Human Life Alliance, advertising supplement (2001), 10.

[35] E-mail message from a father to Human Life Alliance (humanlife.org).

[36] Rachel Winer et al., "Genital Human Papillomavirus Infection: Incidence and Risk Factors in a Cohort of Female University Students," *American Journal of Epidemiology* 157, no. 3 (2003): 218–26.

Chapter 12

[1] Sir. 6:14–15.

[2] Eccles. 4:12–13.

[3] Prov. 27:17.

[4] Heb. 10:25 (NAB).

[5] Prov. 27:6.

[6] James 5:16.

[7] Mark 9:29.

Chapter 13

[1] Sir. 7:27–28.

[2] Pier Giorgio Frassati, *Pier Giorgio Frassati, Letters to His Friends and Family* (New York: St. Paul's, 2009), 190.

[3] Ibid., 224.

[4] Nanci Hellmich, "Bad Hair Day Can Hit Women's Self-Esteem, Wallet," *USA TODAY*, April 12, 2010.

[5] Harris, *Boy Meets Girl*, 43–62.

Chapter 14

[1] Larry Bumpass and Hsien-Hen Lu, "Trends in Cohabitation and Implications for Children's Family Contexts in the U.S.." *Population Studies* 54 (2000): 29–41.

[2] Whitehead and Popenoe, "Why Men Won't Commit."

[3] Ibid.

[4] Gen. 2:24.

[5] Susan Brown and Alan Booth, "Cohabitation Versus Marriage: A Comparison of Relationship Quality," *Journal of Marriage and the Family* 58 (1996): 668–78; Larry Bumpass and James Sweet, "National Estimates of Cohabitation," *Demography* 26 (1989): 615–30.

[6] Centers for Disease Control and Prevention, "Cohabitation, Marriage, Divorce, and Remarriage in the United States," July 2002, Table 21.

[7] Bumpass and Lu, "Trends in Cohabitation and Implications for Children's Family Contexts in the U.S."

[8] Whitehead and Popenoe, "Why Men Won't Commit."

[9] Ibid.

[10] Ibid.

[11] Jill Murray, *But I Love Him* (New York: ReganBooks, 2000), 91.

[12] Whitehead and Popenoe, "Why Men Won't Commit."

[13] Jay N. Giedd, "Structural Magnetic Resonance Imaging of the Adolescent Brain," *Adolescent Brain Development: Vulnerabilities and Opportunities* 1021 (June 2004): 77–85; Medical Institute for Sexual Health, "Maturation of the Teen Brain," *Integrated Sexual Health Today*, Spring 2005, 2–9.

[14] Centers for Disease Control and Prevention, "Cohabitation, Marriage, Divorce, and Remarriage in the United States," Table 21.

Chapter 15

[1] Ambrose Hollingworth Redmoon, "No Peaceful Warriors!" *Gnosis* 21 (Fall 1991).

[2] Often attributed to Jim Elliot, Journal entry for October 28, 1949.

Chapter 16

[1] Michael Collopy, *Works of Love Are Works of Peace: Mother Teresa of Calcutta and the Missionaries of Charity* (San Francisco: Ignatius Press, 1996), 197.

[2] Song of Sol. 4:9.

[3] Luke 7:44–48.

[4] Karol Wojtyla, *The Way to Christ* (San Francisco: Harper & Row Publishers, 1984), 34, 35.

[5] Lam. 3:22–23.

Chapter 17

[1] Oliver Berton et al., "Essential Role of BDNF in Mesolimbic Dopamine Pathway in Social Defeat Stress," *Science* 311 (February 2006), 864–868; McIlhaney and Bush, *Hooked*, 85.

[2] C. Pacifici, et al., "Evaluating a Prevention Program for Teenagers on Sexual Coercion: A Differential Effectiveness Program," *Journal of Consulting Clinical Psychologists* 69 (2001): 552–59; M. Blythe et al., "Incidence and Correlates of Unwanted Sex in Relationships in Middle and Late Adolescent Women," *Archives of Pediatric Adolescent Medicine* 160 (2005): 591–95; A. Biglan, et al., "Does Sexual Coercion Play a role in the High-Risk Sexual Behavior of Adolescent and Young Adult Women?" *Journal of Behavioral Medicine* 18 (1995): 549–68.

[3] Psalms 27:10 (NAB).

[4] C. S. Lewis, *The Four Loves* (Orlando, Fla.: Harcourt Brace & Company, 1988), 121.

[5] Mother Angelica Live, EWTN (Nov. 9, 1993).

[6] Rev. 21:5.

Chapter 18

[1] Frans de Waal, "Sex Differences in the Formation of Coalitions Among Chimpanzees," *Ethology and Sociobiology* 5 (1984): 239–55; F. B. M. de Waal,

"Sex Differences in Chimpanzee (and Human) Behavior: A Matter of Social Values?" In: *The Origin of Values*, M. Hechter, L. Nadel and R. E. Michod (eds.) (New York: Aldine de Gruyter, 1993), 285–303; Frans de Waal, "Coping with Social Tension: Sex Differences in the Effect of Food Provision to Small Rhesus Monkey Groups," *Animal Behavior* 32 (1984): 765–73.

[2] M. Eugene Boylan, *This Tremendous Lover* (Allen, Tex.: Christian Classics, 1987), 224.

[3] Sir. 19:5–15 (NAB).

[4] Matt. 12:36–37 (NAB).

[5] St. Maria Faustina Kowalska, *Diary: Divine Mercy in My Soul* (Stockbridge, Mass.: Marians of the Immaculate Conception, 2002), 234.

[6] Marc Foley, *The Love That Keeps Us Sane: Living the Little Way of St. Therese of Lisieux* (Mahwah, N.J.: Paulist Press, 2000), 39.

[7] *The Life of the Blessed Paul of the Cross: Founder of the Congregation of the Barefooted Clerks of the Most Holy Cross and Passion of Jesus Christ*, Volume II, Book II (1853), 55.

[8] Rom. 12:14, 17–21.

[9] Sir. 8:3.

Chapter 19

[1] T. G. Morrow, *Christian Courtship in an Oversexed World* (Huntington, Indiana: Our Sunday Visitor, 2003), 38.

[2] Emily Stimpson, "A Mother's Tears," *Franciscan Way* (Winter 2008), 20.

[3] www.chinalittleflower.org.

[4] Frederick Buechner, as quoted in John and Stasi Eldredge, *Captivating*, 213.

[5] Jenny Lugardo, as quoted in Father Peter Mitchell, *John Paul II, We Love You!* (Cincinnati: St. Anthony Messenger Press, 2007), 53.

[6] Eden, *The Thrill of the Chaste*, 22.

[7] Pope John Paul II, Address to Astana, Eurasia University, September 23, 2001.

Chapter 20

[1] Matt. 6:33.

[2] Léon Bloy, as quoted in Fulton Sheen, *The World's First Love* (San Francisco: Ignatius Press, 1996), 83.

[3] Von Hildebrand, *The Privilege of Being a Woman*, 65.

[4] 1 Thess. 5:17.

[5] Fr. Augustine Donegan, as quoted in Emily Stimpson, "Donegan's Wake," *Franciscan Way*, Autumn 2009, 14.

[6] St. John Vianney, *On Morning Prayers*, as quoted in *Thoughts of the Curé D'Ars* (Rockford, Ill., TAN Books and Publishers, 1984), 18.

Chapter 21

[1] Shalit, *Girls Gone Mild*, 40.

[2] Esther 4:14.